THE ETERNAL WAY

The Author

The
ETERNAL
WAY

THE INNER MEANING
OF THE BHAGAVAD GITA

ROY EUGENE DAVIS

CSA PRESS, *PUBLISHERS*
CENTER FOR SPIRITUAL AWARENESS
Lakemont, Georgia 30552

ISBN 978-0-87707-248-5

CSA Press
P. O. Box 7
Lakemont, Georgia 30552-0001
706-782-4723   Fax 706-782-4560
info@csa-davis.org
www.csa-davis.org

The Publishing Department of Center for Spiritual Awareness
International headquarters and meditation retreat center at
151 CSA Lane, Lakemont, Georgia

This book is also published in India
by Motilal Banarsidass, Delhi.
mlbd@vsnl.com   www.mlbd.com

PRINTED IN THE UNITED STATES OF AMERICA

I salute the supreme teacher,
the truth, whose nature is bliss;
who is the giver of the highest
happiness; who is pure wisdom;
who is beyond all qualities and
infinite like the sky; who is beyond
words; who is one and eternal,
pure and still; who is beyond all
change and phenomena and who
is the silent witness to all our
thoughts and emotions—I salute
truth, the supreme teacher.

– Ancient Vedic Hymn –

The Author's Books Published by CSA Press

Paramahansa Yogananda As I Knew Him
Absolute Knowledge That Liberates Consciousness
Seven Lessons in Conscious Living
Self-Knowledge: Adi Shankaracharya's Treatise on Nondualism
The Science of Self-Realization: Patanjali's Yoga-Sutras
Mystic Reflections
Satisfying Our Innate Desire to Know God

United Kingdom Gazelle Book Services sales@gazellebooks.co.uk

Italy Italian Language: Marco Valerio www.marcovalerio.com

Germany German Language: Kriya Yoga Center www.kriya-yoga.de

India English Language Editions:
Motilal Banarsidass www.mlbd.com
B. Jain Publishers www.bjainbooks.com
Indian Books Centre www.indianbookscentre.com

English and Hindi: Full Circle Publishers www.atfullcircle.com

Tamil: mahadevan101@gmail.com

Turkey Turkish Language: Bilyay Vakfi www.bilyay.org.tr

Spanish Language
download free books and articles at:
www.csa-davis.org
Also articles in English, German, Italian,
French, and Turkish Languages

Preface

One of the earliest commentaries on the *Bhagavad Gita* was written in India in the ninth century by the philosopher-seer Adi (the first) Shankaracharya. Others have since endeavored to explain the message of the *Gita*, including advocates of sectarian religious beliefs who claimed to have found in it support for their own opinions and philosophers who honestly tried to portray its significance for readers of their times. In this book I explain the inner meaning in the light of Kriya Yoga.

The *Bhagavad Gita* is a guide to understanding the reality of God, the processes of universal manifestation, and how every aspiring soul can have awareness restored to higher knowledge and spiritual wholeness. Its seven hundred verses encourage the reader to acquire Self-knowledge and to intentionally engage in constructive performance of personal duties along with dedicated spiritual endeavor—to practice Kriya Yoga. The Sanskrit word *kriya* means "action." *Yoga* can mean to yoke or unite individualized soul awareness with God; practice of procedures for this purpose; or *samadhi*, the soul's realization of spiritual wholeness, the culmination of successful practice.

The central theme of the *Gita* is that everything we do should be done to serve God's will: to serve the cause of evolution and facilitate the awakening and liberation of soul consciousness. By living like this, we can be in harmonious relationship with nature, purify the ego (the illusory sense of independent existence), and fulfill our spiritual destiny.

It was my good fortune to be guided and blessed by my guru, Paramahansa Yogananda, whom I met in 1949 and who ordained me to represent the Kriya Yoga tradition in autumn of 1951. From him, by words and the example of his life, I learned how to know

God, discern truth from untruth, live with insightful purpose, and teach others how to facilitate progressive unfoldment of knowledge which is innate to every soul.

I wrote this book as a spiritual exercise for myself, and for readers who are sincerely interested in learning how to live effectively and experience rapid, authentic spiritual growth. Effective living is as important to our total well-being as is subjective meditative contemplation. Soul unfoldment can be rapid when attention is directed to matters which nurture it. Spiritual growth is authentic when unfolded soul knowledge is demonstrated by functional freedom.

For assistance in defining many of the Sanskrit words, I used the translation of the *Bhagavad Gita* prepared by Winthrop Sargeant (State University of New York Press) and Judith Tyberg's *Language of the Gods*. Also helpful were the commentaries by S. Radhakrishnan (Harper & Row, New York) and Adi Shankaracharya (Samata Books, Madras). Of special value were a few published notes and comments by Swami Sri Yukteswar and Lahiri Mahasaya.

Frequent study of this book can be both intellectually and spiritually beneficial. It is my hope that each reader will find in these pages that which is most helpful to nurturing the unfoldment of their highest good.

Roy Eugene Davis

Lakemont, Georgia (U.S.A.)
Spring, 1996

Publisher's Note

A hardcover edition of *The Eternal Way* was first published by CSA Press in 1996 and by Motilal Banarsidass, Delhi, India, in 2001. This quality paperback edition will serve a wider readership.

Contents

INTRODUCTION

The Inner Meaning of the Bhagavad Gita

The Bhagavad Gita, one of the great literary classics of the ages, has spiritually nurtured and inspired millions of its readers for over two thousand years. The common translation of the title is descriptive of a holy or divine song: Sanskrit *bhaj*, reverence or love, to share wealth and glory; and *gita*, from the verb-root *gai*, to sing. The prefix *srimad* (or *shrimat*), from the verb-root *sri*, to flame, to spread or pour out light, is usually used in the title.

The two central characters in the story are Arjuna and Krishna. *Arjuna* represents the seeker of knowledge and experience of God. *Krishna*, Arjuna's cousin, friend, teacher, and the personification of divine power and grace in human form, represents the indwelling Spirit of God. In eighteen chapters, a broad range of philosophical views are explored and practical instruction about how to live skillfully and fulfill personal destiny is methodically expounded. The inner message of the Gita explains how to awaken to Self-knowledge and God-realization.

Although many devotees presume the text to affirm God to actually be a cosmic person whose name is Krishna, a more insightful analysis reveals that, what is pointed to, is a supreme or transcendent Reality which, because formless and nameless, is beyond all categories, therefore, indescribable although knowable or realizable.

In the first ten chapters, *Jnana Yoga*, the way of knowledge; *Karma Yoga*, the way of selfless work or action; and *Bhakti Yoga*, the way of surrendered devotion to God, are described along with mind-freeing philosophical ideas. In the eleventh chapter, Arjuna, by Krishna's grace, is enabled to perceive the reality of the one Consciousness expressive as all things. The story does not end there; a cosmic conscious episode is but the beginning of a new and higher stage of life during which knowledge has to be applied and integrated into the fabric of existence. The concluding seven chapters are devoted to explaining how to apply in daily life what has been learned.

When read superficially, the text tells of a great war that occurred between opposing factions, who were cousins, on a battlefield north of the present-day city of New Delhi, India. When interpreted as an allegory—a story in which characters, objects, and events symbolically illustrate ideas or moral and spiritual principles—the esoteric meaning portrays a drama far more significant than any transitory historical event. The insightful reader is provided with the following helpful information: (1) the progress of the soul's awakening from self-conscious involvements with physical and psychological circumstances to realization of its true nature as pure consciousness; (2) the challenges commonly confronted during the process; (3) the liberating knowledge which removes awareness from all that is suppressive and restrictive.

The truths explained have great value to every person who sincerely aspires to clear understanding of life's processes and of ways to facilitate rapid, authentic spiritual growth that culminates in illumination of consciousness and soul liberation. Mind-clouded, sense-bound existence characteristic of ordinary human experience is often painful and sometimes seems to be devoid of meaningful purpose. What is needed, is for the mind to be illumined by the soul's innate light and for the senses to be subject to the soul's will or capacity to freely choose. Self-consciousness is then transcended and life flows smoothly under the direction of soul-originated impulses referred to as grace. The actions of grace are the effective influences of the inclination of the Spirit of God indwelling Nature to fulfill the purposes of life.

As soul-mind-body beings relating to the physical realm, we are instinctively and intuitively directed to fulfill basic desires and to satisfy needs essential to our survival, security, well-being, and continued growth. To this end, we innately want to live in harmony with Nature's processes, have life-enhancing desires easily fulfilled, experience spontaneous satisfaction of needs, and know of and unfold our spiritual potential. When soul awareness is not yet pronounced, we may be inclined to direct most of our attention to satisfying our physical and emotional needs and to ignore or neglect our spiritual growth. While this behavior may result in marginal human happiness, it will not satisfy the deep-seated desire of the heart (real essence of being) to awaken to that Self-knowledge which allows God-experience and transcendent realizations.

In Sanskrit literature, the first chapter serves as the introduction to the main body of the text. To have access to the core message, we have to carefully examine this chapter to acquire an understanding of the author's purpose for writing the Bhagavad Gita and learn the esoteric meanings of the names of the main characters of the story. In the lengthy Mahabharata epic, of which the Gita is but a small part, tradition and folklore are interwoven with symbolism in narrating the history of Bharata, an ancient King, and his descendents. The main characters of the drama are introduced in the following unusual ways:

In ancient India, at Hastinapur, there lived a king of the solar dynasty whose name was Santanu. The first of his two queens was named Ganga. When she deserted him under unusual circumstances, he wed Satyavati.

While walking beside the Ganges River, King Santanu met Ganga and asked her to be his wife. He did not then know that she was actually a manifestation of the river in human form. Ganga agreed to his proposal only after the King promised not to interfere with anything she might do after they married. If he ever questioned her actions, she declared, she would forsake him immediately.

When their first son was born, Ganga carried the infant from the palace and threw it into the river. The King, although much disturbed by her behavior, because of his prior promise not to interfere did not attempt to prevent it.

Six more sons were born, and each of them was given to the Ganges by the Queen. When the eighth son was born, the King implored her not to do with that infant as she had done with the first seven. True to her word, Ganga left her husband and her eighth son. Rushing to the Ganges River, she threw herself into it and merged in the waters.

King Santanu lavished affection upon his remaining son, Devavrata, providing for his education and training in all arts and skills befitting a prince and heir.

One day, the King went hunting in the forest. Resting under the shade of a tree by a river, he saw lotus petals floating on the waters. Following the stream of petals to their source, he saw a charming damsel, Satyavati, putting them into the river as a ritual offering.

Remaining out of the young woman's sight, the King followed her when she returned home, where she lived with her father, Dasa Raja, known as the fisher-king because his main activity was fishing. Santanu talked with Dasa Raja, requesting consent for Satyavati to be his wife.

Dasa Raja agreed, insisting, however, that his daughter must be the principal wife and that her son must be the successor to the throne.

King Santanu refused the terms of marriage and returned to his palace. As time passed, everyone around him became aware of his unhappiness. Prince Devavrata decided to do something about the situation. Without telling anyone of his plan, he went alone to Dasa Raja and asked him to consent to the marriage of Satyavati to his father. To reassure Dasa Raja about his daughter's future and that of any future sons, Prince Devavrata promised that he would not himself claim the throne, and that he would never marry or have any children. Because of these two awesome vows, Prince Devavrata thereafter became known as Bhishma (the formidable).

King Santanu and Satyavati were married. Two sons were born of their union: Chitrangada, who died at an early age, and Vichitravirya, who was peculiar and weak. After Santanu's demise, Vichitravirya became King, but because he was weak, the kingdom was really ruled by Bhishma.

When Vichitravirya grew to adulthood, Bhishma decided that he should have a queen. With this plan in mind, he went to the court of the King of Kashi, where a gathering of royal families assembled for the purpose of having their daughters choose husbands from among the princes who were invited to be there. The King of Kashi had three marriageable daughters. In keeping with the tradition of that time and culture—of sometimes kidnapping women for the purpose of marriage—Bhishma waited until the King's three daughters wandered away from the larger group, put them into his chariot, and rushed back toward Hastinapur.

The princesses' names were Amba, Ambika, and Ambalika. Amba prayed to be released because, in her heart, she had already promised herself to another. Bhishma let her go and continued on with the two remaining sisters.

King Vichitravirya, because of his weak constitution, died soon after marrying Ambika and Ambalika. His two widowed wives were then introduced to the sage Veda Vyasa, and by him each had a son. Ambika's son, Dhritarashtra, was born blind. Ambalika's son, Pandu, was of light complexion.

Bhishma continued to rule the kingdom. When the sons grew to adulthood, Pandu was put on the throne because Dhritarashtra, his older half brother who would have otherwise ruled, was blind.

Pandu had two wives, Kunti and Madri. Before her marriage, Kunti, testing the power of a mantra she had learned from a sage, inadvertently invoked the blessings of the sun and gave birth to a male child. Because it was considered to be illegitimate, the child was adopted by a carpenter and later became known as Karna, a hero of the Kaurava clan. After her marriage, Kunti invoked the gods who controlled *dharma* (righteous actions), *prana* (vital forces), and *Indra* (the god of fire, the power of transformation). From these unions were born Yudhisthira, Bhima, and Arjuna. Kunti then taught the mantra to Madri, who could only use it once. Madri invoked twin gods and begat twin sons, Nakula and Sahadeva. Because they were considered to be the progeny of Pandu, the five sons were known as the Pandavas.

When the five Pandava brothers grew to adulthood, they participated in a contest arranged by King Drupada for the purpose of having a husband chosen for his daughter, Draupadi. Participants in the contest had to lift a heavy bow, string it, and shoot an arrow through the eye of a fish that was hanging above a revolving wheel with a hole in the center. More, they had to aim at the target by looking into a reflection pool below. Arjuna, among all of the contestants, was successful. Returning to their home with Draupadi, the brothers asked Kunti, their mother, to come outside of the house to see what they had brought. She said, "Whatever you have brought, share among yourselves." Draupadi thus became the wife of the Pandavas.

The blind Dhritarashtra, half brother to King Pandu, fathered one hundred sons and one daughter, cousins to the five Pandava brothers. When King Pandu died, Duryodhana, the firstborn son of Dhritarashtra, sought the throne which he felt was rightfully his because his blind father had been denied it. When Yudhisthira, the eldest Pandava, was put on the throne instead, Duryodhana conspired to remove him from rulership of the kingdom. To do this, advised by a conspirator in the plot to use loaded dice, he challenged Yudhisthira to a dice game. It was agreed that whoever should lose would have to go into exile for twelve years, plus retire into seclusion for one year. Yudhisthira lost the game, and with his four brothers and their wife, Draupadi, departed for the agreed upon period of time. Duryodhana assumed rulership of the kingdom.

After thirteen years, the Pandava brothers returned to Hastinapur to reclaim their rights, but were refused them. Civil war was declared. All of the royal families of that region of India took sides and gathered their armies. Krishna, a king, and cousin of the Pandavas, asked the opposing factions to choose either him or his army. He would not participate in the battle, but would put his army at the disposal of whoever wanted it, while remaining with the other side.

What are we to think about this amazing story? We learn of a

Inner Meaning of the Progenitors of the Pandavas (*Chakras*)

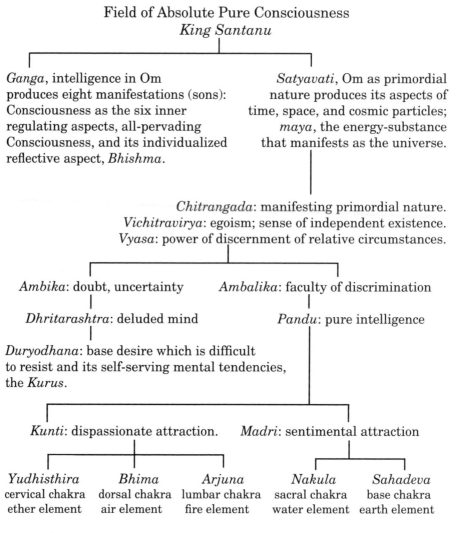

Field of Absolute Pure Consciousness
King Santanu

Ganga, intelligence in Om produces eight manifestations (sons): Consciousness as the six inner regulating aspects, all-pervading Consciousness, and its individualized reflective aspect, *Bhishma*.

Satyavati, Om as primordial nature produces its aspects of time, space, and cosmic particles; *maya*, the energy-substance that manifests as the universe.

Chitrangada: manifesting primordial nature.
Vichitravirya: egoism; sense of independent existence.
Vyasa: power of discernment of relative circumstances.

Ambika: doubt, uncertainty   *Ambalika*: faculty of discrimination

Dhritarashtra: deluded mind   *Pandu*: pure intelligence

Duryodhana: base desire which is difficult to resist and its self-serving mental tendencies, the *Kurus*.

Kunti: dispassionate attraction.   *Madri*: sentimental attraction

Yudhisthira	*Bhima*	*Arjuna*	*Nakula*	*Sahadeva*
cervical chakra	dorsal chakra	lumbar chakra	sacral chakra	base chakra
ether element	air element	fire element	water element	earth element

Draupadi: *Kundalini shakti* that vitalizes the five *chakras*.

Note: The expressive aspects of Consciousness which manifest and enliven the universe also manifest and enliven the human body and all other biological forms. Pure Consciousness pervades the universe and is individualized as souls. The soul's unfolded Self-revealed knowledge returns its awareness to cosmic consciousness, realization of oneness, and liberation.

King who weds an embodiment of the Ganges River, who, for reasons of her own, throws her first seven sons into the water and merges into the river when she is not allowed to dispatch her eighth son as she did the first seven. We learn of plural marriages, children conceived by the power of mantra, manipulative behaviors, intrigue, deception, and finally, a decision to engage in battle. An interesting story! What can we learn from it? The key to understanding the drama is to discover what the names of the characters mean and what their actions and experiences reveal. To accomplish this, we have to examine the mythical genealogy and the unique behaviors of the participants in accord with the concepts of the philosophical system known as *Samkhya* —the precise numbering and classification of the categories of the emanations and manifestations of Consciousness:

Santanu, (pure Consciousness) interacted with *Ganga* (the conscious intelligence of Om). From this interaction, eight aspects of Consciousness were produced. The first seven always remain hidden or subjective; the eighth is objective.

The seven hidden aspects which regulate subjective cosmic processes are: two aspects, cosmic and individualized, at the level of causal or fine cosmic forces of creation; two aspects, cosmic and individualized, at the level of astral or subtle life forces; two aspects, cosmic and individualized, at the level of gross physical creation; and one all-pervading aspect. Although in some religious traditions these are referred to as gods, they are not independent beings; they represent the various intelligence-directed influences and powers of Consciousness.

In Vedic scriptures, the two aspects at the causal level are, together, referred to as *Vishnu*, that which preserves or maintains. The two aspects at the astral level are referred to as *Brahma*, that which expands and causes manifestation. The two aspects at the physical level are referred to as *Shiva*, that which causes change and transformation; also *Maheshvara*, the "great lord" or ruler. The seventh unseen aspect is the Spirit of God pervading the cosmos without itself being confined to or limited by it.

The eighth aspect, which does not remain hidden, is cosmic individuality or *Bhishma* (the witness or perceiving aspect of Consciousness which participates in outer affairs but is not itself the determining factor. Because it is unmarried (aloof from creation), it does not produce anything. It and the Spirit of God are like two faces of Consciousness: the former looks outward into the realm of objective Nature, the latter remains hidden. The Sanskrit word for the all-pervading Spirit, the consciousness of God aspect, is *Kutastha Chaitanya*, "the one on the summit." It is sometimes referred to by Hindu devotees as Krishna Consciousness. Some devotees personalize it in order to feel themselves to be in close relationship to it.

Interacting with the unconscious side of Nature, *Satyavati* (the intelligent principles of primordial Nature — Om expressive as fine cosmic forces, space, and time — which embodies *sat* or truth), the enlivening aspect of Consciousness causes the primordial field of Nature, *maya* — that which is form-building and truth-veiling — to undergo changes which cause outward manifestation of itself. The first to manifest (the first child of Satyavati) is the aspect of the field of primordial Nature undergoing mutation from fine to gross expression which does not last long (*Chitrangada*). Satyavati's second son, *Vichitravirya* (the false or deluded sense of independent existence, ego consciousness) which, although peculiar (different) and weak, is necessary for the processes of creation to occur. Because it is contractive, it is relatively powerless. It conceals knowledge but is not possessed of knowledge.

The two wives of ego consciousness (*Vichitravirya*) are doubt (*Ambika*) and the power of discrimination (*Ambalika*). The other sister, *Amba*, chose not to marry because she was promised to another (involved with sensation through the lower chakras). In the story, Vichitravirya weakened and died soon after marrying his wives. It was then arranged for them to have children by the sage *Veda Vyasa* (wisdom-knowledge). From knowledge and doubt (*Ambika*) blind mind (*Dhritarashtra*) is born. From knowledge and the power of discrimination (*Ambalika*) pure intelligence (*Pandu*) is born.

In the Mahabharata story, it is said that Dhritarashtra and his wives had one hundred sons and a daughter. This means that blind or deluded mind, influenced by sentiment or feeling, produces numberless self-serving tendencies. The first of these was *Duryodhana* (passion, lower desire that is difficult to fight or resist, which causes many problems). Although Dhritarashtra and Pandu belonged to the Kuru clan, only Dhritarashtra became known as the chief representative of the clan because, with Bhishma's help, he ruled the kingdom.

Pandu (pure intelligence) with his two wives: *Kunti* (kundalini's power of attraction, dispassionate compassion, and discernment which banishes error) and *Madri* (intellect influenced by sentiment) secluded himself in the forest and was, therefore, away from the kingdom (of the mind). Yogis teach the front part of the body to be the realm of mental and physical impulses and tendencies. The back, the spinal pathway, rules spiritual inclinations. Dhritarashtra's children are referred to as

Kauravas (representative of the self-serving, destructive or trouble-causing tendencies and habits rooted in the mind) which are considered to be enemies of the soul's aspiration to enlightened understanding. Pure intelligence, like Pandu in the story, remains aloof, while the mind, like Dhritarashtra, rules material affairs.

By the power of mantra, the two wives of Pandu produced five sons, referred to as the *Pandavas* (the products of pure intelligence). *Kunti* (kundalini's power of attraction, dispassionate compassion, and discernment which banishes error) produced three sons: Yudhisthira, Bhima, and Arjuna. They symbolize the true essences (*tattvas*) of the subtle elements of the three higher chakras in the spinal pathway.

Yudhisthira (righteousness, dharma, steadfast and firm) represents the ether element essence of the throat chakra at the cervical section of the spine: *Vishudda*, the pure. The sound frequency is of the ocean's roar, the mingling of all of the sounds of prana frequencies of the chakras. The color is misty grey with sparkling points of light. The taste is sour. The seed (*bija*) mantra, is *Ham* (pronounced "hum").

Bhima (dauntlessness, pranayama, control of vital forces, endless strength, formidable) represents the air element essence of the heart center at the dorsal section of the spine: *Anahata*, unstruck sound—like the peal of a gong. The color is blue. The taste is salty. The seed mantra is *Yam* ("yum").

Arjuna (purity of mind and heart, the aspiration to excellence, fiery self-control) represents the fire element essence of the lumbar chakra, midway between the higher and lower chakras: *Manipura*, the city of gems. The color is red. The sound frequency is as of a harp. The taste is pungent. The seed mantra is *Ram* ("rum").

Pandu's second wife, *Madri* (spiritual intellect influenced by sentiment), gave birth to twins, which symbolize the element influences of the two lower chakras:

Nakula (the stillness of the mind, the power to adhere) represents the water element essence of the chakra at the sacral region of the spine: *Swadisthan*, the abode of the Self. The color is of a white crescent moon. The sound frequency is of a flute. The taste is astringent. The seed mantra is *Vam* ("vum").

Sahadeva (the power of resistance) represents the earth element essence of the chakra at the bottom of the spine: *Muladhara*, foundation. The color is yellow. The sound frequency is like the buzzing of disturbed bees. The taste is bitter. The seed mantra is *Lam* ("lum").

Draupadi, the common wife of the five Pandava brothers, represents *kundalini shakti*: the flowing, harmonizing, enlivening actions of the creative power of the soul expressive in the body. The five sons of

Draupadi are the sound and light frequencies perceived in the chakras when they are energized by the actions of kundalini shakti.

The eldest Pandava brother, *Yudhisthira* (righteousness, tranquility) the fifth chakra state of consciousness, gambled with his eldest cousin, *Duryodhana* (egotism, lower desire, jealousy, pride), lost the match, and was banished. When righteousness plays with unrighteousness, when soul awareness gambles with conditioned mental tendencies and sense attractions, errors in judgment can occur, causing clouding of awareness. To reclaim the former status, one must withdraw for a duration to become grounded in the virtues, engage in spiritual practices, and again confront that which restricts the soul's freedom of expression and the fulfillment of its destiny; hence, the symbolism of the Pandavas having to be exiled, going into seclusion, and returning to engage in battle.

When Krishna (enlightened consciousness) offered his services to one of the opposing factions and his army to the other, the *Kauravas* (the self-serving mental tendencies) chose the army. The Pandavas chose Krishna, who agreed to drive Arjuna's chariot. The outcome of the forthcoming contest was then already decided, for where there is Krishna (enlightened consciousness), victory is certain.

Translating and commenting on the Bhagavad Gita requires alert attention to details regarding the intent of the original author[s]. It is believed by some scholars that, through the years, minor changes were made in the text and perhaps some additional material included. Also, for many centuries before the invention of the printing press, the entirety of the Mahabharata, which includes the eighteen chapters of the Gita, was communicated by storytellers who had memorized it. The elaborate, colorful, and often dramatic narration made it easy to remember and popular with people in all walks of life. Even without knowledge of its inner meaning, listeners (and, later, readers) could derive benefit at whatever level the message was comprehended. At an exoteric level, there is much of value to be learned in regard to meaningful human existence, the well-being of society, and the importance and usefulness of sustained spiritual aspiration. The esoteric message has value to those who are perceptive enough to understand and benefit from it. Because the concepts set forth in the story were already well-known when it was composed, the information is considered to be traditional, or remembered, knowledge rather than a new revelation. It is, however, accepted as an authentic Scripture of Yoga.

The story begins as a great war between rival factions is about to start. The incidents described and the dialogue provided for the symbolic characters, portray the drama of individual psychological transformation and spiritual growth. The words attributed to Arjuna and Krishna, and of the few other characters who are given lines to speak, were written for the purpose of describing timeless truths.

Dhritarashtra represents unenlightened mind, the father of the physical aspects of Nature and ruler of the kingdom of the senses. Knowledge of transformative processes cannot be apprehended by a mind governed by partial understanding devoid of discernment. In the story, Dhritarashtra is blind and at a place distant from where the armies have gathered; he relies on his counselor, Sanjaya, to report on what is transpiring. Sanjaya, with powers of clairvoyance which enable him to see with inner vision, represents every person's faculty of impartial intuitive perception that, when called upon during interludes of introspection, provides insight. The story begins with Dhritarashtra's question:

Assembled on dharmakshetra-kurukshetra, desirous to fight, what did my sons and the sons of Pandu do, Sanjaya?

Dharma is righteousness, virtue, morality: that which upholds or supports evolution's inclination toward transformation, growth, and expression. The impulses of Consciousness which enhance life are dharmic. *Kshetra* is the field (place) where actions occur. The word *kuru* is used to refer to the characteristics and tendencies of the deluded mind. This first verse sets the stage for the drama which is to take place in the field where righteousness confronts unrighteousness. Where is this field? Since the story describes the soul's return of awareness to wholeness, the place where righteousness must overcome unrighteousness is the devotee's individualized awareness.

Arjuna's questions and comments testify to the soul's aspiration to awaken to Self-knowledge and realization of God, and of its conflicts, struggles, and endeavors to learn what is true and how to actualize it. In the story, Arjuna is portrayed as a warrior who must fulfill his duty in a responsible manner. He represents the soul at a critical stage of spiritual growth, still somewhat grounded in physical and mental awareness and its concerns (third chakra characteristics), yet beginning to awaken to higher understanding. The progression of unfoldment is from confusion to the fourth chakra devotee stage devoid of ego-fixation; the fifth chakra stage of apprehension of truth; the sixth chakra stage of revelation; and final unfoldment of innate knowledge that culminates in permanent illumination of consciousness.

Krishna represents the accessible, grace-imparting reality of God that, while ever omnipresent, omniscient, and omnipotent, is also the indwelling reality of every soul and creature. Krishna's words are not to be thought of as the actual words of a historical personage; they represent Self-revealed knowledge that unfolds from the innermost level of being when one is prepared to recognize and comprehend it.

When reading the Gita, instead of thinking of the events described in the story as having occurred at another place and time, or the characters as real people, remember that what is described is every person's quest for understanding and personal endeavor to experience the unfoldment of innate potential. When reading the words attributed to Arjuna, you may recognize some of your own characteristics and attitudes. When reading statements attributed to Krishna, you are being reminded of the mind-cleansing, soul-liberating knowledge you already have within you.

To facilitate easier reading, I have not italicized Sanskrit words except in special instances where a word definition is given. More comprehensive definitions of some common Sanskrit words used in the body of the text are provided in the glossary at the end of the book. Because an understanding of the meanings of the names of some of the characters in the story can be helpful, the following list is provided:

Abhimayu. High-minded, above passion.

Amba, Ambalika, and Ambika. Three daughters (products) of the King of Kashi who represents shining qualities, who were kidnapped by Bhishma to be wives of King Vichitravirya (ego consciousness). Amba refused to wed because in her heart she was pledged to another. Ambalika (power of discrimination) and Ambika (doubt) are the two "wives" or companion-characteristics of ego consciousness. Ambalika (power of discrimination) gave birth to Pandu (pure intelligence). Ambika (doubt) gave birth to Dhritarashtra (blind or deluded mind).

Anantavijaya. Power that eternally subdues, unfolded spiritual qualities, endlessly conquering.

Arjuna. Purity of mind and heart, fiery energy, the lumbar chakra.

Asvatthaman. Worldliness, superficiality, love of transient things, fantasy, imagination, that which will not last until the dawn.

Bhima. Dauntlessness, control of breath (prana), control of the forces of nature, endless strength, the formidable, the dorsal chakra.

Bhishma. Reflected Consciousness, cosmic individuality; corresponds to individualized soul awareness, the cause of egoism.

Bhurisravas. Irreverence, lack of devotion, frequent movement.

Chekitana. Higher intelligence, seeing through the illusory veil of nature, intensely shining.

Chitrangada. First son of Satyavati and Santanu. Om manifesting as the mutation stage, which does not last long. *See Satyavati.*

Devadatta. Devotion, the power to abide in the Divine, the gift of God.

Dhrishtadyumna. Self-control, leader of spiritual forces, intense light or splendor.

Dhristaketu. That by which obstacles are banished, restraint, the first step in yoga, intense flame.

Dhritarashtra. Blind mind, delusion, the firm kingdom.

Draupadi. Loyalty, the child of keen perception, energy of kundalini, common wife of the five Pandava brothers (the chakras).

Drona. Revolution through experience in material realms, active support of lifestyle to complete destiny. Samskaras or mental impressions because of experience which can be either constructively or destructively influential until regulated, neutralized, or transcended. When they are influential they contribute to mental fluctuations and transformations.

Drupada. Keen penetration, concentration, pure love, swift-footed, omniscience.

Duryodhana. Passion, lower desire which fights insistently to accomplish its ends and is difficult to overcome, jealousy, pride, egotism.

Gandhari. Dhritarashtra's wife, mother of the Kauravas (self-serving mental tendencies); that aspect of the mind which acquiesces to its actions and their results.

Gandiva. Bow or bridge to divinity, a present given to Arjuna by Agni, the god of fire. Some yogis say that the steady, upright spine of one sitting in meditation is the bow that overcomes the enemies of restlessness and subconscious resistance to practice.

Hanuman. The spiritual light, principle of discernment.

Ganga. In the *Mahabharata* epic, the personification of the Ganges River, the first wife of King Santanu who threw her first seven sons into the Ganges, then herself merged in the waters of the river after the birth of her eighth son, Devavrata, whose name was later changed to Bhishma. Ganga represents the creative force of God, Om, endowed with guiding or governing intelligence.

Karna. Selfishness, bigotry, immoral or unrighteous desire which has become an opposition to spiritual growth and which can, if one has the resolve to overcome it, be a stimulus to growth.

King of Kashi. Divine pleasure, enthusiasm, a sun-quality, the shining, inner light of knowledge.

Kripa. Kindliness and pity without discrimination, sentiment, emotion, resignation.

Krishna. The Universal or Supreme Self which produces, enlivens, and maintains the universe—and is the indwelling true Self or Being of every person and living thing.

Kunti. Kundalini energy with power to attract, dispassionate compassion, discernment which banishes error, mother of the first three Pandava brothers (the three upper *chakras* in the spinal pathway).

Kuntibhoja. Peace and pleasure derived from the removal of negative tendencies, power of attracting spiritual experiences.

Kuru. Ancestor of both the Kauravas and the Pandus. The Kauravas represent the dark, heavy, or tamasic forces, the undeveloped thus destructive or trouble-causing tendencies. The Pandus or Pandavas represent the sattvic and rajasic forces, the unfolded thus constructive or life-enhancing influences.

Kurukshetra. The field of individualized soul awareness, the body, the plane or field of self-conscious awareness and of mental activity where ego-directed influences are confronted by the soul's aspiration to actualize its innate spiritual qualities which are *dharmic*: supportive of orderly unfoldments of evolutionary actions. The field of individualized soul awareness where righteous inclinations are in a contest with unrighteous tendencies is named dharmakshetra-kurukshetra.

Madri. Pandu's second wife, mother of the Pandava twins (the two lower chakras), spiritual intellect which is compassionate.

Manipushpaka. The spiritual powers of one with higher understanding, a wise person.

Nakula. One of the Pandava twins (the second chakra), the silence of the mind, night. Inward resistance to unrighteousness.

Panchajanya. The power of Krishna (Divine Consciousness) that extends over all creation, represented by the sound of Om.

Pandu. Pure intelligence, inner knowing of divinity, the father of the spiritual side of nature. The Pandavas represent the virtues and are related to the five chakras in the spinal pathway.

Paundra. Courage or valor that shatters all that opposes.

Prince of Kashi. Spiritual splendor, light.

Purujit. Control of mind and senses; many-conquering; the fifth stage of raja yoga meditation practice when attention and vital forces are internalized, thus effectively removing awareness from involvements with mental and sensory processes so that contemplation of transcendent realities can flow smoothly.

Sahadeva. The other Pandava twin (first chakra), spiritual awareness, devotion.

Saiva. Blessedness, the enlightenment that brings liberation.

Sanjaya. Reflection, introspection, the completely victorious.

Santanu. Eternal tranquility, Pure Consciousness which "weds" or interacts with Ganga (Om) to produce eight sons or aspects of expressive Consciousness. The first seven aspects are subjective, merged with Om (the Ganges, the river of life), and regulate cosmic processes. The eighth remains objective as reflected Consciousness, Cosmic Individuality or Bhishma.

Satyaki. Truth; Krishna's charioteer. Also known as Yuyudhana: truth, faith, (wishing to contest the opposition).

Satyavati. Om, expressive as primordial nature which embodies truth or Spirit, second wife of Santanu. Her first son, product of interaction between eternal Pure Consciousness and Om in the manifesting aspect, was Chitrangada, the aspect of mutation from fine to gross manifestation, which is why, in the story, it soon died. Her second son was Vichitravirya, the false or deluded self-sense, egoism, *ahamkara* or false sense of independent existence, which is why it was peculiar and weak.

Sikhandin. Illumination, halo of spirituality, bearing a crest.

Somadatta. Inconstancy, gift of the moon.

Subhadra. Auspiciousness, happiness due to kindness. Beautiful, fortunate; one of Arjuna's wives.

Sugosha. The power of harmony, pleasing sound.

Uttamaujas. Highest valor, highest strength.

Vichitravirya. Second son of Satyavati and Santanu. *See Satyavati.*

Vidura. Realized state of pure consciousness.

Vikarna. Heresy of hatred, repulsion, dislike, a strong helm.

Virata. Spiritual eye vision, insight, revealing.

Yudhamanyu. The quality of dispassion.

Yudhisthira. Righteousness, *dharma*, tranquil while firm in battle, the first Pandava brother, the throat chakra.

Each chapter title includes the word *yoga* to indicate an

approach to knowledge and experience of God. *Yoga* can mean
practice or procedure, unification of the individualized field of
consciousness with Universal Consciousness, or samadhi—realization of wholeness experienced when the mind is devoid of
fluctuations which are characteristic of its restless condition.
Because wholeness is the natural state of soul consciousness, it
is not considered as a state to be created or a goal to be achieved.
When soul awareness is removed from all that is transient and
restored to pure consciousness, wholeness is experienced.

THE BHAGAVAD GITA
With Interpretation and Commentary

CHAPTER ONE

The Yoga of the Despondency of Arjuna

As the story begins, the unenlightened soul is confronted by a challenge which it perceives as being of immense proportions, yet which affords an exceptional opportunity to learn of the dynamic processes of life and to outgrow conditioned limitations. Because the confusion and despair that some devotees experience during early stages of spiritual growth may indicate that necessary transformative changes must occur if the devotee is to be restored to right understanding, this temporary phase of despondency is also called yoga.

Dhritarashtra [deluded mind] asked:

1. **Assembled in dharmakshetra-kurukshetra, desirous to fight, what did my sons and the sons of Pandu do, O Sanjaya?**

   Assembled in the field of righteousness-the field of unrighteousness, alert and prepared for confrontation, what did the self-serving mental tendencies and the virtuous soul qualities do? Introspective discrimination, reveal to me the outcome.

The soul, realizing that it is incapable of perceiving the facts of prevailing circumstances while identified with the unenlightened mind (Dhritarashtra), resorts to introspection and inquires: What is happening in mind-body awareness (dharmakshetra, the field of virtue-kurukshetra, the field of unrighteousness) where multitudes of ego-driven mental tendencies (the sons of deluded mind) confront righteous impulses (the sons of Pandu), with both sides intent on being victorious?

Superconsciousness is the basis of soul awareness. When the waking state, sleep with dreams, and dreamless sleep are experienced, pervading these conditioned states is our awareness that is ever observing what is occurring at all levels. Even when confused or in the throes of emotion, we can still be aware that we are other than the dominant mental and emotional states. We also intuitively know that at our innermost center of being are all the answers to our questions, the source of solutions to all problems, and the perfect peace that remains regardless of our temporary surface involvements.

Sanjaya [introspective intuition] replied:

2. **Seeing the army of the sons of Pandu ready for battle, King Duryodhana, approaching his teacher [Drona] spoke these words:**

    Aware that virtuous qualities were fully prepared to confront and eliminate all the self-serving tendencies and characteristics, passionate desire to ensure their survival [Duryodhana] directed the mind to its "teacher," its storehouse of memories: impressions [samskaras] of prior perceptions and experiences which support the karmic or conditioned, material lifestyle.

3. **Behold, O teacher, this mighty army of the sons of Pandu, arrayed by the son of Drupada who is wise because of your instruction;**

    O storehouse of memories, see the great assemblage of the virtuous qualities [the sons], born of pure intelligence [Pandu], which are directed by the inner light [Dhrishtadyumna, a quality of kundalini] supported by knowledge based on experience.

Duryodhana represents self-serving desire, the first son or impulse of Dhritarashtra, deluded mind which is difficult to overcome, nurtured in this instance by thoughts of superiority because of memories of past accomplishments. When this kind of desire is strong, even though virtuous impulses in opposition to it are acknowledged, it feels as though it is able to persist and prevail. The son of Drupada (penetrative concentration and omniscience) is Dhrishtadyumna, the inner light, the leader of the forces of virtue. Duryodhana, self-serving desire, supported by its memories, falsely assumes that the inner light is wise because of having been trained by the same teacher. In the *Mahabharata* epic the Kauravas (mental sentiments and tendencies) and the Pandus (virtuous qualities of the soul) were trained in the art of accomplishment by Drona, mental impressions of experience.

However, the deluded mind tends to become increasingly conditioned and restricted by memories of its perceptions and experiences, while the impressions upon the mind made by the inner light have entirely constructive influences.

4. **Here are heroes, mighty archers. In battle they are equal to Bhima, Arjuna, Yuyudhana and Virata, and the great warrior Drupada;**

   Here are heroic qualities, skillful in action. In any contest they are equal to innate strength and life force control, fiery will power, faith-based determination, and equanimity in all circumstances;

5. **Dhristaketu, Chekitana, the King of Kashi, known for valor, Purujit, Kuntibhoja, and Saibya who is strong among them;**

   Restraint which removes all obstacles, higher intelligence, enthusiasm, mastery of mental and sensory impulses, peace and satisfaction when overcoming obstacles, and concentrated discipline giving superior strength;

6. **And the powerful Yudhamanyu, valorous Uttamaujas, the son of Subhadra and the sons of Draupadi, all of them are indeed great warriors.**

   And dispassion, bravery in actions, happiness arising from kindness, and the enlivened powers of kundalini expressing through the chakras, all of them extremely effective.

When we are simultaneously aware of our ego-centered desires and of our soul-impelled inclinations, we may feel that we are willing to do the right thing but the conditioned behaviors are also compelling. We may be aware of our virtues and soul qualities while, at the same time, want to fulfill the impulses and urgings of the senses and restless mind. Even when aware of our potential for choosing the right course of action, we may feel ourselves to be at the mercy of our desires, whims, and habitual behaviors which are rooted in the memory of past experiences. If we are mentally perverse (inclined to twist valid information to suit our self-centered interests) or willfully inclined to perform actions which are life-restricting rather than life-enhancing, we may actively resist our nobler impulses, choosing the darkness of ignorance and its consequent painful effects to the light of knowledge and its redemptive influences. At such times we may review our ego-supported qualities, as described in the following verses.

7. **Know now our own distinguished warriors, O highest of the twice-born! I describe the leaders by their proper names;**

    Be aware of whom our army consists! I shall name and describe them;

8. **Yourself, Bhishma, Karna, and Kripa, Asvatthaman who is victorious in battle, Vikarna, also the sons of Somadatta;**

    Memories of experiences which support change and transformation, strong sense of individuality, worldliness which is attached to superficial and transient things and circumstances, hatred or strong dislike, and inconstancy;

9. **And many other heroes willing to risk their lives for my sake, with various weapons at their command and all of them skilled in battle;**

    And the many other psychological tendencies with addictive drives to protect and support strong desires, with their many ways of expressing and all of them effective in their actions.

10. **Our army, guarded by Bhishma, is sufficient; the army guarded by Bhima is insufficient.**

    The psychological tendencies and drives, defended by a strong sense of individuality, are sufficient to meet the challenge; the virtuous qualities, defended by life force control are insufficient.

11. **Therefore, during the progress of this contest, let each of you be in your assigned place, and protect Bhishma!**
    In this contest about to begin, let each of you play your specific role. Protect individualized awareness!

When egocentric self-consciousness, with its firmly structured psychological nature, gathers its forces to protect itself against unwanted change or transformation, all of its habits and conditioned characteristics rally to its defense. Then, feeling smug and falsely secure, one may endeavor to actively resist useful or constructive change for the better. In verse seven, the words "twice-born" are used to flatter, to attempt to strengthen and encourage the memories (samskaras) which support the mind's actions. In actuality, one who is twice-born is awake to spiritual realities.

When in a self-centered, decided, and defensive mode, one may, under the spell of delusion and illusion, mistakenly presume to be more powerful and capable than all of the soul qualities. Thus, in the narration, passionate desire impels the thought: "Because we (the array of instinctive drives and conditioned tendencies supported by memories of experience) are many and strong, our forces are sufficient while the forces of virtue and righteousness are not sufficient—not equal to the task of overcoming us." There is seldom any chance that reason can be brought to bear to transform the deluded mental condition. What is needed is to introduce into it the transformative influences of awakened soul awareness.

12. To encourage and give happiness to Duryodhana, the aged Kuru, [Bhishma], roaring like a lion, powerfully blew his conch.

To rally the psychological tendencies and drives, and to stimulate and nurture desire to prevail, individualized self-sense aroused vital forces to stir and energize the senses.

13. Suddenly, the conch horns, kettledrums, cymbals, small drums, and trumpets all tumultuously sounded.

Immediately, the intensity of stimulated desires and energized senses became more pronounced.

When ego-based, false, and insubstantial confidence neutralizes our attempts at rational thinking, we may erroneously believe that we are capable of fulfilling our personal desires. Pseudo-confidence may result in a release of energy that somewhat empowers us to proceed in the direction we have chosen or to endeavor to obtain the object of our urgent desire.

14. **Then, standing in the great chariot yoked to white horses, Lord Krishna and Arjuna the son of Pandu, also sounded their glorious conches.**

The indwelling Spirit of God that commands the senses and the soul's ardent aspiration to prevail, also manifested signs of evidential powers.

15. **Krishna sounded his Panchajanya; Arjuna sounded his Devadatta; Bhima, of mighty deeds, blew the great conch horn Paundra.**

The Spirit of God manifested as the sound of Om; the sound of the prana frequencies of the lumbar chakra also resounded, as did that of the dorsal chakra.

16. **Yudhisthira blew Anantavijaya; Nakula and Sahadeva sounded Sugosha and Manipushpaka.**

The prana frequencies at the cervical chakra, and at the sacral and base chakras also manifested.

17. **The King of Kashi, the supreme archer, and Sikhandin, the great warrior; Dhrishtadyumna, Virata, and Satyaki the invincible:**

Enthusiasm, spirituality; self-control, the virtue of equanimity, and invincible truth consciousness, were enlivened and manifested.

18. **Drupada, and the sons of Draupadi, and the son of Subhadra, O Lord of earth, all sounded their respective conches.**

Concentrated pure love and omniscience, kundalini shakti's chakra manifestations and their qualities, were also expressive.

Krishna, as the driver of Arjuna's chariot with white horses, symbolizes the indwelling Spirit of God as the soul in control of the purified senses.

When the devotee's attention turns inward during meditation, Om, the primordial sound may be heard. Om is evidence of the reality of God because it flows from the Field of God. It is heard internally, flowing from the soul. Here, Om is portrayed as Krishna's horn or trumpet, with which he produces a commanding sound to make his presence known to both the qualities of virtue and the tendencies of the deluded mind.

Before the sound of Om is heard, other sound frequencies emanating from the kundalini-enlivened chakras may be perceived: buzzing like disturbed bees from the base chakra, the note of a flute at the second chakra, the resonance of a harp at the third chakra, the peal of a gong at the fourth chakra, and the mixture of sounds at the cervical chakra. A variety of sounds may be discerned as various prana influences interact and their forces manifest. By merging awareness in these sounds until the clear stream of Om is heard (and is eventually transcended), the accomplished meditator successfully withdraws feelings and attention from physical and mental phenomena and experiences progressive stages of superconscious perception:

- Preliminary superconscious (samadhi) experiences related to the base chakra are of somewhat clear comprehension mixed with mental confusion and doubt about the validity of the perception.
- Superconscious experience related to the sacral chakra is characterized by steadier concentration and improved comprehension of what is being experienced.
- Superconscious experience related to the lumbar chakra is characterized by improved concentration and a sense of elation because of emerging signs of Self-mastery.
- Superconscious experience related to the dorsal chakra is characterized by awareness of egocentric self-consciousness dissolving to allow apprehension of oneness or wholeness.
- Superconscious experience related to the throat chakra is characterized by awareness and knowledge that all conditions which formerly obscured realization of the soul nature are being overcome or transcended. This allows true Self-knowledge or realization.
- Superconscious experience related to the spiritual eye and crown chakra allows spontaneous unfoldment of knowledge of God and of cosmic processes, and realization of pure consciousness.

19. The great noise burst asunder the hearts of the sons of Dhritarashtra, and reverberated through the earth and sky.

The overwhelming sounds of the prana frequencies of the chakras severely disturbed the psychological tendencies and drives rooted in self-consciousness, and spread throughout the devotee's body, mind, and field of awareness.

As Om contemplation becomes more concentrated, the superior influences of the primordial sound disrupt the coordinated, conditioned actions of the mind, weakening and dissolving destructive drives while constructively impressing the mind with entirely beneficial characteristics. Eventually, darkness and heaviness (tamasic influences) and restlessness (rajasic influences) are eliminated and only luminous (sattvic influences) remain. Thus, for mastery of sensory impulses and mental processes, alert practice of pranayama followed by contemplative meditation is far superior to internal dialogue or superficial endeavors.

20. Arjuna, his chariot bearing the banner of Hanuman, seeing the sons of Dhritarashtra at their battle stations, as the clash of weapons [almost] began, took up his bow.

Concentrated aspiration reinforced by soul-will, under the sign of victory, aware of the impulses of self-serving psychological tendencies and their resistance to change, prepared to confront them.

The banner of Hanuman, the monkey-god devotee of Rama in the *Ramayana* epic, signifies one who will be victorious. Confident of victory, seeing what must be done, the devotee takes up the arms of righteousness, fully willing and prepared to successfully engage in life's processes and awaken through the stages of spiritual growth. For the God-surrendered devotee, the banner of Hanuman symbolizes the radiance of the soul that protects one from being unduly reactive to destructive mental tendencies and weakens their influences.

Arjuna's taking up of his bow indicates that the devotee, aware of the need to confront obstacles which oppose spiritual unfoldment, with inspired determination sits to meditate.

21. Then, Arjuna spoke these words to Krishna: Imperishable One, put my chariot between the two armies,

Concentrated aspiration reinforced by soul-will chose to be aware of pure consciousness positioned between the contesting forces,

Arjuna continues to speak:

22. So that I may see those whom I must fight.

So that obstacles to accomplishment can be apprehended.

23. I now behold those who are assembled, eager and willing to serve the material-minded son of Dhritarashtra.

All of the tendencies and actions resulting from mental delusion, which are obstacles to spiritual growth and illumination of consciousness, are now clearly seen and known.

When we take our stand for right action, we center ourselves spiritually by establishing ourselves in awareness of our true nature as an individualized expression of pure consciousness. This is the explanation of why Arjuna (the aspiring devotee) asked Krishna (innate pure consciousness) to be positioned between the opposing factions. As Krishna did not take part in the battle but only remained on the side of righteousness, so pure consciousness does not directly act, but makes possible all actions. When we are established in soul awareness, we can clearly see what our duty is and know how to effectively perform it.

Sanjaya said:

24. Thus directed by Arjuna, Krishna, driving the most magnificent chariot, placed it between the two armies.

In response to the soul's urge to clearly perceive the facts of conditions as they are, innate knowledge along with intuition unfolds to enable the devotee to examine both sides of the situation.

25. In front of Bhishma, Drona, and all the other leaders, Krishna said: Arjuna, behold these Kurus here assembled.

Aware of reflective, individualized consciousness, memories, and other influential conditioned tendencies, soul consciousness chose to analyze the various psychological conditions restricting its expression.

Distinct from individuality (Bhishma), the causes of actions which contribute to transformational experiences (Drona) and the various other influential characteristics of mundane spheres, knowledge and intuition enable the devotee to be aware of all obstacles to spiritual growth and the tendencies which support them, as well as to apprehend the soul's innate, constructive life-enhancing qualities. In the story, the cousins on both sides of the contest are members of the Kuru clan descended from common ancestors, just as individuals have psychological and spiritual characteristics derived from common causes. Egoism, the false sense of selfhood which causes a soul to feel itself to be independent of God, is the progenitor of the self-conscious condition with its diverse characteristics. Even though God's Consciousness is the origin of souls and their characteristics, the effects of egoism are apparent because consciousness expresses through clouded awareness and mental conditionings.

26. **Arjuna saw fathers, grandfathers, teachers, maternal uncles, brothers, sons, grandsons, and their friends standing there.**
27. **He saw fathers-in-law and companions in both armies. When he saw all these kinsmen thus arrayed,**
28. **Overcome with pity and sadness, impelled by excessive compassion, Arjuna said: O Krishna, having seen my own kinsmen desiring to fight,**

Arjuna continues to speak:

29. **My limbs grow limp, my mouth becomes dry, my body trembles, and my hair stands on end.**
30. **My bow slips from my hand, my skin burns as with fever; I am unable to stand firm, my mind wavers.**

On the opposing side delusion is perceived, the father or cause of births and deaths and of known and unknown actions; the grandfather [Bhishma], reflective or individualized consciousness; the teachers, mental impressions, the basis of memory; the maternal grandfathers, the mental waves of restlessness and material desire [vrittis]; brothers, surges of egoism; sons, the products of egoism; grandsons, random waves of desires; and their friends, among them Asvatthaman, wishful thinking and fantasy. On the righteous side is perceived Drupada, omniscience, the father of kundalini; and many other mental waves [vrittis] of helpful inclinations.

When the devotee becomes simultaneously aware of the characteristics and influential tendencies of the self-conscious (egocentric) condition and of the innate soul qualities and capacities, and understands that, because they are often in opposition, the self-conscious characteristics will have to be eliminated or transformed, lethargy and despair may be experienced. The challenge may seem awesome, and attachment to personality traits may cause excessive, unreasoned compassion to be expressed as blind, emotion-based sentiment. One may feel weak, insecure, and afraid. A self-conscious person may have become so accustomed to personality-based views and circumstances that the very thought of having to modify attitudes, psychological traits, and behaviors may represent a formidable challenge even though aspiration to spiritual growth is present.

Arjuna's bow, which his hand releases, represents the weapon of firm resolve and will-to-accomplish without which neither meditative concentration nor purposeful living are possible. The weak-willed devotee is unstable because the mind is dominated by restlessness and confusion. What is needed is improved understanding, alert curiosity about the possibilities of apprehending higher realities, and undiminished aspiration to spiritually awaken. Arjuna's bow is also said to represent the upright spine of the meditator who is alert and intent on discovery. The bow falling from Arjuna's hand indicates inattentiveness to meditation practice.

The Sanskrit word *vritti* refers to fluctuations that occur in the unsettled mind, causing thoughts to ripple through the mind that incite tendencies to action or stimulate desires. These wave-like actions are to be calmed and returned to a dormant state so that awareness can be clear and undisturbed. The samadhi of pure consciousness is then experienced. When pure consciousness is not the constant experience, soul awareness is inclined to be involved with the effects of the actions of the vrittis, the modifications of the mind described as either afflicted, painful, impure, and restrictive—or not afflicted, not painful, pure, and not restrictive.

In this verse, the soul is described as being able to apprehend mental influences which are in opposition to its aspiration to spiritual growth and the mental waves of helpful inclinations.

31. I perceive omens of misfortune, O Krishna; nor can I see any good resulting from the slaying of my kinsmen in battle.

32. I do not desire victory, nor royal status, nor pleasures. What is the value of such kingship [self-mastery and Self-realization]

to us, or enjoyment, or life itself?

When one's reason is overcome with emotion, rational thinking is impaired. One may then speculate about the challenges that lie ahead and predict difficulties. Clouded intelligence may result in unreasoned attempts at self-justification for the purpose of preserving existing circumstances, and may cause one to assert that eliminating discomforting psychological characteristics is wrong; that no good can come of it. It may seem that without the companionship of thoughts, feelings, and opinions which have become habitual, life is not worth living. Arjuna is portrayed as saying that he cannot see any worthwhile outcome by going ahead with the contest. The higher life which can be realized by application of knowledge cannot be apprehended by the devotee whose mind is overcome with conflict and heaviness (tamas guna). Arjuna's words reveal but a limited view of life and its possibilities, as we will soon learn.

33. **Those for whose sake we desire rulership, enjoyments, and pleasures, are arrayed here before us, having renounced their lives and their riches.**
34. **Teachers, fathers, sons, and also grandfathers, maternal uncles, fathers-in-law, grandsons, brothers-in-law, and others who are related.**
35. **Though they are intent upon killing me, I do not desire to kill them, not even for sovereignty of the three worlds; how much less then for the earth?**
36. **What happiness can we have by striking down the sons of Dhritarashtra, O Krishna? Having thus banished these aggressors, misfortune would be our lot.**
37. **Therefore, it is not right for us to kill our kinsmen, the sons of Dhritarashtra. Having done so, how could we be happy, O Krishna?**
38. **Even if those whose thoughts are overpowered by greed do not see the wrong caused by the destruction of the family or the crime of treachery to friends,**
39. **Why should we not have the power of discernment to see the unwisdom of destruction of the family and turn away from this contest?**

As is characteristic of one who is depressed, emotional, and somewhat irrational, Arjuna continues to defend his point of view. The devotee at this stage is still attached to the human condition and wants to defend it. Addressing his own higher consciousness (Krishna), Arjuna naively states, "It is not right for us to do away with the characteristics (the sons or products) of blind mind (Dhritarashtra). The devotee is fully aware of the existence of nonuseful and harmful psychological tendencies but cannot exercise enough power of soul-will to directly confront and dominate them. The problem is twofold: complacency (intellectual laziness), and passivity. One in this confused state of mind may mistakenly think that some arrangement can be worked out whereby negative, destructive conditions can coexist with positive, constructive conditions. One may naively think that turning away from the problem is the easiest solution.

40. **With the destruction of the family the ancient laws are destroyed. When the laws perish, the entire family goes to ruin.**
41. **When lawlessness increases, O Krishna, the women of the family become corrupt; when women are corrupted, confusion of duties occurs.**
42. **Confusion brings conflict and disorder to both the family and the destroyers of the family; no longer nourished, the ancestors of the family also suffer.**
43. **By the misdeeds of those who destroy the family and create confusion, the timeless laws which sustain life are destroyed.**
44. **We have often heard, O Krishna, that those whose family laws have been done away with, dwell in a condition of continual misfortune.**

The devotee erroneously believes that when the family of sense desires and urges are quieted during contemplative meditation as the result of internalizing attention, or intentionally regulated in the course of everyday circumstances, the governing influences that make desires possible may be permanently vanquished. This is not true, of course, but the idea provides an excuse for a superficially motivated devotee to avoid spiritual practices. The aimless fear is that, when sense urges are regulated, their functions will be disorganized and the capacity for feeling (referred to here as a feminine characteristic) will be disturbed, causing confusion that creates conflict and disorder to both the host of desires and to the field of individualized consciousness in which they find expression. At this stage, a person lacking higher knowledge does not know that rational control of physical and mental urges removes destructive drives, constructively modifies habitual behavior, conserves vital forces, strengthens mental powers, and purifies both mind and senses so that life can be more enjoyable and productive.

The subtle sense faculties, the subjective, true essences (tattvas) or root-causes of the physical sense faculties which make possible sight, hearing, seeing, touching, and smelling in the objective realm, are nurtured by intelligence and by experiencing refined perceptions. The senses become used to gross perceptions and sensations when allowed to be overly used to gratify unregulated physical desires. When one allows strong emotion and urge for sensation to determine desires, problems can arise. Desires should be regulated by the so-called masculine (assertive) characteristics of inclination to purposeful accomplishment and productive, creative expression. Even when meditating, desire for novel perceptions or for serene, blissful states which are pleasant to experience but are not accompanied by insight or expansion of soul awareness, should be transformed into pure aspiration for Self-knowledge and God-realization.

The ancestors of desires are egoism (the false sense of independent existence) and the soul. When egoism is not nourished by attention, it fades—a spiritually beneficial outcome for a devotee of God. When the soul nature is not nourished by Self-remembrance, prayer, devotion, meditation, and samadhi, its awareness tends to overly identify with mental transformations and changes, sense perceptions, and objective circumstances.

The timeless laws which sustain life are the principles of causation which support orderly processes of evolution. If their actions are unable to be harmoniously expressive, orderly unfoldment of both the natural processes which make life worthwhile and of spiritual growth is impeded. The mistaken notion that disciplined regulation of impulses and actions characteristic of unenlightened consciousness might produce unfavorable results is unfounded. While the conditioned personality will certainly be challenged and transformed, the benefit will be that of providing ideal circumstances for progressive soul unfoldment. In Patanjali's

Yoga Sutras 2:1, self-discipline is stressed as a prerequisite to mastering behaviors, mental states, and states of consciousness:

> Regulation of sensory and mental impulses, self-analysis, profound metaphysical study and meditation, and surrendering self-consciousness (egoism) in favor of God-consciousness, are the practical means of accomplishing perfect concentration. This is the path of Kriya Yoga.

A God-surrendered devotee does not waste energy in idle daydreaming, purposeless talk, or useless action of any kind. Instead, concentrated attention is focused on matters essential to psychological transformation and spiritual growth.

45. Alas! We are resolved to perform unrighteously because we are willing to slay our own kinsmen because of greed for our own happiness.

A devotee is sometimes so confused that self-conscious awareness, with its delusions, illusions, and rigid psychological characteristics, is considered to be not only normal but ideal. Because of this, a spiritually unawake soul, preferring the darkness of ignorance to the light of knowledge, will often actively resist any change that might disturb its habit-bound routine of thoughts, moods, relationships, and behaviors. Such a one may assert that it is wrong—because it appears greedily self-serving—to go against the tide of conditioned human nature; that to desire higher knowledge and spiritual freedom is a selfish aspiration.

46. I would therefore be happier if the sons of Dhritarashtra, armed with their weapons, should slay me, unresisting and weaponless.

The devotee, overwhelmed by mental conflict, emotionally depressed, deficient in aspiration and will-to-accomplish, and awed by the seeming awesomeness of the transformational process to be undergone, may be temporarily resigned to a fate of passive acquiescence to the perverse tendencies and drives (weapons) of the unenlightened mind (Dhritarashtra). At a deeper level, however, one knows that unconsciousness and suppression of innate soul qualities will not be a permanent condition. One will

eventually have to confront the obstacles that inhibit the unfoldment of true knowledge and either intentionally banish them or
agreeably allow grace to dissolve them.

Sanjaya said:

47. **Having thus spoken in the midst of the battlefield, throwing
    down his bow and arrows, Arjuna sank down on the seat of
    the chariot, his heart overwhelmed by sorrow.**

Before, Arjuna's bow slipped from his hand because his grasp
was weak. Now, the devotee, dramatizing sadness and despair
characteristic of self-pity, intentionally discards his bow (his determination to meditate) as a gesture of futility. The act may also
be seen as one of defiance grounded in emotional immaturity and
neurotic self-centeredness; a display of resistance to that Higher
Good which must inevitably be acknowledged.

It should be remembered that in this story the conversation
between Arjuna and Krishna represents the soul's observation
of conditioned feelings, thoughts, and inclinations along with its
aspirations and intuitive apprehension of higher knowledge. The
contest is between the compulsion to remain identified with outer
circumstances because of restlessness and confusion, and the innate impulse to have awareness restored to wholeness. These two
drives can be apparent to us whenever we reflect upon the matter
of who we are and our relationship with life, whether absorbed
in meditative contemplation or routinely involved in ordinary
activities and relationships.

*In the Upanishad of the Bhagavad Gita, the science of the
Absolute, the scripture of Yoga and the dialogue between
Sri Krishna and Arjuna, thus ends the first chapter,
entitled Arjuna Vishada Yoga: The Yoga of the
Despondency of Arjuna*

CHAPTER TWO

The Yoga of Knowledge
of the Imperishable

In the second chapter, instruction in matters essential to understanding the facts of life and awakening to Self-realization and liberation of consciousness begins. The original title of this chapter is *Samkhya Yoga*. Samkhya philosophy enumerates the categories and aspects of cosmic manifestation, explaining the difference between imperishable Consciousness and transient cosmic manifestations and forms of nature. When knowledge of Supreme Consciousness is flawless, erroneous beliefs are banished, enabling soul awareness to be restored to its normal state of wholeness. This chapter has been called the heart of the *Gita*.

Sanjaya said:

1. **To him who was overcome by self-pity and despair, whose downcast eyes were filled with tears, Krishna spoke these words:**

The devotee in this state of mental confusion and unrest continues to be preoccupied with matters which, while they seem to be important, really are not. The dramatization of sadness is an immature, emotional display of self-indulgence. However, revelation of truth is about to unfold.

Krishna spoke:

2. **From whence has this weakness come to you at this difficult time? It is not befitting you who are of noble character. It does not lead to heaven [the state of spiritual fulfillment], and can only cause you disgrace.**

During moments of introspective reflection, when confronted by challenge and when choices need to be made, our common sense and intuition may remind us that our behavior is inappropriate. We may inwardly know that the course of action we are inclined to take, because of allowing our moods to determine it, cannot result in constructive ends; that the outcomes will be unfortunate. Indecisiveness, lack of knowledge of meaningful purpose, a negative self-image, flawed awareness of ourselves as spiritual beings, fear of failure, fear of what others will think of us regardless of our actions, fear that it is not right for us to exercise free will, and other considerations, may impair our ability to function.

3. **Yield not to this immature behavior; it is not suitable for you. Abandon this show of weakness and faintheartedness. Stand up, Arjuna!**

The practical advice is to renounce passivity which is not appropriate when what is needed is decisiveness and constructive action to accomplish worthwhile purposes. As spiritual beings, we are supposed to be insightful and creatively functional. Petty self-centeredness and dramatizations of weakness and cowardice are not soul characteristics; they are symptoms of neurosis and dysfunction. The command "stand up" means to confront what needs to be examined and analyzed, make the right choice, and decisively act with clear, focused intention.

All aspects of Kriya Yoga practice should be given our alert, involved attention. During every waking moment we should be aware of the need to regulate physical and mental urges and impulses and to live appropriately, skillfully, and successfully. When meditating, we should lay aside mundane concerns, withdraw attention from physical, emotional, and mental processes, and contemplate God and transcendent realities without distraction. When contemplating the truth of ourselves, and of God and universal processes, we should use our intelligence and intuition to see through outer appearances and through our own beliefs and illusions to what is actually real or true. When aspiring to awaken in God we should renounce all thoughts and concerns about anything other than God. At all times we should be impelled by willingness to awaken from unconscious states so that complete Self-knowledge and illumination of consciousness can spontaneously unfold.

Arjuna spoke:

4. **O Krishna, how can I kill Bhishma and Drona in battle? How can I fight with my skills against these two venerable beings?**

   O my Divine Self, my true Reality, how can I eliminate this sense of independent existence, along with memories and habits? How can I use my skills against these two long-standing conditions?

When we are not yet Self-realized, when we are still looking at the enlightened state from the deluded viewpoint of being a self-conscious creature, we may turn to our higher, true nature as a source of knowledge and inspiration. We may ask how we can possibly remove the error of belief of independent existence which keeps our awareness removed from direct experience of wholeness, and how our mental conditionings and memories of prior experience may be ignored. Conditions which have long persisted may be venerated or respected by us because of our long familiarity with them and their seeming indestructibility. Bhishma is a code word for both cosmic individuality and the personal sense of individuality. The appearance of cosmic individuality makes possible universal manifestation. The personal sense of individuality causes the soul to unconsciously identify with mind and matter. Memories, impressions (samskaras) of experience of all kinds, are often tenacious, clinging to the mental field because it is characteristic of them to do so and because of the deluded soul's identification and attachment to them. To transcend these two long-standing conditions (egoism and mental conditionings) the devotee needs only to withdraw attention from them. To struggle to overcome the false sense of individuality and the influences of mental impressions is to presume them to have power which they do not really have—to consider them to be formidable when they are not.

5. **Indeed, rather than to slay these noble teachers, it would be preferable for me to be a beggar here on earth. Having slain the teachers with desire for personal gain, I would only enjoy on earth delights tainted by my actions.**

The sense of individuality and one's memories are referred to as teachers because they support the self-conscious condition.

They provide continuity of individualized existence, a sense of personal history of passage through time, and information about mundane circumstances. The devotee, because of lack of clear insight into higher possibilities, may feel that it would be better not to eliminate these two conditions, and remain at their mercy. At this stage, one may feel or think that dissolving the strong sense of individuality and being free from the influences of trouble-causing memories might be cause for regret. This consideration exists only because the devotee has not yet experienced illumination of consciousness which makes possible higher understanding based on true knowledge.

6. **And I do not know which is preferable; whether I should conquer them or they should conquer me. If I slay the sons of Dhritarashtra now standing here before me, I would not wish to live.**
7. **My very being is overcome by pity and weakness. My mind is confused as to my duty. I implore you: correct me, teach me, tell me for certain what is the better way. I am your pupil. I seek refuge in your guidance.**
8. **I do not see what will dispel this sorrow which dries up my senses, even if I should obtain on earth unrivaled personal power and prosperity, or even godlike dominion.**

Indecision and irrational thinking continue. The devotee feels that life without the companionship of the tendencies of the unenlightened mind (Dhritarashtra) would be devoid of familiar meaning. Now, however, there is hope! The devotee, weary of fruitless mental quandary, surrenders, and asks for help in the form of right knowledge while admitting that no solution has thus far been found.

Sanjaya said:

9. **Thus having addressed Krishna, Arjuna proclaimed: I will not fight. Having spoken, he was silent.**

The devotee, though still somewhat self-consciously willful, and resistant to the earlier invitation to engage in righteous action, finally does the right thing by deciding to be quiet. Mental stillness and receptivity to learning are necessary conditions if the way of discipleship is to be apprehended and lived.

10. O Dhritarashtra, to Arjuna, who was dejected, Krishna smiled, and in between two armies he spoke these words:

Krishna's smile implies that no real problems exist; that the matter at hand can be addressed with objectivity.

Krishna spoke:

11. You have been mourning those that need not be mourned, and yet you speak some words as if with wisdom. The wise mourn neither for the dead nor for the living.

12. Never was there a time when I was not, nor you, nor these others; and never will there be a time when we shall cease to be.

13. As one passes through childhood, youth, and old age in the body, even so, beings acquire another body; the wise person is not deluded about this.

You have been grieving about those that need not be a cause for sorrow, and yet you speak some wise words. The really wise do not grieve for that which has gone nor for that which is present. Never was there a time when Supreme Consciousness and all that is real did not exist. Just as one moves through the stages of incarnated life, so souls attract to themselves bodies or coverings as needed in their journey through space and time; wise people know this.

Arjuna's problem is that of attachment to the false idea that he is other than a radiant, God-expressed being. When this error of the intellect is corrected, the products of ignorance cease to exist. Arjuna is told that he has been indulging in unnecessary concerns about the welfare of those forces which represent obstacles to his spiritual fulfillment. He is told that One Life prevails while objective circumstances are transient. He should see the One Life behind the panorama of appearances and go forward to accomplish a noble purpose. Just as the true Self which enlivens bodies is not them, so the One Life that enlivens mental tendencies remains independent of them. Arjuna has been grieving over transitory changes instead of seeing beyond conditions to Reality. Only people deficient in knowledge mourn the passing of bodies, things, and circumstances, which, by their nature, have temporary existence. Delusion and grief attach the soul's awareness to mind and matter, keeping it involved with causes and effects in the field of nature.

14. **Material sensations of cold, heat, pleasure, or pain [unpleasantness], are transient and impermanent. Endure them while you seek knowledge.**

That which is impermanent, even if temporarily uncomfortable, can be patiently endured until knowledge of how to improve conditions is acquired. True patience is other than complacent agreement to unpleasant circumstances; it is being soul-centered, mentally peaceful, and emotionally calm regardless of outer circumstances. Because thought processes and feelings are also external to the soul, we can be patient even when mentally conflicted or emotionally challenged, until conflict is resolved and emotional stability is restored.

15. **The devotee who is not troubled by these sensations, who remains unmoved during episodes of transient displeasure or pleasure, who is wise [because of being knowledgeable], becomes receptive to realization of eternal life.**

When we are spiritually aware we can be undisturbed by any outer condition. Such equanimity is not the result of disinterest, but of superior understanding which makes us receptive to spontaneous soul unfoldments, illumines our consciousness, and provides direct experience (realization) of immortality. No longer addicted to circumstances of minor significance, soul awareness can expand and reclaim omnipresence.

16. **That which is nonexistent does not come into manifestation; that which truly exists never ceases to be. Seers know this to be true.**
17. **Know the life that pervades the universe is indestructible; no one can change it or cause it to be nonexistent.**
18. **Bodies inhabited by the eternal, indestructible, immeasurable embodied Self come to an end. Therefore, engage in righteous endeavor.**
19. **Those who think the Self [the true essence] can slay or be slain fail to discern the truth; no one slays or is slain.**

Consciousness alone exists. It manifests by self-referring processes which express as various categories and aspects. From the Field of Pure Consciousness an impulse arises which produces the Godhead with attributes or qualities (gunas): *sattva*, illuminating; *tamas*, which contributes to inertia; and *rajas*, transformative processes resulting from sattvic and tamasic interactions. From the Godhead the Word (Om) flows to express as modifications of itself: space, time, and primary cosmic forces—the field of primordial nature, the substance which manifests as all forms. Interaction between the Spirit of God and the field of primordial nature produces cosmic individualization (Bhishma). A Cosmic Mind is emanated, which produces the subtle essences (tattvas) of the five sense organs, five organs of action, and the five elements which interact to produce the causal, astral, and physical realms. Rays of God's light shining on the field of primordial nature reflect as individualized expressions of Consciousness, or souls. Supreme Consciousness is the true Self of every person and creature.

Because Consciousness alone exists, there is no other essence or thing. This fact can only be directly known. Endeavors to prove or disprove it by any means other than intuitive perception will fail. Even intellectual inquiry, while useful in providing a degree of insight, will fall short of realized knowledge because the intellectual faculty is a material organ of determination. The Field of Pure Consciousness is without origins or endings. Its self-manifestations—as the field of nature and as the aspects which regulate nature's processes—are subject to transformations and changes; although they come and go, Consciousness remains ever what it is. Bodies and other manifest forms (including thoughts and mental tendencies) enlivened by Consciousness are impermanent. That is why one should aspire to authentic spiritual growth while the opportunity to do so is compelling.

Consciousness, being eternal, cannot be diminished or made to be nonexistent. Therefore, belief that Consciousness can be killed is a delusion based on faulty understanding.

20. The true Self is never born, nor does it die at any time, nor having once come to be will it cease to be. The true Self is unborn, permanent, and ageless. It does not die when the body dies.

21. One who knows that the true Self is indestructible and eternal, uncreated and unchanging; how can one possessed of this understanding kill anyone. Whom can he kill?

As rays of God's light we are expressed, not created. When initially involved with primordial nature, mind, and matter, the soul's awareness is diminished, causing temporary, partial unconsciousness and tenacious identification with objective phenomena. This results in the primary clouding of awareness and the delusion (erroneous belief) of independent existence which gives rise to the false notion of "I-ness" or egoism. The deluded soul then becomes attached to further self-generated delusions (erroneous beliefs), experiences perceptual errors (illusions), identifies with sensations and thought processes, and becomes somewhat forgetful of its true nature. The soul's awareness then becomes fragmented, mixed, or conflicted. However, because the soul was never born (created), it will never die (cease to be). Nor will conscious awareness of existence cease once the soul's awareness is completely restored to wholeness. Responding joyously to the soul's innate urge to have awareness restored to conscious wholeness or oneness assures rapid, authentic spiritual growth which can be spontaneously demonstrated as unrestricted creativity and orderly unfoldments of supportive events, conditions, and relationships in everyday circumstances.

Whom can be killed? Even though we know that the true Self of a person or creature cannot be slain, we are to be so established in harmlessness that no harmful thoughts arise in our minds and no harmful actions are performed. Because the habits and psychological tendencies which are obstacles to our spiritual growth and effective functioning are conditions and not creatures, they can be eliminated as necessary.

The direct way to banish unwanted or troublesome mental influences and psychological conditions is to immediately determine their nonusefulness and renounce them. If this cannot be done, concentrated self-training to modify mental and emotional states and behaviors can be adopted. To do this, the *yamas* (restraints) and *niyamas* (intentional practices) of yoga are effective. The devotee's lifestyle should be chosen—including daily routine, selection of foods, how one obtains money and other resources, social relationships, time for regular philosophical reflection and spiritual practices—so that it fully supports the fulfillment of personal needs and spiritual growth. Nurturing devotion to God and regular superconscious meditation should be the basis of the devotee's spiritual practices. Cultivating flows of life force in the spinal pathway during meditation practice, and centering awareness at the spiritual eye and the heart chakra at other times, will help one maintain inner balance and prevent excessive outward flows of life forces and attention.

22. **Just as a person casts off worn-out garments and later acquires new ones, so after casting away worn-out bodies the true Self acquires new ones as needed.**
23. **Weapons do not harm the true Self, fire does not burn it; water does not wet it; nor does the wind cause it to dry and wither.**
24. **The true Self cannot be harmed; it is eternal, all-pervading, stable, unmoving, and primeval.**
25. **The true Self is unmanifest, cannot be defined by the mind, and is unchanging. Knowing this, you should not mourn.**
26. **Even if you think that the true Self is perpetually born or eternally dies, you should not mourn.**
27. **For that which is born, death is certain, and certain is birth for that which dies. Therefore, for what is unavoidable, you should not grieve.**
28. **Creatures and human beings are at first unmanifest, manifest when they appear in form, and are unmanifest at the end of their term of manifestation. Why should this be cause for discontent?**

The author of the *Gita* compares the changing of garments to the soul's casting off of bodies and the taking on of new ones until awakening in God removes the necessity for undergoing these episodes. The doctrine of reincarnation is here taught as a philosophical concept that can be verified by personal, intuitive discernment. No attempt is made by the author (or authors) to prove the process; it is simply acknowledged as (usually) being necessary for souls according to their states of consciousness, karmic condition, desires which support fate, or soul destiny. Just as God pervading the universe is not influenced by anything in the field of nature, so the embodied soul, when fully enlightened or liberated, need not be influenced by its relationship to mind or body. However, the awareness of unenlightened souls may be somewhat modified because of identification with the mind, body, and environmental circumstances while the reality of the soul is not flawed. The true Self of us is an individualized unit of the true Self of everything. We are endowed with all of the characteristics, qualities, capacities, and full knowledge of God.

Even if we were to erroneously believe that the true Self is frequently born or will eventually die, since there is nothing we could do to change the facts, to grieve about what is inevitable would be an act of foolishness. Creatures and human beings are born and they die because they are formed of impermanent flesh. This is not cause for sorrow because the soul is superior to the physical form it temporarily animates.

Mental and emotional states, tendencies, thoughts, and desires are also born and they die (they are produced and they cease to exist). Knowing this, we have freedom to nurture constructive mental and emotional states and to renounce and vanquish those which are detrimental to our well-being.

29. **One person considers the true Self to be wondrous, another declares it likewise, still another hears of it as being marvelous; but having heard of this, no one knows it.**
30. **The embodied true Self is eternally indestructible. Therefore you should not mourn for any creature or person.**

Regardless of how unusual we may consider the true Self to be, until we are insightful and knowledgeable because of being spiritually awake, we cannot accurately know its reality. Hence, no one in a state of self-consciousness really comprehends the truth about Absolute Consciousness, God, and the one Self expressing as the soul. To be accomplished on the spiritual path and happy in life, it is useful to remember the soul's real nature and live from that understanding without compromise.

31. **Knowing now the duty before you, you should not hesitate; indeed, there is no higher good for a warrior-spirit than righteous endeavor performed as duty.**
32. **Happy are such devotees to whom such a fortunate endeavor is presented as an open entrance to spiritual fulfillment.**
33. **Now, if you will not undertake this righteous endeavor, and**

thereby avoid your own duty, you shall incur misfortune.
34. **Also, people who know you will talk about your weakness; and for one such as you who has been held in high esteem, disgrace is worse than death.**
35. **Great warriors will think that you have abstained from your duty because of fear, and those by whom you were esteemed will consider you to be superficial.**
36. **Unkind words and slander will be uttered by your foes. Could anything be more grievous than that?**
37. **If you are slain, you shall attain spiritual fulfillment; if you are victorious, you will enjoy life in the world. Therefore stand up, resolved to do your duty.**

The true Self's innate inclination to unfold its potential urges the devotee not to hesitate in engaging in spiritual practice performed as sacred duty. Of all duties we might have, none is more important than that which nurtures soul qualities, makes us skillfully effective, and facilitates rapid spiritual growth. When we have such an opportunity that assures the fulfillment of soul destiny, we should immediately respond in the affirmative.

Arjuna is portrayed as one whose duty it is to uphold and defend, when necessary, the *dharma*: the eternal way of righteousness, the orderly processes by which evolution is able to effectively fulfill its purposes. It is, therefore, of interest to us that he, a warrior presumed dedicated to duty, shrinks from it when the challenge seems to him to be too great. In this, we see human nature at its most vulnerable. It is easy to do what we are capable of doing or what seems worthwhile. It is not always so easy to commit ourselves wholeheartedly when confused about the issues or uncertain of our skills.

When we are rightly resolved and effectively engaged in worthwhile endeavors, we are certain of success of one kind or another because we are working out our fate (karma) and fulfilling our soul destiny. Not to do this, when we know we should, is to invite unhappiness and misfortune. Therefore, we should courageously dedicate ourselves to intentional right actions for the purpose of putting an end to all troubles common to the self-conscious condition. By so doing, we ensure our awakening to Self-knowledge in this present life cycle.

If soul resolve is weak, the great warriors (the self-serving mental tendencies) will be free to grow stronger and more influential. Could they but do it, they would rejoice to know of the soul's unwillingness to actualize its potential.

38. **Considering pleasure and displeasure, gain and loss, victory and defeat, with even-mindedness, engage in righteous endeavor. Thus you shall not incur misfortune.**
39. **This is the wisdom of the ancient seers. Now hear it, and apply it by dedicated practice. With this yoga of knowledge, Arjuna, you shall rid yourself of the bondage of karma.**
40. **In this righteous way no endeavor is wasted and no obstacle prevails; even a little of this practice protects one from great dangers.**

Our approach to Self-knowledge and its actualization should be selfless, with focused resolve devoid of anxiety regarding the outcome. With right endeavor and by God's grace, fulfillment is assured.

This teaching emphasis is the core theme of all enlightened seers. The knowledge that is acquired lights the way. The knowledge that is self-revealed removes the soul from mundane actions of cause and effect, from karma. Progress is steady and obstacles are banished. Even a little right practice facilitates spiritual growth that brings the soul into a harmonious relationship with the actions of grace and the currents of evolution. Fear of present and future circumstances, including transition from the body and other-realm conditions, is dispelled.

41. **On this path, those who are firmly decided are resolute; the thoughts of the uncommitted branch out in many directions and in endless variations.**
42. **The undiscerning people who rejoice in the letter of the scriptures, who contend that there is nothing else, whose nature is driven by desire and who are intent upon heaven, proclaim flowery words that result in rebirth as the fruit of actions.**
43. **They prescribe various specialized rituals for the attainment of enjoyment and power.**
44. **Of those whose minds are enchanted by these words because of their craving for enjoyment and power, intellectual ability is flawed and meditative insight is not possible.**

It is characteristic of conditioned human nature to be confused and distracted. One is then often enchanted by glamorous promises and impelled to actions for the purpose of gratifying whims. Such a life often concludes with little or no spiritual progress having been actualized.

The *Gita* makes a distinction between worthwhile spiritual activity and ritualistic piety or self-serving religious practices. Some people pray, fast, and outwardly observe rules enjoined by their chosen scripture, hoping to acquire merit (good karma, perhaps, or the favor of God or of imagined gods) or gain of some kind: health, prosperity, or various soul powers or abilities (siddhis). Devotees intent upon Self-knowledge and God-realization should know that enlightenment naturally provides all that is needed for spiritual fulfillment, which is the highest soul happiness. Everything needed for well-being is present when we are established in conscious experience of wholeness.

A discerning devotee should know that endless speculation about various heavens, pointless discussion about scripture, blind adherence to rules which are not understood, and glib talk about abstract metaphysical concepts, are a waste of time and energy— a waste of one's life—as are involvements in magical practices to control the elements or to manipulate the lives of others for self-serving purposes. If the devotee is not discerning, even the meditation routine can be performed as a rehearsed ritual that is unproductive of soul-freeing results. There can be no soul contentment, mental peace, or effective use of intellectual powers so long as one's field of awareness is clouded, restless, and conflicted. Only when the devotee is surrendered in God can meditation practice be satisfying and samadhi be experienced.

45. The qualities [gunas] of nature are described in scriptures. Become free from these qualities of nature; be firmly established in purity, not caring for acquisition and preservation, and be Self-realized.

The purity in which to be established is the transcendent state of consciousness devoid of the characteristic qualities of nature. Thus established, resting in realization of wholeness, desire for acquiring things, and concern about self-preservation, cannot exist. These characteristics are only possible while egoism, a sense of independent selfhood, remains. While there is yet striving, even for that which is deemed desirable or good, the self-conscious soul is perceiving and relating to the world through its delusions and illusions. Even one's obsessive quest for union with God can be a barrier to realizing that which is already true—that God, being the only manifesting Reality, is always where one is, and is also the soul seeking experience of oneness.

A devotee of God should learn to discern the difference between the soul and the mind and its processes, and to discern the influences that gunas, the influential, constituent qualities of nature, can have on the mind and body. Tamas guna contributes to mental dullness and inertia. Rajas guna contributes to restlessness as well as energizes the will to purposeful action. Sattva guna contributes to mental poise and life-enhancing aspiration. Tamas guna is neutralized by intentional right actions (kriyas). Rajas guna is neutralized by the cultivation of even-mindedness and repeated episodes of superconsciousness. Sattva guna is transcended by nurturing Self-realization which results in permanent enlightenment (full knowledge) and liberation of consciousness. While we are yet in relationship to the field of nature and still "working out our salvation," we have a relationship with nature's qualities or gunas. When we are grounded in Self-knowledge, nature's qualities are supportive of us but they no longer restrict.

In the *Yoga Sutras* 4:32 and 34, the final stages of spiritual awakening are described:

> With the dawning of knowledge, the cosmic forces [gunas], having served their purposes, cease to be influential. When the expressive cosmic forces, having no further purpose to serve, return to their origins [the realm of primordial nature, where they become dormant], the soul experiences absolute freedom.

This liberation is described: (1) when cosmic forces no longer influence soul awareness; (2) when soul awareness is established in Being, referred to as the Supreme Self.

46. As is the value of a pond in a place flooded by water, so is the value of scripture for one who is Self-realized.

A devotee established in flawless Self-knowledge does not have to look to another source for knowledge, nor engage in further spiritual practice. While appearing to be good, a Self-realized person no longer has to endeavor to be good.

47. **You have a right to actions only, not to the results of actions. Let not the results of actions be your motive, neither let there be any attachment to inaction.**
48. **Firmly established in Self-realization, do the work at hand; giving up attachment to it, be even-minded in both success and failure, for, truly, mental poise is yoga.**
49. **Mere action alone is inferior to the discipline of intelligence. Those who work for results alone are to be pitied.**
50. **One who has realized the true Self abandons both the good and the ungood. Therefore, aspire to the yoga of Self-knowledge. Skillful action is yoga.**
51. **The wise who have actualized enlightenment, who have renounced the results of actions and are free from compulsion to be reborn, are beyond sorrow because established in soul-bliss.**

So long as our awareness is clouded or fragmented, psychological transformation and spiritual growth endeavors are our necessary duties. The results of our right endeavors are due to unfoldments of soul qualities and are not the direct effects of our actions. The ideal approach is to do what must be done without anxiety about the outcome and without claiming the results to be of our own doing. Because right endeavor contributes to success on the awakening path, our role is to do what is necessary as a disinterested observer of both the actions and their results. The key is to be established in yoga, the samadhi of Self-knowledge. The mechanical or rote performance of spiritual practices, devoid of disciplined exercise of intelligence, cannot produce desired results. Conscious, knowledgeable performance of useful actions is itself fulfilling because it removes delusions, and illusions of separateness from the mind. One experiences a degree of unity or harmony, of life as oneness, and is aware of causative actions occurring without psychological compulsions or inner resistance. When enlightenment (full knowledge of Consciousness and its operations) is actualized, it is permanent. The soul, then established in Self-realization, is completely liberated from involvements with causes and effects which have only to do with the interactions of nature's qualities (gunas) and their influences in relative spheres.

52. **When your intelligence transcends all delusions, you shall be indifferent to what has been heard and is yet to be heard.**
53. **When your intelligence, which was bewildered by conflicting [philosophical or scriptural] information, is stable and unshaken in realization of oneness [samadhi], then shall you awaken to flawless, insightful knowledge.**

Established in Self-knowledge one is contentedly unconcerned about various philosophical or religious opinions and theories which may be propounded or discussed now or in the future by others who are not yet spiritually awake. When the devotee's intelligence is firmly established in pure consciousness, innate soul knowledge spontaneously unfolds of its own accord.

Arjuna asks:

54. **What is the description of one who is firmly established in Self-knowledge? How does such a one speak and behave?**

For a devotee new on the path, it can be helpful to know what will be the results of attentive spiritual practice. How does an enlightened person think, speak, and relate to others? What motivates their actions? How do they view themselves in relationship to others? What is it like to be Self-realized?

Krishna answers:

55. **When one has put away the desires of the mind, and is content in Self-knowledge, such a one is said to be established in wisdom.**

Because misdirected impulses and desires supported by delusions and illusions are in opposition to the heart's (soul's) aspiration to awaken to Self-knowledge and higher realities, they should be renounced by the resolved devotee. Soul contentment based on true Self-knowledge should be nurtured until soul qualities are actualized by direct realization. One is then stable in clearly comprehended true knowledge (wisdom).

56. **One whose mind is untroubled in the midst of misfortune and is free from cravings in the midst of pleasurable circumstances, from whom passion, fear, and anger have departed, and whose meditative concentration is steady, is said to be a sage, to be wise.**

Soul contentment enables one to be calm in the midst of discordant circumstances and devoid of even a trace of desire in the presence of opportunities for experience which might overwhelm the average person's self-control. The driving force of passion, fear, and anger (and other symptoms of mental and emotional immaturity) are entirely absent in the personality of one who is established in peace of soul. Because the various characteristics of psychological unrest are absent, meditative contemplation is easy, spontaneous, and steady (uninterrupted). A comparison is described in the *Yoga Sutras* 4:26:

> Having overcome identification with the body, senses, and mind, consciousness becomes serene and calm, and awareness flows in the direction of absolute freedom.

57. **That one who is without sentimental attachment, who does not rejoice because of pleasant circumstances or feel aversion toward that which is unpleasant, is firmly established in understanding.**

Sentimental attachment is based on feeling or emotion rather than reason. A discerning person, while able to have and enjoy relationships, is not blindly attached to them, nor is such a one uncontrollably reactive to either pleasantness or unpleasantness. Insightful understanding prevails in all circumstances.

58. **One who withdraws sensory awareness from temptations, as a turtle withdraws its limbs [into a shell], is firmly established in wisdom.**

The wise person does not *suppress* physical and mental urges. Instead, awareness is *withdrawn* from things and circumstances which might otherwise tempt the senses or energize desire. An easy first stage of accomplishment is to be soul-centered, dispassionate, and disinterested. Intellectual discernment can enable us to determine what may be the unfortunate outcome of unreasoned behavior in contrast to what would be the outcome when wisdom is allowed to govern behavior. It is easier to regulate sensory inclinations and desires when our aspiration to spiritual growth determines our sense of purpose in life. Also, regular practice of contemplative meditation turns soul forces inward to the source of being, neutralizes prana flows, calms the mind, and produces a condition of mental, emotional, and physiological balance which allows soul awareness to remain constant.

59. The objects of the senses turn away from the one who abstains from them but the taste [memory and desire] remains. Even this turns away when the Supreme Reality is apprehended.

The subjective, causative law or principle of correspondences determines that our states of consciousness and mental states attract circumstances which conform to them. We tend to attract what we are agreeable to experiencing or what we desire and can accept. When we have no agreements, feelings, or thoughts about a thing, experience, or circumstances, these objects of the senses are no longer attracted by us—they seem to "turn away." We may, however, still have memories of past experience or desire for that which is not compatible with our aspiration to awaken to our highest good. As spiritual growth continues, memories no longer influence us and all nonuseful desires cease.

60. Even though a discerning devotee may continuously strive for perfection, the impetuous sense urges may forcibly influence the mind.

Until illumination of consciousness purifies the mind, while one is intent upon spiritual growth, emotion-driven urges, sometimes nourished by memories of past experience, may influence the mind to produce desires, fantasies, and even hallucinations of various kinds. These should be resisted, restrained, and transformed by disciplined endeavor and repeated meditative superconscious experiences. Superconscious experience produces constructive mental impressions (samskaras) which weaken and neutralize destructive impressions. *Yoga Sutras* 1:33:

The mind is calmed and purified by cultivation of feelings of friendship, by compassion, joy, and neutrality [indifference toward matters of no consequence to the devotee's higher purposes], and by examining and contemplating ideal [alternative] possibilities.

61. **Having controlled the sense urges, the devotee should remain firm in yoga [superconscious meditative contemplation], intent on Supreme Reality. For that one whose senses are mastered, intelligence is firmly established.**

Mastery of states of consciousness and of mental and emotional states gives one control of sense urges. It is then easy to rest in contemplation of the Infinite when meditating and to sustain aspiration for God-realization in all circumstances when engaged in necessary or chosen relationships and duties. Spontaneous samadhi, comprehensive awareness of the truth of life and its processes is then constant.

62. **When one mentally dwells on objects of the senses, attachment to them is produced. From attachment comes desire and from desire anger is born [when desire is frustrated].**
63. **From anger confusion is produced; because of confusion memory is impaired. When memory is impaired, powers of discernment are diminished and one wanders aimlessly.**

Preoccupation with sense objects may result in obsession which dominates awareness. Obsessive desires then may become so overwhelmingly important that anger immediately arises when desires are thwarted. Anger creates mental and emotional confusion and interferes with memory. A powerful surge of anger may cause one to confuse the present situation with a similar one experienced at an earlier moment in time; thus even one's sense of time and place may become disoriented. Powers of discernment are weakened, common sense is abandoned, and one tends to behave erratically and inappropriately.

64. **But the devotee whose mind is disciplined, who moves in the world with the senses under control and is free from attachments and aversions, is established in tranquility.**
65. **And that purity of spirit removes one from all sorrow. The knowledge of the devotee is soon firm in permanent peace.**

When the mind is disciplined by soul-will and superconscious influences, when the senses have been mastered and sentimental attachments and feelings of aversion are absent, the impulses (vasanas) which cause mental and emotional disturbance are quieted and inner calm prevails. When inner calm is established, the soul rests in flawless Self-knowledge that removes it from the causes of discontent and unhappiness.

66. For the uncontrolled person, discriminative intelligence, power of concentration, and inner peace are absent. How can there then be happiness for such a one?
67. When the mind pursues the inclinations of restless sense urges, it carries with it one's understanding, as a wind carries away a ship on the water.
68. Therefore, the intelligence of one whose senses are withdrawn from their objects is firmly established.

Insistent desires can be as compelling as powerful external influences. Constructive desires inspired by aspiration to excel may elevate us to the heights of self-discovery. Misdirected desires may cause us to abandon our reason and result in pain and disgrace. Who has not, at one time or another, felt the strong urge to give up all that has been accomplished in order to possess the present object of desire? The direct way to master physical and mental urges is to assume an attitude of objectivity, to view them as other than ourselves. The soul is neither mind nor body; it is the immortal unit of individualized awareness that enlivens mind and body and is superior to them.

Observed with indifference, the inclinations of the restless sense urges are seen for what they are: mere effects of a deeper discontent. It is only when desires, attachments, and addictive behaviors are claimed as one's own that they have power to dominate awareness. When they are allowed to be a problem, it is only because one lacks the will to decisively exercise freedom of choice. Because right choices can be difficult to make when reason is clouded by emotional unrest, the more effective way to overcome the problem of restlessness and compulsive desire is to remove attention from externals—including from moods and thoughts, which are external to soul awareness—in order to perceive conditions from an objective point of view. To do this, all that is needed is to be self-reminded of the fact that we are other than mind and body; we are immortal spiritual beings.

An immediate way to soul contentment is surrendered prayer and meditative contemplation. By remaining calm during everyday circumstances, one can implement other helpful actions. These might include regulation of personal behaviors; decisive choosing of supportive relationships and circumstances; cultivation of optimism, courage, and will-to-live and to excel; intentional constructive thinking; intentional constructive verbal expression; a balanced, nutrition-rich food plan; a balance of activity and rest; and an awareness and conviction of a sense of meaningful purpose for living.

A primary cause of mental confusion, emotional conflict, and other personality disorders, is narcissism: self-admiration, arrested emotional growth at, or regression to, the infantile developmental stage during which one's body (and personality) is the object of erotic or sensual interest. (In Greek mythology, Narcissus was a youth, who, enamored of his own image in a pool of water, was transformed into a flower that today bears his name.) The cure for this soul awareness-confining condition is agreement to the necessity of allowing emotional maturity to unfold and be actualized. Ego-based self-centeredness is rooted in the illusion of independent existence, which is the cause of delusions: erroneous ideas and beliefs.

69. What is night for all [spiritually unawake] beings is the time of wakefulness for the disciplined devotee; for the one who sees clearly, what is the time of wakefulness for ordinary people, is night.

While self-conscious people, asleep to knowledge of higher realities, are enchanted by and attracted to objects (including relationships, circumstances, and experiences) which stimulate the senses, devotees of God are awake to truth. That condition in which self-conscious people think of themselves as being truly awake to what is real, devotees of God know to be unconsciousness, or night.

70. That devotee unto whom all desires enter as waters enter the seas, which though ever filled are ever undisturbed, realizes

peace. This is not so for one who clings to desires.
71. **One who abandons all desires and lives free from their influences, without possessiveness or egotism, attains to peace.**

Established in Self-knowledge, the devotee of God is unmoved by the stream of impressions which flow through the field of awareness during the course of daily life. Having renounced all desires, attachments, and the illusional sense of independent existence while intent upon awakening to complete knowledge of Reality, a devotee who surrenders self-consciousness in favor of Self-realization experiences spontaneous illumination of consciousness because the soul's innate urge to have awareness restored to wholeness is no longer suppressed.

72. **That is the divine state; having realized it, one is never again bewildered. Established in that state at the time of passing from the body, one can awaken to the bliss of God-realization.**

The soul as individualized pure consciousness is divine. This state of being, when permanently realized, removes the soul from all conditions which formerly clouded its awareness. After necessary purposes and soul destiny have been fulfilled, when the soul discards the physical body, it can awaken to the joyousness of spiritual freedom. To be established in Self-knowledge while embodied is to be liberated while continuing earth-life existence. Yoga literature refers to this condition as *jivanmukta (jiva,* soul; *mukta,* liberation), a state of salvation (Latin *salvatio;* Greek *soteria),* to be safe because saved from troubles and misfortune. A wise devotee aspires to awaken to truth-consciousness as soon as possible; to enjoy knowledgeable freedom of expression long before demise of the body. However, if Self-knowledge unfolds and is sustained at the very moment of departure from the body, soul liberation is also assured.

*In the Upanishad of the Bhagavad Gita, the science of the
Absolute, the scripture of Yoga and the dialogue between
Sri Krishna and Arjuna, thus ends the second chapter
entitled Samkhya Yoga: The Yoga of Knowledge
of the Imperishable*

CHAPTER THREE

The Yoga of Action

Although the final state of spiritual practice is soul tranquility because awareness has been restored to wholeness, to awaken to liberation, actions are necessary to ensure harmonious relationships with life's processes and to facilitate necessary adjustments of states of consciousness. Well-intentioned but misguided actions often only further complicate our lives. What is needed is enlightened or knowledgeable action.

Arjuna said:

1. **If you consider the path of knowledge to be better than the path of action, why do you urge me to engage in this awesome endeavor?**
2. **With words that seem [to me] to be contradictory, you confuse my intelligence. Tell me clearly: What should I do to attain the highest good?**

In early stages of discipleship experience, the new devotee may find it difficult to immediately comprehend the complete meaning of what is being learned. Partial information about categories of cosmic manifestation was included in chapter two of this text; now the emphasis is on the way of necessary actions, the path of karma yoga. The devotee asks why, since acquisition of knowledge has been emphasized, is it necessary to also engage in actions.

Krishna answered:

3. **A twofold way of devoted life has been taught by me since ancient times; the path of knowledge for contemplative devotees and the path of right action for practitioners of yoga.**

    A twofold way of devoted life has ever been revealed to the soul by innate intelligence; the way of knowledge for those capable of pure contemplation and the way of appropriate, constructive action for those who should engage in spiritual practices.

The way of knowledge is that of intellectual and intuitive examination of a subject for the purpose of having insight into it. Very few truth seekers are able to engage in the subtle discerning processes necessary for success on the pure knowledge path. Most need to implement processes or actions for the purpose of eliminating psychological, physiological, and behavioral obstacles to the spontaneous flows of soul awareness so that innate knowledge can unfold. They need to nurture transformative changes that will allow direct experience of their true nature and of the all-pervading Consciousness which is the Reality of everything.

4. **Not by abstaining from actions does one awaken to that freedom which is beyond karma, nor by renunciation alone does one realize perfection.**

Karma refers to actions and their effects, the principle of causation. Actions may be constructive, destructive, or neutral. They may be as overt as a physical movement or as subtle as an impulse of an intention. In the material realm—all realms this side of the Field of Pure Consciousness are material; nature's qualities (gunas) are their constituents—effects have causes. Events do not occur without causative influences being instrumental to their happening. When souls identify with mind and matter because of delusion grounded in a false sense of being independent of God, they become confused. They make errors in determination, experience mental conflict and emotional unrest, assume erroneous beliefs about themselves and the processes of life, become further bewildered by their misperceptions, and develop attachments, aversions, desires, and memories of pleasure and pain. These conditions comprise the individual karmic condition, which is not of the soul, but of the mind and the sheaths or bodies used by the soul when relating to material realms.

When aware of the karmic condition, a wise person discerns it as something to which to relate for the purpose of working with, overcoming, and transcending, rather than to claim as one's own. Mental conditionings and emotional conflicts can cloud or obscure soul awareness, interfere with rational thinking, distort perceptions, influence behaviors, and attract circumstances which correspond to them. So long as karmic conditions are a determining factor in our lives, soul freedom is thwarted. That is why the devotee is encouraged to awaken to states of consciousness beyond karma. So long as soul awareness is identified with the conditioned mind, neither actual avoidance of necessary actions nor false renunciation of necessary actions by refusal to implement them, will result in spiritual growth which allows soul liberation.

5. **No one can remain even for a moment without doing some kind of work; every being is caused to act by impulses innate to its nature.**

In the *Gita*, work and action refer to what is done to accomplish purposes. Work can be accomplished by physical means, by mental means (constructive adjustments of mental states, thinking, planning, choosing, deciding, visualizing desired outcomes, and holding fast to an intention that will cause desired effects), and by spiritual means such as constructive adjustments of states of consciousness to restore awareness to Self-knowledge and maintain it. So long as the qualities (gunas) of nature are influential, we are impelled to experience action of some kind.

6. **One whose mind is deluded, who sits [to meditate], forcibly restraining the organs of action while continuing to mentally dwell on objects of the senses, is said to be hypocritical, a person of false conduct.**

Unskilled, aggressive, or naive endeavors to suppress feelings and impulses while remaining mentally preoccupied with desires are characteristics of a person who is still personality-centered; whose behaviors are determined by tamasic and rajasic influences. While one may present an appearance of being self-controlled, the outer facade is but a pretense. When meditating, the devotee should be fully attentive to the purpose of practice, disregarding physical and psychological conditions while giving complete attention to contemplation of higher realities. Concentrated practice of meditation techniques—prayer, pranayama, listening to one's mantra, absorption in inner sound and light, and surrender to the soul's impulse to have awareness restored to wholeness—effectively removes the devotee's attention from causes of distraction. During meditation one should intentionally adjust the viewpoint from self-conscious preoccupation with personality characteristics to soul awareness which is tranquil.

7. **But that devotee who mentally controls the senses and, without attachment [to the results of practice], engages the organs of action in the yoga of action is superior.**

Especially when engaged in intentional meditation, sensory impulses should be restrained and practice should be without desire for any experience but that which contributes to increased spiritual awareness. The senses can be regulated by will, mental and emotional detachment, pranayama which cools and balances the body and mind, prayer, and superconscious meditation.

8. **Do the work that is your duty, for [this kind of] action is better than nonaction; even the maintenance of your body cannot be accomplished without [necessary] action.**

The work that is the devotee's duty is that which contributes to total wellness, harmonious relationships with life processes, and rapid spiritual growth. Unless intentional constructive actions are implemented, one's life is inclined to be at the mercy of environmental influences, the influences of unconscious and subconscious tendencies, and the actions of the gunas. A sincere devotee of God is encouraged to transform inertia (tamas) into constructive rajasic action until soul unfoldment allows spontaneous, intuitive, appropriate sattvic behaviors.

9. **Except for work performed for the purpose of sacrifice, this world is in bondage to [causative] work. Therefore, do perform your actions for the purpose of sacrifice, remaining free from attachments.**

Except for actions freely offered to support the processes of evolution, in the mundane realm the necessity of performing actions to cause effects prevails. Therefore, for your highest good, perform all actions as an offering to evolutionary processes, remaining free from attachments to your actions and their results.

The Sanskrit word for sacrifice (*yagya*) is commonly used in reference to ceremonies or rituals, during which material substances and or prayers are offered to God or to various governing aspects of nature (the gods) for the purpose of establishing communication, orderly relationships, and other desired benefits on behalf of an individual, a particular community, or social group. The emphasis in this verse is upon intentional offering of all actions for the support of evolution for the individual and collective good, to assist in inviting transcendent influences into the mundane sphere, and to hasten the actualization of enlightened consciousness. Actions performed in this way remove the devotee from unconscious involvement with mundane causes and their effects, liberating soul awareness.

10. **Having created humankind along with sacrifice, the Lord of Creatures said, "By this [sacrificial actions] may you bring forth; may this bring unto you the fulfillment of your just desires."**
11. **By this [sacrificial actions] may you nourish the gods and may the gods nourish you; by nourishing each other you shall attain to the highest good.**
12. **Nourished by sacrifice, the gods will indeed give you the enjoyment you desire. One who enjoys these gifts without offering them in return is a thief.**
13. **The good [devotees] who eat [absorb] the remainder of the sacrifice are released from all misfortunes; the wicked [egocentric, mentally perverted] who endeavor to nourish only themselves, consume their own ignorance.**
14. **Beings exist because of food [nourishment]; food is produced by rain; rain is produced by sacrifice; and sacrifice is produced by work [actions].**
15. **Know that the principle of causation [karma] originates in the Field of God, and the Field of God emanates from the Imperishable [the Field of Absolute Pure Consciousness]. Therefore, the all-pervading Reality is present in sacrificial actions.**

The realms of nature, creatures, and human beings are manifested within an omnipresent Field of Consciousness which has given of itself to express in diverse ways. In like manner, our experiences and circumstances are manifested within our field of consciousness and within the Infinite Field as we give of ourselves to express in accord with our desires and choices in harmony with nature's processes. The gods to which sacred texts refer are not entities; they are the influential forces which determine the actions of nature. They nourish us and we nourish them when our awareness is clear and our actions are appropriate. If we do not offer ourselves and our actions to life, life cannot nurture us because our choice to withhold what we have to offer restricts the flow of the currents of nature in relationship to us. Healthy-minded people are able to accept the blessings bestowed by nature. People who, because of psychological unrest or conflict, choose to be self-centered, often engage in self-destructive actions and further injure themselves.

Creatures are nourished by the food nurtured by the freely offered rain which, in turn, is produced by the actions of nature. A devotee should know that the origin of causative actions is the Field of omnipresent Consciousness (God) which emanates from the eternal Field of Absolute Pure Consciousness. God is present in all offerings to support evolution.

Meditators whose awareness is immersed in the aftereffects tranquility ("the remainder of the sacrifice" or devotional ritual mentioned in verse 13) are eventually "released from all misfortunes" because of the purifying influences of superconscious realizations.

16. **That one who does not, in this world, help to turn the wheel of causation thus set in motion [from the beginning of world manifestation], lives maliciously, sensually, and in vain.**
17. **For that devotee whose delight is only in Self-knowledge, whose satisfaction is in Self-knowledge, and who is content in Self-knowledge only; there is no further work to be done.**
18. **Similarly, for such a devotee there is nothing more to be gained in this world by actions performed in the past or by those left undone. There is no further dependence upon other beings or sources of causation.**
19. **Therefore, without attachment [to actions or their results], perform always the work [duty] that is essential, for the highest good results by doing work [performing constructive actions] without attachment.**

A person who chooses not to participate in nature's creation and renewal processes is unaware of the real purpose of life, remains sense-oriented, and experiences a self-centered, desire-driven, purposeless existence.

For the Self-realized devotee there are no compulsory actions to perform because all necessary actions spontaneously occur: either as one is intuitively impelled to act or as life processes flow in the field of nature to support the devotee in response to wisdom-chosen desire or to provide primary needs. Established in comprehensive awareness of the fullness of life, the devotee is nurtured by the inexhaustible Source of everything. All actions should be chosen for their entirely constructive outcomes. This is the righteous (dharmic, right, correct, supportive) way to live.

20. It was by right works [actions] alone that ancient kings [like Janaka] realized perfection. You should perform right actions for the maintenance of the world.

Centuries ago, in India, King Janaka was renowned because, while fulfilling his royal duties, he remained established in Self-knowledge. His primary right action was remembrance of God in all circumstances. Even when enlightened, most devotees have personal responsibilities to fulfill and relationships to nurture. One should be aware of the interconnectedness of society, understanding that if the common life is to be decent and orderly, the processes of life must flow harmoniously from subtle to gross levels through enlightened members of society and those who are not yet enlightened.

21. Whatever a great [accomplished, respected, therefore influential] person does, others will emulate.

Our states of consciousness, mental states, and behaviors can influence others by blending with the collective social and planetary consciousness. Our mental states interact with the subjective level of Universal Mind, the mind-stuff common to all embodied souls. Our behaviors, when known to others, can adversely or beneficially influence their own. Others who respect us for our accomplishments, may especially be likely to follow our positive example.

22. For me, there is nothing whatever to be done in the three worlds, nor is there anything to be accomplished which has not been accomplished; yet I am engaged in action.
23. For if I did not engage in tireless action, humankind would follow my example.

24. If I should cease from actions, these worlds would perish and I would be the cause of the confusion and destruction of the people.

For transcendent Supreme Consciousness there are no required actions because it is self-complete; yet it continues to provide the impulses which nurture and maintain the manifested realms. Without the disinterested actions of the various specialized aspects of all-pervading Consciousness, creation would revert to a formless condition.

For Self-realized souls, God is known as an omnipresent, manifested aspect of Supreme Consciousness, out of which the realm of nature is emanated and by which it is nurtured because of a primordial impulse which began the process of world manifestation and maintains it. The impulse to self-manifestation, and to maintain the field of nature and its operations, is referred to as God's will or result-producing intention. God's will should not be compared with willfulness of egocentric human beings.

25. As the unlearned perform work attached to their deeds [because they are being true to their conditioned nature], so wise people should work without attachment to maintain the realm of nature.

26. Let not the person of knowledge unsettle the minds of those who are attached to their actions. The wise should inspire others to enjoy right actions while themselves performing disciplined actions.

Just as people who lack understanding are impelled to function in accord with their conditionings and habits to accomplish what they perceive to be important, so devotees should be responsive to soul inclinations for the purpose of fulfilling their known duties and supporting evolution. Devotees are advised to attend to their own duties and allow friends and associates who are not on the awakening path to live their lives without unduly challenging or disturbing them. The best way to help others to a healthy, functional life is to set a positive example and, when possible, share helpful words of encouragement. Regardless of what others do, the devotee should be consistently engaged in the yoga of knowledge and right disciplined actions.

27. Actions of all kinds are performed by the qualities [gunas] of nature; a person whose mind is confused by egoism [deluded self-sense] mistakenly thinks, "I am the doer."
28. That devotee who knows the truth about the two roles—of the Self which is removed from involvement and of the qualities [gunas] which produce actions—and understands that it is the qualities which interact, is not attached to their actions.
29. Those who are deluded by the qualities [gunas] of nature are attached to those actions. One with higher knowledge should not disturb the minds of people whose knowledge is incomplete.

The key to understanding our relationship with life's processes and to knowing what actions we should perform, is to remain stable in awareness of our true nature as spiritual beings. It is only when soul awareness becomes identified with disordered thought processes, sentiment, and shifting moods that it becomes clouded and confusion reigns.

30. Surrendering all actions in me, established in Self-knowledge, being free from desire and egoism, delivered from your confusion, engage in right endeavor!

Surrendering all actions to the Infinite, established in Self-knowledge, being free from desire and egoism [mistaken self-identity], delivered from your [former] confusion, engage in right endeavor!

31. Faith-filled devotees who steadfastly practice this teaching are released from the bondage of actions.
32. But distrustful and disrespectful people who do not practice this teaching, know *them* to be confused about wisdom, lost and devoid of reason.

Devotees who have faith in God and in this enlightened teaching find it easy to remain committed to practices they know to be beneficial. Those who doubt the value of spiritual practices and who are cynical, lack clear understanding of the purpose of life and its possibilities, and are irrational.

33. One acts according to one's own nature. Even the wise do so. When people follow their own material nature, what can [attempts at] restraint accomplish?

Success in yoga practice requires total dedication to it. If dedication is not total, one is merely indulging in metaphysical speculation and engaging in halfhearted endeavors to meditate to avoid having to confront the facts of life and the need to grow to emotional maturity. The rhetorical question is asked: When people are intent upon letting their lives be dictated by habits, of what value are their feeble attempts to regulate physical and mental impulses or to aspire to higher understanding? If people claim to be devotees of God without living up to their highest potential for excellence, we can assume them to be either lacking in knowledge about what is required on the spiritual path, or insincere.

34. Attachment and aversion to objects are seated in the senses. One should not come under the power of these two tendencies for they are indeed opposed to the soul's well-being.

The way to transcend attachment and aversion is to: (1) avoid considering either to be a problem; (2) remove attention from these inclinations and their objects by being so intent on awakening to higher knowledge and being freely functional that they are easily renounced.

35. Better is one's own duty [dharma] though imperfectly performed than the duty of another performed well. Better is defeat in one's own duty, for to follow another's path is to invite difficulty.

Ask: What am I here to do? Having discovered what it is, do it to the best of your ability. In this way will you steadily grow in knowledge and in grace. To endeavor to emulate the destiny of another is to live a shallow life, devoid of soul satisfaction. Materially minded people often think only of surviving until they are placed in a grave. Because they believe death to be inevitable, they fear it and distrust life. A devotee should know, "I am an immortal, spiritual being," and live with that understanding. Life can then be lived fearlessly, skillfully, and successfully.

Arjuna asked:

36. By what influence is a person impelled to commit error, as if by a force contrary to personal will?

Krishna replied:

37. It is desire, and anger born of rajas guna, all-consuming and greatly injurious. Know this to be the enemy [of good intentions and of attempts at right endeavor].
38. As fire is obscured by smoke, as a mirror by dust, as the embryo is enveloped by the membrane, so the intellect is obscured by passion.
39. The knowledge even of the wise is obscured by this adversary, insatiable desire, O Arjuna.
40. The senses, the mind, and intelligence are said to be the abode of desire which veils wisdom and deludes the embodied being.
41. Therefore, control your senses and banish this destroyer of discrimination and wisdom.

The soul's individualized field of awareness is capable of apprehending sensation, is identified with an individualized mental field which is a fragment of Universal Mind, and uses the faculty of intellectual determination to discriminate between truth and untruth. When tamas guna prevails, awareness is clouded and mental and intellectual faculties are sluggish. When rajas guna prevails, there may be willingness to live with purposeful intention but conflicting, compelling desires driven by strong emotions impair powers of intelligence and incite one to energetic actions which do not always result in happy outcomes.

42. The senses, some say, are superior. [In truth] superior to the senses is the mind; superior to the mind is the power of intellect; and superior to the intellect is the Self.
43. Thus, knowing that which is superior to the intellect, sustaining [steadying] self-consciousness by Self-knowledge, eliminate the obstacle of insistent desire [that is often so difficult to overcome].

Personality-centered people assert that sense perceptions, satisfaction of sense urges, and emotional comfort are the dominant characteristics which determine knowledge of ourselves and motivate our behaviors. By such testimony they reveal their limitations. The mind is superior to the senses because the senses can be regulated by choice and intention. Intellectual determination is superior to the mind because it provides the means to discern truth from untruth. The Self, the soul or individualized field of awareness, is supremely superior to mind and body because it is instrumental in their production, can regulate them, and continues to exist when they cease to exist.

Knowing the truth about the senses, mind, intellect, and soul, the devotee is encouraged to remain calm while choosing to discard obsessive and useless desires so that attention and soul forces can be liberated and allowed to flow for the fulfillment of worthwhile purposes. When obstacles to flows of soul awareness and the soul's subtle, creative force (shakti) are removed—which is the real purpose of learning to knowledgeably perform right actions (kriyas)—necessary psychological transformations and spiritual awakening processes proceed without interruption. Whether one is engaged in meditative contemplation, involved with actions and relationships, enjoying interludes of leisure, or when asleep, when physical and mental obstacles to the free flow of soul awareness and soul force are absent, innate qualities and capacities spontaneously unfold.

*In the Upanishad of the Bhagavad Gita, the science of the
Absolute, the scripture of Yoga and the dialogue between
Sri Krishna and Arjuna, thus ends the third chapter,
entitled Karma Yoga: The Yoga of Action*

CHAPTER FOUR

The Yoga of Knowledgeable Renunciation of Action

While the devotee is encouraged to perform necessary actions, attachments to actions and their results are to be renounced so that a more cosmic understanding of life's processes can be apprehended. The purpose of spiritual practice is not to produce a condition of human fulfillment and happiness—although this side-benefit is acceptable if it does not detract from spiritual growth endeavors. It is to provide the means for ultimate discovery of the soul's relationship with the Infinite. In this chapter it is explained that knowledge of The Eternal Way is revealed from the core or heart of Consciousness.

Krishna said:

1. **I proclaimed this imperishable yoga to Vivaswat; who communicated it to Manu; who imparted it to Ikshvaku.**

    Supreme Consciousness imparted this knowledge of Self-realization to its manifesting light, from which it passed to Cosmic Mind and to radiant cosmic life force.

While the opening verses of this chapter seem to speak of religious mythology and historical events, the inner meaning can be intuitively discerned. Knowledge of Consciousness is innate to it at all levels and in every aspect of its expression. Souls, expressed units of God's light, are innately endowed with complete knowledge of Consciousness and its processes. The names used to designate the categories of manifesting Consciousness are actually code words, which, when intuitively understood, reveal the inner meaning of the verses.

From the Field of Absolute Pure Consciousness an impulse to express resulted in its "shining forth" (*Vivaswat*) as light, the first objective manifestation of Supreme Consciousness. Because manifested expressions of Supreme Consciousness are inseparable from their origin, the essences of manifestations have characteristics of their cause. Light expressed as sound (Om) and primordial nature along with Cosmic Mind (*Manu, manas* or mind: the progenitor of man or humankind and that which processes perceptions. Cosmic Mind is the field in which cosmic processes occur). Radiant, manifested cosmic life force (*Ikshvaku*), is infused with knowledge which governs its processes, and enlivens and animates nature.

This imperishable yoga—of knowledge of categories of cosmic manifestation and its actions—was described in the second and third chapters. It is now further explained that knowledge is innate to every aspect of Consciousness. Comprehension of this *yoga of knowledge* provides understanding of the *yoga of actions* or *processes*, which make possible the experience of the *yoga of unification* of the individualized field of awareness (soul) and the universal field of awareness (God), so that the *yoga of oneness* (wholeness, samadhi) can be reclaimed or realized.

2. **Thus transmitted by succession, the royal sages knew this [truth] until, after a long duration of time, it was lost to the world.**

    Thus receiving this knowledge by direct transmission, realized souls knew this truth until, after an extended duration of time, it was forgotten by most people.

There is an inner meaning to this verse. The radiance of Consciousness can be perceived in the spiritual eye as a brilliant sun-like light (Vivaswat) which energizes the mind (Manu) and vitalizes the subtle and gross bodies by flows of life force through the chakras (the royal sages). When the soul's attention constantly flows outward and attachments obscure awareness, causing misperceptions or illusions, the truth of one's being is temporarily forgotten and has to be unfolded.

Because localized processes reflect cosmic processes, the flow of knowledge of Consciousness, along with its progressive stages of manifestation, can be discerned within the field of individualized awareness.

Lahiri Mahasaya, commenting on these verses, said that the

flow of knowledge of Consciousness is revealed within the individual from the inner Self to the inner light, to the still state of breath (prana), to the tranquil or desireless state.

When the devotee is established in soul peace and life forces are harmonized and stilled, the fluctuations and transformations that ordinarily occur in the field of awareness are calmed and the impulses which empower them are dormant, allowing the light of the soul or true Self to shine.

Many souls experience a clouding of awareness, become deluded, and forget the truth of themselves and God as they become progressively identified with mind and matter. Subjective facts of life are known to very few people during a Dark Age, to about one-half of the population during the second ascending cycle, to about three-quarters of the population during the third ascending cycle, and to almost everyone during the fourth, culminating cycle, an Age of Enlightenment when knowledge of God is comprehended. At all times there are souls with characteristics corresponding to these four time-cycles. Some souls are asleep to truth; others are partially awake to it; many are almost fully awake to it; and a few are fully awake. In our solar system, the Ages progress and decline in 12,000 year time-phases divided into 1,200, 2,400, 3,600, and 2,400 year segments: 12,000 years ascending and 12,000 years descending cycles, or 24,000 years to complete the process. Human beings, acted upon by celestial influences, experience a clearing of their faculties of perception during ascending cycles and a clouding of perceptual faculties during descending cycles. Individuals, however, can remove their awareness from external influences and choose to facilitate rapid spiritual awakening regardless of external circumstances. Advanced meditation techniques enable an initiate of Kriya Yoga to transform the body's brain and nervous system so that soul awareness can more easily flow and mental restrictions can be eliminated, allowing spontaneous unfoldment of Self-knowledge.

Just as knowledge of Consciousness is directly conveyed from its source into and through all levels of manifestation, so this knowledge, along with transformative spiritual power (shakti), is transmitted by succession from enlightened teachers to their receptive disciples who, in turn, when sufficiently enlightened, can represent the soul-liberating tradition.

3. **This same ancient yoga is today declared by me to you, because you are my disciple and friend. This is indeed the supreme secret knowledge.**

This same knowledge of Consciousness and its processes, inaccessible to the undiscerning, is immediately Self-revealed when the devotee is prepared to apprehend it.

Arjuna spoke:

4. **You were born after those ancient ones. How am I to understand that you declared this truth to them?**

Although now interested and attentive, the devotee errs in presuming that its innermost reality, the true Self, emerged after the manifestation of light, mind, and expressive life forces.

Krishna replied:

5. **I have had many embodiments, and so have you; all of them I know, but yours you know not.**

Supreme Consciousness has often been in relationship to manifested forms, as has each individualized unit of awareness or soul; Supreme Consciousness is aware of all of its relationships, but souls confined to self-consciousness are not thus aware.

Manifesting aspects of Supreme Consciousness are many, as are the relationships the soul has with mind and matter. The difference is that Supreme Consciousness, though manifesting to express in various ways, is never diminished or confined by its interactions with mind and matter. While regulating cosmic processes, it transcends them. Souls, individualized fields of awareness, tend to overly identify with mind and matter because of egoism (a false sense of selfhood), delusions, and illusions. Therefore, memories of their past experiences in space and time are hidden in the recesses of the subconscious mind.

6. **Although I am unborn and my true Self is imperishable, although I am the lord [governing influence] of all creatures, yet established in my own nature, I manifest by my own power.**

Although Supreme Consciousness is unborn, imperishable, and the ruler or determining influence of all creatures, yet established in its transcendent state, it expresses by its limitless potential and innate impulse to do so.

Forever transcendent Supreme Consciousness manifests as light and vibrating energy (Om) endowed with intelligence that interacts to produce primordial nature. The light of Consciousness reflected from the field of primordial nature manifests as units of individualized consciousness or souls. The self-veiling characteristic of primordial nature (maya) makes possible the categories of cosmic manifestation.

7. **Whenever there is a decrease of righteousness and an increase of unrighteousness, I come into manifestation.**
8. **For the protection of the virtuous, for the removal of non-virtue, and to establish righteousness [dharma], I come into manifestation from Age to Age.**

Whenever there is a decrease of righteousness [sattva guna influences] and an increase of unrighteousness [tamas guna influences], then Supreme Consciousness is impelled to express. For the protection of constructive conditions and aspiring souls, for the removal of impediments to orderly unfoldment and to establish harmonious, constructive actions, it expresses whenever necessary.

In the field of individualized soul consciousness and in the field of planetary consciousness, whenever the impulse of evolution contends with resistance and disorder increases, a new spiritual impulse originates in the Field of Pure Consciousness that restores the momentum of evolution. This happens for the nurturing of souls and of nature, for the removal of obstacles to evolutionary actions, and to restore supportive actions.

In the collective field of consciousness shared by all living beings, the trend of evolution is always toward growth and completion of impelled purposes. Although there may be occasions of stress and even of conflict and disaster, the inexorable creative force of the Supreme Self, God, will have dominion. In our current Era, evolutionary currents are resulting in mass soul awakening and the emergence of the *universal avatar*—a more obvious expression of God's Consciousness expressing through human beings and nature. From time to time enlightened souls are born into the world, to teach anew the eternal truths, implement constructive actions, be an example to others of what life can be like, and to provide collective consciousness a fresh infusion of transformative, vitalizing, redemptive spiritual energy.

While the presence and blessing-actions of enlightened souls are to be acknowledged and appreciated, the devotee must be self-responsible for his or her own right choices and spiritual growth. One is foolish to remain passively complacent in the face of obvious personal need to wisely act—or to plead weakness and ineptitude while hoping for an avatar, savior, or messiah to come to the rescue and make everything right.

Knowledge is imparted to us that we might learn and apply it. All knowledge of God and life's processes is available to us, to be acquired from valid sources and self-revealed from the innermost core of our eternal being.

9. One who knows in truth my divine manifestations and actions, upon departing the body is not born again; that soul comes to me.

One who comprehends the reality of Supreme Consciousness and its expressions and actions, awakens from delusions and illusions of births and deaths because permanently established in flawless realization of wholeness.

10. Contemplating me only, resorting to me, many whose greed, fear, and anger have departed, purified by the discipline of knowledge, have awakened to my state of being.

With attention absorbed in pure consciousness, turning to it at all times, many souls with all obstacles to awakening having been overcome or removed, and devoid of error because established in knowledge of the truth of life, have realized absolute liberation.

When we choose to identify with self-conscious states and their characteristics, we play an egocentric role in time and space. When we choose to flow our attention to the Absolute, we facilitate our awakening from limitations to realization of complete knowledge and freedom.

11. In whatever way devotees take refuge in me, I provide them grace. Devotees everywhere [of various psychological temperaments and in various ways] follow my path.

However devotees turn to God, God provides them grace. Regardless of the outer form of endeavor or practice, rightly resolved souls with knowledge and devotion adhere to the eternal way of righteousness.

We apprehend the reality of Consciousness according to our capacity to do so. When new on the Self-discovery path we may have traditional ideas about what God is. Our endeavors to know God may be limited by our conditioned mental concepts and immature, emotion-based aspirations. Even so, if we are sincere, if we turn our attention to higher realities, we open ourselves to the actions of grace which express as awakened, transformative soul impulses from within and as supportive circumstances in our everyday experience.

12. Those who desire the results of their actions here on earth offer sacrifice to the gods, and quick indeed are such actions productive.

People wanting immediate fulfillment of their personal desires in this mundane realm learn and use creative principles of causation that provide quick results.

The "gods" are the causative principles which determine the effects of applied actions. When we want to have our desires fulfilled and our needs met, we have only to learn how to cooperate with the causative principles which determine these outcomes. By ridding the mind of beliefs of limitation and by rational use of creative mental processes—supplemented by effective actions when necessary—our desires can be easily fulfilled and our needs spontaneously met. We should learn to function skillfully in order to fulfill our primary aims in life, including that of awakening to God-realization. If our interests and actions are primarily personality-centered, we may successfully demonstrate a comfortable human existence devoid of God-knowledge and soul peace. To fulfill our spiritual destiny we need not completely withdraw from mundane relationships—indeed, we cannot. We need only to put spiritual growth first in our order of priorities, then live a natural, orderly life. The same creative skills—imagination, intention, the cultivation of faith, and expansion of awareness to apprehend and feel comfortable with new or alternative circumstances—that enable us to accomplish our mundane purposes can be used to facilitate spiritual growth.

Mahavatar Babaji, the first guru in the Kriya Yoga lineage I represent, told disciples, "Few people in mortal (conditioned) states of consciousness know that God's reality extends fully to this earth plane." We should live freely in this world. Complete freedom includes soul freedom.

13. **The fourfold kinds of human endeavor were created by me according to the divisions of qualities and actions in the field of nature. Although I am their maker, know me to be eternally transcendent and beyond actions or change.**

Four categories of human psychophysiological types are expressed according to the characteristics caused by the influences of sattva guna, rajas guna, tamas guna, and karma or individual causative influences. Although these characteristics are made possible by Supreme Consciousness from which the gunas are produced, Supreme Consciousness remains removed from them.

The four kinds of human behavior in relationship to accomplishment of purposes correspond to the stages of personal mental and spiritual development characteristic of the four Ages or electric time-cycles. They are in accord with how the influences of the qualities of nature are expressive, modified by the individual karmic condition.

When tamasic influences result in apathy and mental dullness, individuals tend to be capable of but routine survival behaviors. In society, these characteristics are evident in the behavior of the majority of the planet's human inhabitants. During the period of history and in the culture when the *Bhagavad Gita* was written, people with these characteristics were referred to as *sudras*, the working class.

When tamasic and rajasic influences are both influential, individuals are more capable of independent thinking and action. In society, these characteristics are evident in the behaviors of planners, organizers, and executives. People with these characteristics and duties were referred to as *vaisyas*.

When rajasic and sattvic influences are more dominant, individuals are inclined to be active in preserving the values and circumstances favorable to the common good. In society, these characteristics are evident in the behaviors of representatives and custodians of government, education, science, the arts, religion, and philosophy. People with these characteristics and duties were referred to as *kshatriyas*. In the *Gita* story, Arjuna belonged to this category.

When sattvic influences prevail, individuals are more insightful, intellectual powers are pronounced, and spiritual qualities are more obviously actualized. In society, these characteristics are evident in the idealists, visionaries, discoverers, prophets, enlightened philosophers, and custodians and teachers of spiritual values. People with these characteristics and duties were known as *brahmins*.

These four categories are broad because of the mixed influences of the gunas, genetic predisposition, degrees of intelligence and soul awareness, and individual karmic conditions. Because people are capable of changing, learning, and growing, with the exception of the mentally incompetent, no one is confined to a social class or station in life except by choice and behavior.

Devotees on a spiritual path exhibit the characteristics of the influences of the qualities of nature as well as unique characteristics in relationship to their emotional, mental, intellectual, moral, and spiritual development.

Devotees strongly influenced by tamas guna tend to be difficult to teach because of their clouded intellect, and may be lax in their endeavors because of feeble aspiration to improve and a general sense of heaviness or inertia. If they are religious, they tend to be blind believers of doctrine, with little or no interest in learning, or ability to do so. If they meditate, they tend to be passive, inclined to unconscious states or to create a pleasant mood that provides emotional comfort or mental satisfaction.

Devotees influenced by a mixture of tamasic-rajasic characteristics tend to be enchanted by phenomena and magical possibilities, interested in the strange and mysterious, and are confused because of their delusions (erroneous beliefs and opinions) and illusions (tendency to err in perception). If they meditate, they tend to be fascinated by visions, symbolic revelations, and psychic perceptions or experiences.

Devotees influenced by both rajas guna and sattva guna tend to be energetic, restless, self-serving, and motivated to personal accomplishment. If committed to a philosophical or religious tradition, they tend to aggressively defend it. When they meditate, they tend to be forceful, endeavoring to cause effects, or to be inclined to create or achieve an ecstatic state or to overly identify with inner perceptions. They sometimes give attention to acquiring proficiency in the practice of meditation techniques and procedures but neglect to remember that techniques and procedures are but the means to the desired end.

Devotees influenced by sattva guna tend to be purely motivated to improve intellectual abilities and to awaken soul qualities and capacities. Their aspiration is to be enlightened and liberated. When they meditate they contemplate their relationship with God and transcendent realities.

All of these kinds of devotees can improve their practices and their circumstances by becoming better informed, applying what they learn, choosing an entirely wholesome, constructive lifestyle, emulating role models whose behaviors are superior, and living up to their highest potential to the best of their ability.

14. **Actions do not defile me, nor do I desire the results of actions. The devotee who [truly] knows me is [likewise] not bound by actions.**

Cosmic actions influenced by the qualities of nature or by motiveless, creative impulses of Supreme Consciousness do not mar or stain Supreme Consciousness which is transcendent. The devotee established in realization of the Self is likewise untouched by actions.

We are not adversely influenced by our thoughts, feelings, actions, or the results of actions when we do everything while remaining established in Self-realization.

15. **Knowing this, devotees in times past who aspired to liberation of consciousness, performed right actions. Therefore, engage in yoga practice as they did.**

Even though the soul or Self is not directly affected by routine behaviors or spiritual practices, its qualities and capacities are released from identification with mind and matter when helpful actions are implemented for the purpose of removing physical and mental obstacles which cloud awareness or restrict function. Inspired by the example of others who have successfully fulfilled their spiritual destiny, we, also, should fulfill our own.

16. **What is action? What is inaction? These questions confuse even wise people. I will explain to you what action is. Knowing this, you shall be liberated from all bondage caused by ignorance.**
17. **One has to understand what [right] action is, what is wrong action, and the nature of inaction. To understand requires clear insight.**
18. **That one who perceives inaction in action and action in inaction, is wise. Such a one is an accomplished yogi.**

An action is an impulse or causative influence that produces an effect. For a devotee, right actions are those which enhance life, allow successful accomplishment of purposes, and contribute to spiritual growth. Wrong actions, for them, are those which diminish life, contribute to disorder and misfortune, and restrict spiritual growth. An insightful devotee knows that, while implementing actions, the essence of being is always inactive.

19. **That devotee whose endeavors are devoid of willful desire, whose karma is consumed in the fire of knowledge, is referred to by the wise as a sage.**

    That insightful devotee who acts by disinterested necessity, whose actions and their effects are purified by revealed knowledge, is said to be wise.

A devotee's behaviors should be motivated by knowledge. Neither compulsion nor willfulness should be allowed. Compulsion is due to obsessive urges. Willfulness is grounded in emotional immaturity and self-centeredness. Knowledge of higher realities is compared to fiery influence that effects psychological transformation by neutralizing destructive mental conditionings and providing insight that enables the soul to discard delusions and illusions.

20. Having abandoned all attachment to the results of actions, always [soul] content and independent even when performing actions, that devotee actually does nothing at all.

Established in renunciation and Self-knowledge while engaged in right actions, the devotee knows, "I am not the doer."

When established in soul contentment, while being responsible for our clear intentions and constructive behaviors, we can function freely with the understanding that what happens as a result are but effects unfolding in the realm of nature.

21. Without compelling desire, and having renounced all motives for attainment, performing actions by the body alone, that devotee makes no mistakes.

Devoid of compulsions and cravings and without being motivated for the purpose of personal gain, doing in the right spirit whatever needs to be done, that devotee performs flawlessly.

To perform actions by the body alone means to witness all actions from the point of view of being a soul expressing through the body. Necessary actions can then be performed with detached, skillful appropriateness.

22. That one who is content with what comes by providence, who has transcended the dualities [of pleasure and displeasure], who is free from envy and remains even-minded in success or failure, even though implementing action, is not in bondage.

The devotee who accepts the results of personal actions and of grace, who is aloof from circumstances that change, is devoid of psychological disorders and remains calm and undisturbed regardless of what happens, is inwardly free while performing right actions.

23. The actions of one whose attachments are removed, who is liberated, whose mind is stable in knowledge, and who performs actions as sacrifice, are completely dissolved.

The actions of one who is devoid of attachments, who is free from delusions and illusions, whose mind is grounded in knowledge [of Consciousness and its processes], and who performs right actions as an offering to evolution, vanish leaving no trace.

24. God is the sacrifice, God is the pouring out of the offering into the fire of God, God is realized by that one who perceives God in actions.

God is the offering of actions to evolution and the flowing of the actions into transformative processes. By the devotee who clearly comprehends this, God is realized.

When the devotee's knowledge of all aspects and actions of God are clearly known, the ego or self-sense is purified. One is then aware of the fact that the sense of independent existence is but a viewpoint that makes possible the free soul's relationship with the realm of nature. One looks out upon the world through the screen of egoism while remaining inwardly established in Self-knowledge.

25. Some yogis offer sacrifices to the gods; others offer selfless sacrifice into the fire of God.

Some practitioners of yoga make offerings [of their thoughts and actions] to the agencies of nature which can reward their endeavors; others [who are wise] freely offer [surrender] self-consciousness in favor of God-realization.

The necessity of surrender of egocentric self-sense to awaken to Self-knowledge and God-realization is a core teaching of the *Gita* and other yoga scriptures. In Patanjali's *Yoga Sutras* 3:38, although soul abilities (siddhis) are described, emphasis is upon using them for the purpose of facilitating spiritual awakening:

> These abilities, if allowed to flow mainly outward, are obstacles to the unfoldment of soul awareness. If used properly, they become supernatural abilities useful for regulating and neutralizing instinctual and conditioned destructive drives and tendencies.

Yoga Sutras 3:51,52:

> By renouncing these powers, one removes the causes of bondage and completely transcends the relative spheres. There must not be any pride in the use of these abilities or attachment to them, as this can be the cause of reverting to a lower [deluded] state of awareness.

26. Others sacrifice hearing and other senses in the fires of restraint; still others sacrifice sound and other objects into the fires of the senses.

Other devotees discipline sensory and mental impulses; still others regulate their desires and dissolve attachment to externals to purify the sense urges.

Our five senses, along with the mind, allow us to communicate with the objective environment. We do not have to deny ourselves contact with the world or suppress thought processes. The senses need to be purified so that our lives are lived wholesomely and constructively, and mental processes need to be orderly so that rational thinking is natural to us.

27. Others sacrifice all actions of their senses and the actions of the vital force into the fire of yoga of self-control which is kindled by knowledge.

Inspired by a higher order of knowledge and devoted to yoga practice, some devotees internalize their vital forces by self-discipline and various practices such as mantra, pranayama, and meditative contemplation.

The most direct and effective way to master and purify the senses and the mind is to withdraw attention and vital forces into the sushumna, the astral pathway in the spine, and flow it upward into the spiritual eye and higher brain centers. Advanced Kriya Yoga pranayama and supplemental meditation techniques can be used to awaken kundalini energies, enliven the chakras, merge in Om, and experience transcendent states of consciousness. These advanced methods require preliminary preparation by the devotee and personal instruction and initiation from a qualified guru or teacher.

When initiated, the devotee becomes a disciple of God, is given precise instruction about lifestyle routines and meditation practices by the guru, and receives a transmission of spiritual force (shakti) that awakens dormant soul qualities.

28. Some likewise offer as sacrifice their material possessions, or their austerities and spiritual practices, while ascetic devotees offer their study and learning.

> *Some likewise use available material means to nurture their health and well-being to make themselves fit to accomplish their holy purposes, or dedicate their disciplined actions and spiritual practices to God-realization, while completely resolved devotees study authentic truth teachings in order to be established in knowledge, then go beyond acquired knowledge to revelation.*

When we are completely committed to the spiritual growth path, everything we do is for the purpose of improving our understanding of our relationship with the Infinite and facilitating soul unfoldment.

29. Some yogis offer apana into prana and prana into apana to balance and neutralize the flows of vital forces.

> *Some practitioners of yoga use pranayama, regulating exhalation [to influence apana] and inhalation [to influence prana] to make their vital forces tranquil.*

Prana is the soul's vital force distributed throughout the body. Its several modified actions support various physiological functions. Of the five aspects of prana expressive in the body, the aspect involved in downward movements is called apana, influential during exhalation. The aspect directly involved in regulating respiration is called prana, influential during inhalation. These two influences are naturally reduced and their actions neutralized during deep meditation as superconscious states are experienced. Often, however, a devotee is not able to effectively meditate because of stress, restlessness, emotional disturbance, or mental unrest. By practicing pranayama, the meditator elicits profound physical relaxation and experiences slow, refined breathing, emotional calm, mental peace, and internalization of attention so that superconscious contemplation can proceed without interference. Although mental and emotional states may be regulated by an act of intentional will, if this is not possible, a devotee who knows how to practice pranayama will use this approach to directly and quickly remove psychophysiological obstacles to concentration and expanded states of consciousness.

The soul's prana or life force blends with the body at the medulla oblongata at the base of the brain, then flows to the higher brain centers and down through the chakras through which it is distributed and regulated. The three main channels (*nadis*) of prana flow in the spinal pathway are: (1) *ida*, the "moon" current, along the left side; (2) *pingala*, the "sun" current, along the right side; (3) *sushumna*, the central channel, referred to by yogis as "the path of God." The moon or lunar channel (ida) extends from the base of the spine, terminates in the left nostril, and is associated with the right hemisphere of the brain. It is cooling and calming, and is related to more passive, introverted, subjective mental and emotional states. The sun or solar channel (pingala) extends from the base of the spine, terminates in the right nostril, and is associated with the left hemisphere of the brain. It is heating and energizing, and is related to more active, objective, and analytical mental states. The sushumna channel extends from the base of the spine to the uppermost region of the brain. When flows of prana through it are active, the actions of the moon and sun currents are neutralized.

Breathing, prana flows, mental activities, emotional states, and physiological actions are interrelated. When breathing is slower and less forceful, stress is reduced, emotions are calmed, and mental activities are refined and diminished. Usually, rapid, erratic, forceful breathing is associated with emotional instability and mental restlessness and confusion. Slower, smooth, even, refined breathing is associated with emotional calm and mental orderliness and clarity. Intentional regulation of breathing patterns enables one to acquire a degree of intentional control over prana flows for the purpose of regulating physiological, emotional, and mental states so that soul awareness can more easily be experienced.

Five aspects of soul force are active in our bodies. Soul force, blending with the body at the medulla oblongata at the base of the brain manifests as five influential frequencies to facilitate the various functions necessary for our well-being:

- The *primary prana* active during respiration, enabling the body to draw in extra life force from oxygen atoms.
- *Apana*, influential during exhalation and also in eliminating waste matters.
- *Vyana*, the prana influence which governs circulations of fluids and other substances in the body, resists biological decay, and contributes to overall wellness.

- *Samana*, the prana influence which regulates digestion, assimilation, biochemical transformations, and balances the functioning of all physical systems.
- *Udana*, the prana influence which directs vital forces upward to the higher centers. It is also influential when the soul departs the body at the time of physical death.

Four subtle channels (nadis) in the spinal pathway are of particular interest to experienced yoga practitioners:

- *Sushumna* extends from the base chakra to the top of the brain and has within it two astral channels and one causal channel. When we meditate deeply, vital forces circulate more dynamically through the path of sushumna. Vital forces can be encouraged to flow through this channel by nurturing mental calm and practicing alternate nostril breathing and other pranayamas helpful for this purpose.
- Within sushumna is *vajra nadi*, an astral channel with rajas guna characteristics. When the meditator's inward flowing attention pierces this channel a variety of astral perceptions (lights, sounds, expansion of awareness) are possible, although awareness may not be clear and powers of discernment may not be keen.
- Within vajra nadi is *chitra nadi*, an astral channel with sattva guna characteristics. When the meditator's inward flowing attention pierces it, a variety of luminous astral perceptions are possible.
- Within chitra nadi is *brahmanadi*, a fine channel of causal substance. When the meditator's inward flowing attention pierces this channel, astral perceptions are transcended in favor of fine causal perceptions and insights that reveal transcendent realities.

30. **While others, who have moderated their food intake, offer the life breath into the life breath. All these are knowers of sacrifice, and by it their faults and the consequences of those faults have been dissolved.**

While others, who have regulated their diet [and other aspects of their lives], practice more intensive pranayama. All who are self-disciplined for the purpose of awakening to Self-realization are grounded in knowledge of the process of surrendered sacrifice or holy offering. Because of the resulting transcendent knowledge, the mental impressions of their past misguided actions and their effects have been dissolved.

Disciplined regulation of behaviors is essential to success on the spiritual path. One's total lifestyle needs to be conformed to realization and actualization of the heart's (soul's) impulse to reclaim freedom. A moderate, balanced, nutritional food plan is most suitable for physical and psychological health. When adequate but not excessive nourishment is provided, the body's needs are satisfied, the immune system is strengthened, energy reserves are maintained, and overall well-being is nurtured.

The mind, too, should only be fed with wholesome thoughts, mental attitudes, and emotional states, and sensory stimulation should be regulated. Lifestyle and behaviors should be chosen to allow enjoyable, effective living without stressing the nervous system or dissipating vital forces. By right, conscious living, life forces are conserved and are transmuted into finer essences which vitalize and regenerate the body, energize the mind, improve powers of concentration, and liberate consciousness. By offering life forces into their source, the devotee experiences awareness of universal life force and of Universal Consciousness.

The immediate way to pour life forces into their source is to practice *Kriya Pranayama*, a procedure that enables the meditating devotee to direct flows of life force upward and downward through the chakras in the sushumna pathway in the spine. Regular, correct practice of this pranayama technique neutralizes prana flows in the left and right channels, awakens dormant soul forces in the lower chakras and directs them upward to the brain, magnetizes the spinal pathway, cleanses the blood of carbon, vitalizes the body with prana, calms emotions, refines mental processes, empowers concentration, and facilitates adjustments of states of consciousness so that superconscious states are more easily experienced. Dedicated practice enables the devotee to clear the mental field of all distractions. Thought processes are ordered, refined, and diminished because prana flows become balanced and the erratic impulses that are ordinarily the cause of continuous mental fluctuations and transformations are quieted and become dormant.

In the Kriya Yoga tradition, it is taught that movements of vital force upward and downward through the sushumna pathway cleanse the physical, astral, and causal sheaths or bodies. The body's vital forces are balanced, harmful or potentially harmful mental conditionings (samskaras; impressions) are weakened and dissolved, and the subtle organs of perception are purified. It is taught that one complete cycle of mild upward and downward flows of vital force through sushumna contributes to inner transformations equivalent to those normally experienced during the course of a lunar month, a little more than 28 days. When flows are more concentrated, one complete cycle is said to result in transformative changes that normally occur during one solar year (365 days) of stress-free, healthy living supported by entirely natural and wholesome circumstances. By right living and intentional practice of superconscious meditation, the devotee is able to experience a quickening of spiritual evolution, awakening through the stages of soul unfoldment more rapidly than would otherwise be possible. New initiates are advised to practice 14 cycles of this pranayama twice a day. Later, the number can be increased, as can be the frequency of daily practice. When kundalini is awakened, soul-originating life forces (shakti) circulate continuously without the devotee having to perform pranayamas. The impulse of the soul toward liberation impels the appropriate actions which facilitate necessary psychophysiological transformation and regeneration.

Highest knowledge is direct experience: realization of transcendent realities. This knowledge removes one from delusions, illusions, and egocentric self-consciousness, freeing the soul from any relationship with past errors and their consequences (and eventually from involvement with all relative conditions).

31. Those enjoyers of the nectar of sacrificial remnants realize the Absolute. This world is not for one who offers no sacrifice; how then in any other world?

Those who experience soul tranquility, the result of holy offerings [surrendered meditation], realize the transcendent Reality. Since no one can live successfully in this realm without right offering, how can it be otherwise in any other realm?

The "sacrificial remnants" of right actions (spiritual practice) are the aftereffects tranquility (the "nectar" that purifies, enlivens, and confers realization of immortality) and spontaneous enlightenment as a result of self-unfolded, transcendent, realized knowledge.

In this and all realms of nature, actions are necessary to cause desired reactions or, as needed, to remove obstacles to the free flow of creative forces. Even subtle adjustments of mental states, viewpoints, and states of consciousness are actions. Actions can occur at gross, subtle, or fine levels.

32. Thus many kinds of sacrifice are available as means for realizing God. Know them all to be born of action; thus knowing you shall be liberated.

Thus many kinds of holy offerings can be the means for awakening to God-realization. Know them all to result from right action; thus knowing you shall be liberated.

According to need, result-producing or result-allowing actions can be performed. Ordinary actions can *cause* effects or *produce* results; actions which remove obstacles to expression *allow* results. A devotee needs to know when and how to act for best results. Remaining calm as the witness of what occurs can be a matter of choice. Right actions are sacrificial or holy offerings which clear the devotee's field of awareness and provide it access to transcendent knowledge of Consciousness which is liberating.

33. Better than sacrifice of material possessions is the sacrifice of knowledge. All actions without exception culminate in wisdom.

Better than holy offering of rituals, behaviors, and other physical or mental means, is the holy offering of acquired knowledge [to comprehend absolute truth]. All dedicated actions without exception allow wisdom to unfold.

One must work at one's level of need and competence. It is rare that a devotee can disregard preliminary and preparatory practices. Eventually, right practice allows the unfoldment of transcendent knowledge which removes one from dependence upon practices which were formerly necessary and helpful.

34. Know this! By humble submission, by enquiry, by selfless service, wise knowers of truth will be inclined to teach you higher knowledge.

> *Know this! By surrender of egocentric self-consciousness, by astute inquiry, by selfless service, enlightened souls will be willing to teach you knowledge [of God].*

Prerequisites for discipleship—for learning about God and practicing yoga to facilitate soul unfoldment—include humility, alert inquiry into what is to be known and how to know it, sufficient intelligence to enable one to discern what is to be known, emotional maturity, and selfless performance of actions. One may then be blessed to attract the attention of an enlightened guru, a God-realized teacher, who will be willing to share knowledge and instruct in the practical ways to facilitate spiritual growth.

35. When you know it [the truth], you will not again fall into delusion; by that knowledge you will see all beings without exception in the Self, and in me.

> *When you have true knowledge, you will never again be deluded; by it you will see all souls without exception to be within the field of your own omnipresent awareness, and within the Field of God.*

To be established in true or final knowledge is to be stable in realized experience of it. From this state there is no falling back to prior, unconscious, deluded states. Self-consciousness gives way to superconsciousness (degrees of soul awareness) and to cosmic conscious states which allow clear experience of wholeness in which no separation or "otherness" exists.

36. Even if you were the most misguided among the unrighteous, you would cross over the river of delusion by the boat of knowledge.

> *Even if you were the most malicious person, you would transcend all limitations because of the liberating effect of true knowledge.*

Here is the promise that can inspire hope in the heart of the devotee who is attracted to the spiritual path and yet despairs because of memories or present awareness of grievous misdeeds. The redemptive results of right actions and God's grace are sure to be transformative and liberating for the devotee who wholeheartedly devotes all attention and right actions to the yoga of practice and the yoga of superconscious samadhi.

37. As the kindled fire reduces wood to ashes, even so the fire of knowledge reduces all actions to ashes.

As fire transforms wood to ashes, the radiance of knowledge transforms all actions to their most reducible essence.

Illumination of consciousness that reveals all knowledge of God and of the processes of life allows the devotee to clearly apprehend the causes of actions and their effects, enables actions to become progressively refined, and finally removes from the body and mind all traces of causation. Even the qualities of nature (gunas) which are instrumental in actions are transformed and returned to the field of unmanifest nature.

38. Nowhere in the world is anything that purifies that is equal to God-knowledge. That devotee who is perfected in yoga, in the course of time discovers that knowledge in the Self.

Nowhere is there anything that cleanses like God-knowledge. That devotee who is perfected in spiritual practice and the samadhi of superconsciousness, progressively discovers redemptive knowledge to be innate to the soul.

Where there is light, darkness is absent. The emergence of self-revealed knowledge of Reality is progressive until fully unfolded from the innermost essence of the true Self. Until complete enlightenment, incomplete knowledge is recognized as a higher form of ignorance.

39. That one who has faith acquires God-knowledge. Devoted to that, controlling the senses, and having wisdom, the devotee quickly attains the tranquil state.

The devotee with faith acquires knowledge. Devoted to it, regulating the senses, and having mature insight, one rapidly progresses to realization of soul peace.

40. The ignorant person who does not have faith, who is of a doubting nature, perishes. For the doubting person, neither in this world nor the realms beyond, is there happiness.

One who lacks knowledge, who is without faith, and habitually doubts [higher realities and possibilities for spiritual growth], sinks into sense-involvements and apathy. For the [persistently] doubting person there is no possibility of happiness in this world or another.

41. Actions do not bind the devotee who has renounced them by the practice of yoga, whose doubt has been banished by knowledge, and who is ever established in Self-realization.

Right actions do not confine one who has renounced them by practice of superconscious meditation, whose doubts have been eliminated by unfolded knowledge, and who is ever established in Self-realization.

42. Therefore, having cut away with the sword of knowledge this doubt in your heart caused by ignorance, practice yoga! Stand up!

Having with discriminative knowledge removed all doubt born of ignorance, diligently practice yoga [samadhi]. Be firm in your resolve!

In this story, Arjuna is portrayed as a soul awakened to third chakra awareness: skillfully functional and still involved with traditional attitudes and conditioned beliefs while desirous of learning how to live more effectively and to know higher realities. To meet the soul's need, revelations about the Spirit of God and how God's influences act upon the natural world spontaneously unfold. In this chapter, the soul acquires more insight about how to be focused and intentional, and how to explore the inner recesses of mind and consciousness.

In the Upanishad of the Bhagavad Gita, the science of the Absolute, the scripture of Yoga, and the dialogue between Sri Krishna and Arjuna, thus ends the fourth chapter entitled Karmabrahmarpana Yoga: The Yoga of Knowledgeable Renunciation of Action

CHAPTER FIVE

The Yoga of Renunciation

Renunciation is accomplished by seeing ourselves in our true relationship to our thoughts, feelings, actions, and circumstances, and living without compulsions or attachments of any kind. The end result of successful yoga practice is unwavering realization of ourselves as spiritual beings in relationship to the Infinite.

Arjuna inquired:

1. You praise abandonment of actions [for the purpose of spiritual growth] and also their selfless performance. Tell me definitely, which is the better of these two?

The devotee, confused about whether to disregard spiritual practices in favor of seeking knowledge, turns to the source of knowledge within to discover the best way to proceed.

Krishna answered:

2. The abandonment of actions and their selfless performance both result in liberation. Of the two, the performance of selfless actions is better than their abandonment.

A successful outcome of either way results in liberation of consciousness. The way of directly apprehending complete knowledge is difficult for the average person because of: (1) inadequate powers of concentration and intellectual ability; (2) the disturbing influences of psychological conflicts; (3) the devotee's mind and body may need to be refined so that soul awareness can more easily be processed through them. Arjuna's mental state indicates the need to practice yoga. To succeed on the spiritual path, a devotee should adhere to the path which is most beneficial.

3. That one is a true renunciate who neither loathes nor desires, who is indifferent to the dualities. Such a devotee is easily liberated from bondage.

Indifference to what is apparent is not the same as being unconcerned or avoiding the obvious; it is objectivity which enables one to disregard that which presents no challenge and to efficiently relate to and deal with what needs to be confronted. In this way, because there are no disturbing emotional reactions to what is observed or experienced, psychological problems are no longer created. When soul awareness is not restricted by psychological conflicts, restless mental states, erroneous beliefs (delusions), or misperceptions (illusions), keen powers of discriminative intelligence and intuition enable it to perceive flawlessly and function effectively.

4. **Those who are without understanding declare the way of knowledge and the way of yoga practice to be different, but not the wise. When either way is successfully practiced, the fruit [end result] of both is experienced.**

Our approach to discovery and spiritual growth is most effective when we choose the way which is compatible with our temperament and capacity. Some devotees are endowed with keen powers of concentration and intellect. Others are more devotional, have a basic nature which is service oriented, or are incapable of introverted, meditative contemplation when new on the Self-realization quest.

5. **The realization experienced by knowledge is also actualized by yoga practice. The devotee who understands that the way of knowledge and the way of yoga practice are the same, sees the truth.**

While the outer forms of yoga practice differ, the inner way—the process by which knowledge is Self-revealed—is the same. A wise devotee who knows this fact will adhere to the most beneficial path while acknowledging freedom of choice to others. For authentic spiritual growth, one should adhere to the program of study, living, and spiritual inquiry which allows progressive, rapid unfoldment of innate qualities and knowledge.

6. **Renunciation is indeed difficult to perfect without yoga practice. The wise devotee who is disciplined in yoga practice quickly realizes God.**

It is usually difficult to be emotionally settled and free from attachments by endeavoring to come to terms with circumstances and relationships by mental analysis alone. When we have considerable intellectual understanding, emotional states may interfere with honest attempts to think in a rational manner, or the mind may be overcome by a rush of sensory input or be strongly influenced by subconscious conditionings and addictive tendencies. Physical urges may be demanding, dormant desires may become insistent, and memories may flood our awareness and cause mental and emotional confusion. Tiredness may impair concentration. Inadequate nutrition may contribute to weakness or illness. Mood swings may dominate mental processes and influence behaviors. For various reasons, yoga practice based on individual needs and supported by a wholesome, constructive lifestyle, is the most practical approach to spiritual growth. Thus, the *wise* devotee *who is disciplined in yoga practice* quickly awakens to knowledge and experience of God.

7. **The one who is devoted to yoga practice, whose field of awareness is purified, whose soul nature is tranquil, whose senses are controlled, who realizes cosmic consciousness, is not tainted by actions.**

When cosmic consciousness is experienced, a person is no longer confined to former, conditioned viewpoints. Understanding unfolds, enabling one to see circumstances and relationships in perspective. Delusions and illusions are discarded, and soul contentment prevails. Actions are then performed as necessary to produce intended effects or allow life-enhancing results without attachment to either the actions or their outcomes.

8. **Steadfast in yoga practice, whether seeing, hearing, touching, smelling, eating, walking, sleeping, or breathing, the knower of truth should think, "I do nothing at all."**
9. **When speaking, performing necessary bodily functions, holding objects, whatever is done, the devotee knows, "The senses [only] are occupied with their objects."**
10. **Having abandoned attachments, offering all actions to God, the devotee who thus acts is not tainted by misfortune, as a lotus leaf is not wetted by water.**

Steadfastness in yoga practice is the key to being able to accurately discern. We are steadfast when we are committed to the soul awakening path, when we are grounded in understanding of what we are in relationship to God and the realm of nature, and when we practice what we know to be best for us. It is then easy to remember that we are ever a witness to our thoughts, feelings, actions, and to externals. We are in relationship but we are not other than what we are as expressed units of Consciousness.

11. To purify individualized awareness, one who practices yoga, established in renunciation, performs actions with the body, mind, intellect, or merely with the senses.

Purification of the devotee's field of awareness is the purpose of practice. This is accomplished by right understanding and equanimity, using the body as an instrument to accomplish purposes, practicing to refine and diminish mental fluctuations and transformations, improving powers of intellectual discernment, and regulating sensory impulses.

12. One who has renounced the results of actions and is disciplined in yoga practice, experiences peace. The undisciplined person attached to results is bound by actions which are impelled by desire.

The ideal inspiration-to-right-action is to cheerfully do as duty what needs to be done. In this way, we can be inwardly peaceful at all times. Without this kind of discipline, we may be inclined to remain in bondage to desires, to performance of actions which can make possible fulfillment of desires, and to the end results of such actions. The devotee should meditate daily as spiritual duty, disregarding thoughts or feelings which might tempt one to do otherwise.

13. Inwardly renouncing all actions, the embodied soul, having mastered them, dwells comfortably in the body, neither acting nor causing action.

It is not the necessary or wisdom-guided outer actions that must be abandoned; it is mental and emotional attachment to them that must be renounced by the practitioner of yoga. This is entirely an inward process. One then lives at ease, knowing that actions belong to the realm of nature; not to the soul which is stable in Self-knowledge.

14. **Supreme Consciousness is not the creator of the means of action, the actions people perform, nor the relationships between causes and their effects. Nature is the field in which these circumstances occur.**

Although Supreme Consciousness provides the impulse that results in the emergence of the field of nature in which all actions occur, the Field of Pure Consciousness is not modified by what occurs. All-pervading Pure Consciousness is the Field in which relative phenomena manifests.

15. **All-pervading Supreme Consciousness is not influenced by righteous or unrighteous deeds of people. Unenlightened people are bewildered because their innate knowledge is obscured by delusions.**

The omnipresent Field of Pure Consciousness remains ever what it is. The field of awareness of the ordinary person is fragmented and confused because delusions and illusions suppress and veil Self-knowledge. One who hopes to accomplish spiritual growth while clinging to conditioned, self-conscious attitudes and behaviors aspires in vain, for these are the very circumstances that restrict soul awareness.

16. **For those in whom ignorance of the [true] Self is banished by knowledge, their enlightenment allows the Supreme Self to shine like the sun.**

When one's field of awareness is cleared of all obstructing conditions and Self-knowledge is actualized, the full reality of God is spontaneously revealed.

17. **Those who direct their attention to the Absolute, whose total awareness is absorbed in *that*, whose intent is to realize *that*, who aspire to *that* as the highest objective, whose faults and limitations have been removed by knowledge, awaken to full liberation from which there is no return.**

Enlightenment is not caused; it is experienced when restricting influences have been renounced or weakened and banished. Complete liberation permanently removes awareness from all conditions which formerly blinded the soul to Self-knowledge. Note the emphasis on the need for aspiration to the highest good and of having restrictions to soul awareness removed so that knowledge prevails. Some causes of soul limitation, and how to remove them, are described in the *Yoga Sutras* 2:4–11:

> Imperfect perception of the Real is the field of all restricting influences, whether these be dormant or active.
>
> Ignorance is assuming the noneternal to be eternal, the impure to be pure, the painful to be pleasurable, and the ego [sense of selfhood independent of God] as the real being.
>
> Egoism results from the soul's identification with matter.
>
> Dwelling on pleasure and objects of pleasure produces affection [for them] which results in attachments.
>
> Being repulsed by that which may contribute to pain or discomfort produces aversion.
>
> The urge toward death exists along with the inclination toward life, even in the wise. These urges are propelled by their own innate drives.
>
> These restricting influences should be overcome by resolving them into their subtle origins.
>
> The gross modifications of pain-causing influences [life-diminishing mental conditionings and self-defeating tendencies and habits] are to be overcome by calm, introspective self-analysis and superconscious meditation [samadhi].

18. The discerning devotee sees the same Supreme Consciousness in all people and creatures without exception.

Before the emergence of innate knowledge, it is possible to train ourselves to look through and beyond outer conditions to acknowledge the reality which supports their existence. We can then easily relate to all people and all expressions of life with respectful appropriateness.

19. Even here in this realm, the need for rebirth is overcome by those who are established in realization of oneness. They are stable in realization of Supreme Consciousness because of knowledge that it is flawless and the same everywhere.

Even while embodied, souls established in the samadhi of God-realization have transcended karmic conditions which may have otherwise been the cause of their future incarnations. Their realization of God is unchanging because they have experienced absolute oneness or wholeness.

20. One should not rejoice when attaining what is pleasant nor be mentally or emotionally disturbed when confronting what is unpleasant. With unwavering discernment, without delusion, a knower of God is established in God.

The key to being able to enjoy life without creating problems for ourselves or others is to live with enlightened (knowledgeable) purpose without being overly reactive to anything that occurs. While involved in relationships and activities, and when meditating, the yogi's discernment does not waver; awareness of being anchored in the Infinite is constant.

21. That devotee whose awareness is detached from externals, who is content in Self-knowledge and abides in samadhi, knows changeless bliss.

The *bliss* experienced by the Self-realized soul is the pure, serene joy of knowledge and freedom. It does not have a mental, emotional, or physical basis, nor is it any form of ecstasy due to energy flows or superficial happiness based on response to what is perceived.

22. Pleasures resulting from contact with externals are [possible] sources of pain because they have beginnings and endings. The wise devotee is not satisfied with them.

It is not spiritually detrimental for a devotee to experience pleasurable sensations in the course of normal living. The wise devotee is not addicted to pleasurable sensations nor to their causes because of knowing that neither can permanently endure. The pain of loss is certain if strong attachment to an object (or circumstance) of pleasure is allowed to persist, because souls and circumstances are continually flowing and changing. To cling to that which, by its very nature, is subject to change is to invite disappointment.

23. **The one who is able to resist and master the surges of emotion and desire while embodied, that one, steadfast in yoga practice, is fortunate and happy.**
24. **That one who finds happiness, delight, and light [of knowledge] only within, experiences the full reality of God.**

We can appropriately relate to circumstances of this or any realm without losing awareness of our spiritual reality as a flawless ray of God's light. Living like this allows us to be always inwardly happy. Such happiness is not dependent upon any external condition. Awareness of the reality of God can easily blossom when one is happily established in peace of soul. When samadhi is experienced during early stages of spiritual unfoldment, it is usually a temporary episode of transcendence. Samadhi is permanent when awareness is not involved with mental fluctuations or the influential attributes of nature after meditation practice. This is the constant state of spontaneous awareness of truth undisturbed by time or circumstances.

25. **Those knowers of truth, whose errors have been eliminated, who are settled in Self-knowledge, who are happy in the welfare of all beings, are free in God.**

Established in Self-knowledge and God-realization, the enlightened soul rejoices in the highest good of all souls and enjoys the freedom of liberation (salvation) while embodied.

26. **For those dedicated practitioners of yoga who have discarded desire and anger, whose thoughts and mental states are mastered, who are established in Self-knowledge, the happiness of God-realization is undiminished.**

This verse describes the condition realized by souls that have become accomplished by dedicated yoga practice.

27. **Disregarding externals, fixing the gaze inward between the eyebrows, harmonizing the breath within the nostrils;**
28. **The devotee established in knowledge, whose highest aspiration is liberation of consciousness, whose senses, mind, and intellect are controlled, from whom desire, fear, and anger have departed, is forever free.**

The direct way to soul peace is to withdraw attention from externals and from body and mind involvement during regular interludes of focused, meditative contemplation. This should be done until soul contentment and awareness of oneself as pure consciousness is experienced.

The process of meditation will be more fully explored in the following chapter.

29. Having known me to be the enjoyer of sacrifices and austerities, the mighty ruler of the worlds, the friend of all creatures, that devotee who is stable in wisdom is established in the peace of eternal tranquility.

Having comprehended Supreme Consciousness to be the enjoyer of holy offerings, the regulator of occurrences in the field of nature, the nurturing Reality of all life, a devotee whose wisdom is permanent is established in the peace of eternal tranquility.

We are individualized rays of God, the one changeless Being, vitalizing Life, and determining Power, and all that occurs unfolds in the Field of God. Because God is expressing as all souls, our endeavors to awaken to knowledge are divinely impelled. Every soul is destined to realize the truth of what God is. For the majority of devotees, a balanced Self-actualization program that includes essential self-disciplines, wholesome lifestyle regimens, effective spiritual practices, and attentive cultivation of intellectual and intuitive abilities, is most helpful.

In the Upanishad of the Bhagavad Gita, the science of the Absolute, the scripture of Yoga and the dialogue between Sri Krishna and Arjuna, thus ends the fifth chapter, entitled Sanyas Yoga: The Yoga of Renunciation

CHAPTER SIX

The Yoga of Meditation

Meditation is the most helpful spiritual growth procedure for sincere devotees of God. It should be correctly learned and faithfully practiced for the purpose of awakening to superconscious (samadhi) states which allow spontaneous unfoldment of cosmic consciousness, God-consciousness, and transcendence. Some writers who stress the devotional approach to Self-knowledge often overlook the message of this chapter, or err in considering it to be only of minor importance. The story of Arjuna's awakening to truth is the spiritual biography of every soul that aspires to freedom in God. The contest between tendencies and habits rooted in mind and the impulse of the soul to have awareness restored to wholeness, occurs within the body-mind of the devotee.

Krishna speaks:

1. **That devotee who dutifully performs actions without attachments is a renunciate yogi; not one who, without commitment, fails to perform holy offerings.**

    The devotee who selflessly does what must be done to accomplish worthwhile purposes is a practitioner of yoga established in renunciation; a person who is not thus dedicated, who does not surrender egocentric interests and practice meditation, is neither a renunciate nor a yogi.

2. **Renunciation is indeed true yoga. No one can be a practitioner of yoga [samadhi] without renouncing egocentric purposes.**

    Because egoism, the deluded sense of independent existence, is the primary cause of the conditioned self-conscious state, it must be renounced and transcended if authentic spiritual growth is to be experienced. Without surrender of the false sense of selfhood, yoga practice is not productive of satisfying results.

3. **For the wise one who aspires to samadhi, action is said to be the means; for the devotee who has already mastered samadhi, tranquility is said to be the means.**

Until the yoga of oneness is experienced, actions or processes to remove obstacles to Self-knowledge and to facilitate soul-freeing adjustments of states of consciousness are necessary. When the yoga of oneness (samadhi) is experienced, merely consciously resting in the tranquility of Self-knowledge is sufficient to allow further transformations and unfoldments to occur. While still aspiring to spiritual growth, constructive actions must be implemented by the devotee. When mental fluctuations that fragment awareness have been stilled by effective practice, soul unfoldment is spontaneously continuous because of the innate inclination of consciousness to be unrestricted.

Samadhi states and how to experience them are explained in the *Yoga Sutras* 1:15–23:

> One becomes established in dispassionate detachment by mastering compulsions and instinctual urges.
>
> The highest renunciation is the result of Self-realization which enables the devotee to disregard and transcend all cosmic forces [gunas].
>
> The superconscious [samadhi] state of wisdom is accompanied by thoughts, tranquility, and realization of unity with Universal Consciousness.
>
> When the mental field is clear, and its modifications are no longer influential, transcendental superconsciousness is experienced which leaves constructive residues [samskaras, impressions] in the mind.
>
> Superconsciousness devoid of true knowledge may be temporary. From this state one may continue to higher realizations or again become involved with the relative spheres, the realm of manifest nature.
>
> Preceded by Self-knowledge, unwavering self-confidence, self-discipline, enthusiasm, and attentiveness, one can practice meditation and awaken to final liberation of consciousness.
>
> Such devotees, intent upon meditation practice, soon experience superconsciousness.
>
> Devotees who are more intent attain immediate and superior results.
>
> Samadhi can be realized quickly by surrendering in God.

Preliminary samadhi states may be accompanied by subtle thinking, visual perceptions, and feelings produced by the unsettled mind. These may be caused by the actions of the *vrittis*, wavelike movements in the mental field impelled by *vasanas* (impulses of samskaras or mental impressions, as well as by impulses due to restlessness or the influence of desire or instinctual drives and tendencies). Thus a degree of superconsciousness may be experienced, supported by thoughts, visual or auditory perceptions, and feelings of pleasure. So long as the devotee understands that preliminary superconscious states should be transcended, they can be beneficial because they leave constructive impressions in the mental field which resist, restrain, and replace destructive mental impressions.

Preliminary superconsciousness supported by subtle thoughts and perceptions is *savikalpa samadhi* (superconsciousness with support of the object of contemplation, therefore, subject to change). Fascination with or attachments to meditative perceptions and pleasurable sensations is an obstacle to progress in samadhi. Visions (conscious, dreamlike visual perceptions caused by mental restlessness) should be ignored, and inclinations to enjoy prolonged pleasurable sensations, whether caused by energy flows or a sense of delight because of unfoldment of subtle states of awareness, should be avoided. Higher or transcendental samadhi is *nirvikalpa* (without support, not accompanied by objects of perception or influences). Since samadhi is the natural state of soul awareness, it is quickly realized by attentive meditative contemplation and surrender of self-consciousness (the illusion of independent existence) so that wholeness is apprehended and experienced.

4. **When the devotee is not attached to the objects of the senses nor to actions, and has renounced all [egocentric] purposes, that one is said to be an accomplished yogi.**

Realization of oneness (yoga) is not permanent until the devotee is firmly established in it. Until then, attention wavers because of undiscerning involvements with circumstances, egocentric identification with self-generated actions, and the influence on clouded soul awareness by actions or movements which occur in one's field of awareness. All problems are solved by dissolving the false sense of selfhood in favor of apprehending and experiencing unconfined, unbounded awareness.

5. **One should elevate the self-conscious state by Self-knowledge; one should not be sorrowful or depressed; for the Self alone can be a friend of the self-conscious state; and the Self alone can be an enemy of the self-conscious state.**
6. **For that devotee who has mastered self-consciousness by Self-knowledge, the Self is a friend; for the one who has not mastered self-conscious states, the Self will be in opposition.**
7. **When self-conscious states have been mastered and one is tranquil, that devotee is stable in Self-knowledge.**

The devotee should purify the self-conscious (egocentric) state by improving knowledge of the true Self or soul and by cultivating the soul qualities of contentment and optimism. When allowed to do so, soul qualities can constructively benefit the self-conscious state, contributing to psychological health and improved functional abilities. When a person is ego-fixated, willfully self-determined, satisfied with or defensive of the self-conscious state, the wholesome, enlivening, transformative influences of the soul can seem to be a threat to it.

When behaviors are constructive and subtle impulses and tendencies originating in deeper levels of mind and awareness are stilled and soul tranquility is permanent, Self-knowledge is consistent at all times and in all circumstances.

8. **That practitioner of yoga who is satisfied with knowledge and discernment, who is unchanging and has mastered the senses, to whom all observed things are perceived as varied manifestations and expressions of one reality, is said to be established in yoga.**
9. **That one who is equal-minded toward friend, companion, and foe, among those who are in conflict with each other and who are related, and who is impartial among the righteous and the unrighteous, is accomplished in yoga.**

To be equal-minded toward people and circumstances is a helpful first stage of success in yoga practice. To be established in realization of oneness, the devotee must also be equal-minded when aware of friendly subjective tendencies, thoughts, and feelings which are like companions to ordinary states of awareness. One must also be stable in even-mindedness in relationship to subjective tendencies and other characteristics which seem to be in opposition to one's aspirations, the psychological processes which are in conflict and which are interactive, and constructive and destructive inclinations and drives. By observing all situations with objectivity it is easier to relate to them, choose those which are beneficial, or modify or renounce them.

10. **The practitioner of yoga should steadfastly contemplate the Supreme Reality, remaining in solitude, alone, with mind and body controlled, having no cravings for anything.**
11. **Established in a comfortable, steady meditation posture, in a clean and appropriate place;**
12. **There, intent upon practice, with thoughts and senses controlled, one should engage in meditation to purify the mind.**
13. **Holding the body, head and neck erect, motionless and steady, gazing into the spiritual eye with focused attention;**
14. **Serene, fearless, established in self-control, with mental impulses subdued, concentrating on the Supreme Reality, the devotee should sit, devoted to the highest realization.**

Absolute Pure Being is to be meditatively contemplated with unwavering attention by the devotee who aspires to enlightenment. If this cannot be done during early stages of practice, it should be remembered that, as progress results in improved ability to meditate, preliminary perceptions and experiences are to be renounced in favor of experiencing the ultimate, Supreme Reality permanently existing behind changing appearances.

When meditating, the devotee should be in a quiet place devoid of disturbing influences, and alone for the purpose of meditating without distractions. Mental and physical urges should be mastered by self-discipline and desires should be subordinate to the soul's aspiration to awaken to Self-knowledge.

The meditation posture should be pleasant, comfortable, and steady. In the absence of discomfort and of restless physical movements, subjective contemplation can more easily be practiced. Because meditation should be an intentional practice, an upright, seated posture is recommended. Lying down, or slouching in a chair with the head downcast is more conducive to sleep or to subconscious reverie than to alert, superconscious wakefulness.

One should be aware of the purpose of practice: to internalize attention, calm the wavelike fluctuations of the mind, awaken from egocentric self-consciousness to superconsciousness, experience the Self or soul as distinct from the body and mind and their processes, be content in pure soul awareness, and awaken to awareness and experience of transcendent realities. Meditation is not for the purpose of indulging in moods or feelings, nor is it for the purpose of being involved with mental phenomena, mundane problem-solving, endeavors to communicate with souls in more subtle realms to attempt to channel revelations.

It will be helpful for devotees of God to commit to memory the following aphorism in Patanjali's *Yoga Sutras* 1:2:

> Yoga [samadhi, oneness] is the state experienced when the wavelike movements [vrittis] are absent from the field of individualized awareness [chitta] because of having been restrained and returned [nirodha] to their subtle origins.

This describes the primary purpose for practicing meditation. Renouncing feelings and thoughts while remaining established in soul tranquility is yoga (realization of oneness). When absorbed in profound meditation, the devotee is not aware of emotions or thoughts. When not meditating, emotions and thoughts can be experienced and observed with objectivity. Because samadhi is a state in which awareness is removed from identification with external conditions, renunciation of attachments (tenacious identification) is extolled as a necessary prerequisite to experience it. For this reason there is much discussion in the *Gita* about the importance of understanding the operations of expressive aspects of Consciousness and how to effectively relate to them while remaining inwardly free.

To be successful in yoga practice a devotee should endeavor to perfect the restraints (*yamas*) which enable one to master physical actions and mental urges by cultivating the constructive habits of harmlessness, truthfulness, honesty, conservation and transmutation of vital forces, and nonattached attitudes and behaviors. At the same time the intentional practices (*niyamas*) should be implemented: outer cleanliness and inner purity; soul contentment in all circumstances; self-analysis and necessary self-discipline for psychological transformation and elimination of characteristics which restrict soul expression; study to acquire knowledge of God and life processes; and surrender of egocentric self-consciousness to allow awakening to Self-knowledge, cosmic consciousness, God-realization, and liberation of consciousness. Spiritual growth is much faster when the devotee chooses to live consciously, wholesomely, and appropriately at all times, and understands that doing so is just as helpful and necessary as is philosophical reflection and meditative contemplation.

Sitting upright, the meditator withdraws attention from externals and from physical, emotional, and mental involvements; harmonizes flows of prana or life force; internalizes attention; concentrates upon the chosen object of contemplation; continues until the flow of concentration is steady—which is meditation; then either identifies with the object being contemplated or experiences spontaneous superconscious and transcendent states. Concentration upon the chosen object of meditative contemplation, steady-flowing concentration without distraction, and consummation of practice are the three final stages that represent true meditation practice. All that goes before is preparation.

Preliminary and preparatory techniques may be used to elicit physical relaxation and clear the mental field, or meditation may proceed spontaneously. Techniques may include prayer, observation of respiration, listening to a mantra, moving awareness and life force through the chakras, listening to Om, contemplation of inner light, or any other routine that one knows to be helpful. When meditation is spontaneous, the devotee's aspiration to awaken to Self-knowledge and higher realities, supported by the soul's innate urge to be free, will determine meditation processes and unfoldment experiences.

The devotee is advised to aspire to spiritual awakening, attend to necessary, helpful routines and practices, with faith be devoid of anxiety about results, and allow the outcome of practice to be determined by the innate intelligence which governs the awakening process. When restrictions to flows of awareness are removed, grace is influential.

Novice meditators may meditate fifteen to thirty minutes once or twice a day to become familiar with the process and provide themselves opportunities for experiencing constructive results. Then, meditation should be practiced for thirty minutes to one hour, once or twice a day. Intent devotees may meditate more deeply to the extent desired so long as practice is alert and attentive. Passivity, and preoccupation with thought processes, feelings, and moods, should be avoided during meditation.

It can be extremely helpful to have a regular routine for meditation practice. Early morning is ideal, although any time that is convenient is worthwhile. If one can have a private sanctuary—a room or a quiet place set aside for the exclusive purpose of devotional practices—this can be helpful. The important matter is that meditation be learned, and practiced correctly on a regular schedule. Meditating with like-minded devotees on special occasions can be supportive but this is not necessary. Enlightened gurus (teachers) of yoga emphasize that one's dedication to God-realization is a personal, private matter, and that endeavors to socialize the spiritual path can distract one from the purpose of practice.

15. The devotee who, continually self-disciplined, with mental impulses subdued, and who is tranquil, realizes the supreme state of oneness.

To be self-disciplined is to have mastered sensory and mental impulses. When mental impulses (vasanas) have been returned to their subtle field of origin, the meditator experiences soul tranquility and pure consciousness.

16. Yoga practice is not for one who overeats or engages in extensive fasting from food, nor is it for one who sleeps excessively or who does not obtain adequate sleep.
17. For the devotee whose diet and recreation are moderate, whose actions are disciplined, whose routines of sleep and waking are regulated, the practice of yoga removes all unhappiness.

Living in harmony with the rhythms of life nurtures the devotee's total wellness and ensures a natural, supportive relationship with the universe. When spiritual awareness is cultivated and the psychophysiological constitution is balanced, soul-mind-body interactions occur effortlessly. A spiritual aspirant should at all times avoid extremes: choosing a practical, commonsense approach to living, eating, and sleeping on a regular schedule, performing necessary and agreed upon duties, fulfilling family and social obligations, and choosing how much time and energy to devote to other mundane affairs, metaphysical study, and meditative contemplation. Wholesome, orderly living nurtures physical and psychological health, causes one to be affluent, and energizes the mind so that concentration for the purpose of philosophical inquiry and meditative contemplation is easier. Natural living and yoga practice are not only conducive to happiness, they also remove physical, psychological, and circumstantial causes of possible future unhappiness.

18. **The devotee whose awareness is established in pure consciousness alone, whose mental impulses are regulated, and who is free from cravings and desires, is established in wholeness.**

Samadhi is not a temporary state to momentarily experience, or to experience only when meditating. At the innermost level of being, wholeness is the permanent state of soul awareness. When one is established in awareness of pure consciousness at all times, mental impulses are spontaneously regulated and cravings and desires are not demanding.

19. **As a flame in a windless place does not flicker, to such is compared the concentration of the meditator who, with mental impulses calmed, practices the yoga of samadhi.**

When experiencing wholeness with mental impulses at rest, the devotee's field of awareness is clear and concentration is unwavering because awareness is devoid of influences which formerly clouded and conflicted it.

20. **When mental fluctuations and transformations restrained by yoga practice become dormant, when, because of soul perception, the meditator is content in Self-knowledge,**
21. **The meditator experiences that infinite happiness which is apprehended by the intellect and transcends the senses, and established there does not waver from the truth.**
22. **Having realized this, no greater fulfillment can the devotee imagine; established in this, one is not disturbed even by**

[knowing about] profound misfortune;
23. Let this removal of awareness from pain be known as yoga,
to be optimistically practiced with resolved intention.

A devotee should not allow despair to overcome the resolve
to be enlightened when confronted with the obvious fact that the
present stage of spiritual growth seems modest when compared to
the description of realized consciousness outlined in the foregoing
verses. Instruction to enable a devotee to understand how mental
states can be mastered to allow unfoldment of soul knowledge and
capacities is found in the *Yoga Sutras* 1:30-36:

> Some obstacles to success [in practice] are disease, laziness,
> doubt, negligence, procrastination, philosophical confusion, fail-
> ure to progress, attachment to sense pleasure, misperception,
> and distractions.
> Effects which might accompany distractions are grief, anxi-
> ety, unsteadiness of the body during meditation, and irregular
> breathing.
> To control and eliminate these distractions one should prac-
> tice meditation and contemplate Om, the manifesting creative
> force of God.
> The mental field is calmed and purified by the cultivation
> of feelings of friendship, compassion, joy, and neutrality; and
> by analyzing ideal possibilities.
> One may definitely overcome all obstacles to success in
> meditation by practice of pranayama.
> Inner perception and experience of subtle cosmic forces and
> their manifestations cause changes in the mental field, enabling
> the devotee to be stable in meditation practice.
> When the light of Reality is experienced, the mental field
> becomes tranquil, resulting in supreme Self-confidence.

In the Kriya Yoga tradition that I represent through the guru
line of Mahavatar Babaji, Lahiri Mahasaya, Sri Yukteswar, and
Paramahansa Yogananda, the primary meditation techniques
are mantra, a variation of sushumna breathing, and merging in
the inner light and Om.

New meditators are first taught a two syllable mantra, to be
mentally listened to along with the normal breathing rhythm.
Then, breath is ignored and the mantra carries attention inward until meditation proceeds spontaneously. The purpose of

the mantra is to provide an attractive focus for attention so that thoughts and moods can be ignored until they become dormant. Paramahansaji often said that samadhi could be experienced by mantra practice alone, if a devotee practiced until superconscious states emerged.

Kriya pranayama, taught during initiation, is used to direct life forces through the chakras in the spinal pathway.

During the final stages of intentional meditation practice, Om is listened to, merged in, and transcended. When contemplating Om, one may see light in the spiritual eye. It may be like a white, full moon, or it may be gold or blue. This light is reflected from the medulla oblongata at the base of the brain. Golden light in the spiritual eye represents the subtle vibrational frequency of Om. Dark blue represents the subtle vibrational frequency of the all-pervading Consciousness endowed with intelligence. Brilliant white represents that Field of Consciousness which transcends all relationships with the field of primordial nature. Prior to clear, steady light perception, the meditator may perceive in the spiritual eye the vibrational frequencies reflected from the five lower chakras (see descriptions starting on page 19 in the Introduction).

24. Abandoning without exception all desires impelled by ego-centric willfulness, subduing the senses by mental control;

25. Gradually, the meditator should become still. With the intellect firmly concentrated on the reality of the true Self, let nothing else be thought about.

Aspiration for Self-knowledge and God-realization should be pure, devoid of any self-serving inclinations. Subtle sense urges can be regulated by intention, relaxation, and the use of simple meditation techniques. When the devotee's attention is internalized, uninterrupted contemplation of pure consciousness should be attentively practiced.

26. Whenever mental processes fluctuate and attention wavers, let these be restrained and mastered by Self-determination.

When meditation is flowing freely, distractions due to subtle mental changes will be minimal. When they disturb concentration, the devotee should return attention to contemplation of

God. Because the Self (soul) is superior to the mind, it can master mental impulses with determined resolve.

27. **That practitioner of yoga whose mind is peaceful, whose emotions are calmed, who is established in purity and is God-realized, awakens to the highest bliss.**
28. **Thus constantly practicing yoga, the devotee freed from all restraints, easily has knowledge and experience of God that bestows boundless happiness.**

A characteristic of being God-realized is bliss perception: pure soul-joy because free from restraints. This bliss perception is not to be confused with emotions, sentiment, or any other pleasure-producing condition. To constantly practice yoga means to be continually established in the samadhi of God-realization.

29. **The one who is disciplined by yoga practice sees the Self equally in all beings, and all beings in the Self.**
30. **That devotee who sees me everywhere and sees all things in me; I am not lost to him and that one is not lost to me.**

Disciplined by yoga practice, the devotee perceives the One Life everywhere. Thus seeing, the enlightened devotee is constantly aware of all-pervading Supreme Consciousness and knows that it includes all beings in its field of awareness.

31. **The yogi, established in oneness, reverently acknowledging me as abiding in all beings, whatever may be the lifestyle, lives in me.**

The devotee who is established in realization of God knows that God is the innermost reality of all living beings. Thus, whatever one's station in life as determined by duty and destiny, the devotee is conscious of living in God.

32. **The devotee who sees equality in everything, in the image of his own Self, whether in happiness or unhappiness, is to be considered an accomplished yogi.**

The devotee who knows the essence of the soul and the essence of Supreme Consciousness to be the same, and who remains soul-content regardless of transitory perceptions and circumstances, is accomplished in yoga [samadhi].

Arjuna said:

33. **Because of my restlessness, I cannot comprehend the firm basis for this yoga which you declare as evenness of mind.**
34. **The mind is unstable, troublesome, strong and obstinate; it seems to be as difficult to control as the wind.**

Arjuna is symbolic of every person who is skillful and accomplished in matters relating to ordinary, self-conscious life, yet has difficulty comprehending spiritual teachings—especially what samadhi is (unmodified pure consciousness) and how to experience it—and is unaccustomed to mastering thoughts and mental states. However, sincere inquiry unfolds innate knowledge that illumines the mind.

Krishna replied:

35. **Undoubtedly the mind is unsteady and difficult to curb; but it can be mastered by yoga practice and nonattachment.**
36. **I agree that yoga is not easy to accomplish by one whose self-conscious nature is uncontrolled; but by the devotee whose self-conscious nature is subjected to the soul's will, by right endeavor and proper means, it is possible to accomplish.**

Yoga practice includes procedures used to implement constructive psychological and physiological changes, to give mastery of mental states, and to facilitate unfoldments of superconscious states that culminate in samadhi. The self-conscious nature is egocentric. To acquire mental mastery, the devotee is encouraged to learn to exercise soul will or focused intention, and to use other practical means to succeed.

Arjuna inquired:

37. **What about the devotee who is uncontrolled though still has faith, whose mind has fallen away from practice and fails to be accomplished in yoga; what happens to that one?**
38. **Is that soul lost like a cloud that disappears, having fallen from both worlds, confused, and having no safe haven?**

Not every devotee remains steadfast on the awakening path. Some who have faith in God and in the usefulness of spiritual practice, because of their delusions or for other personal reasons become lax in their endeavors or discontinue them altogether. They naturally inquire into the matter of what will become of them. Having experienced, to some degree, higher states of consciousness along with their more usual self-conscious states, they wonder if they will fall from both of these "worlds" of awareness and, perhaps, like a cloud in the sky that dissolves, cease to be.

39. Only you can completely dispel my doubt; there is none other than you who can do it.

Only true knowledge that unfolds from the innermost core of being can completely remove the mind's confusion; nothing but true knowledge grounded in God-realization can do it.

Krishna said:

40. Neither here on earth nor in other realms is there loss for such a one; for no one who is righteous takes the path of misfortune.

The key words in this verse are "who is righteous." There is no field of consciousness in which a devotee who is rightly resolved fails to progress on the awakening path. Even if practice is not consistent, where there is faith in God, the soul's impulse toward awakening is influential. Even if one has no faith and strays completely from the spiritual path, in the course of time that soul will again aspire to awaken.

41. Awakening to the realms of the righteous, and having dwelt there for a long time, the devotee who has fallen from yoga takes a new body in happy, affluent circumstances.
42. Or one may be born in the family of wise practitioners of yoga; though this may be difficult to do in this world.
43. There, memories of past endeavors and acquired knowledge are regained, and the devotee again strives for perfection.
44. Spiritual progress continues irresistibly because of the momentum of prior practice; then even the desire to know God enables the devotee to realize transcendence by merging in Om.
45. By perseverance and self-mastery, purified through many incarnations, the devotee awakens to supreme realization.

After a duration of rest in a congenial astral realm, the soul incarnates into a physical body, perhaps with circumstances which are supportive of rapid learning and spiritual growth. Aspiration for Self-knowledge again becomes influential and memories of prior practices are activated, causing spiritual growth to occur whether or not one is at first conscious of being on the awakening path. The force of constructive, causative influences (karma) propels the devotee until the desire for enlightenment again becomes a conscious, positive driving force. Eventually, the devotee awakens to full realization of God.

46. **The accomplished practitioner of yoga is superior [in realization] to devotees who engage in arduous disciplines, and to others who have merely acquired knowledge about God, or who perform rituals. Therefore, be a practitioner of yoga.**

Because the "accomplished" devotee is established in samadhi, realization of oneness, there is no further need to engage in strenuous practices for the purpose of self-transformation. Nor is there any need to acquire knowledge from external sources, or to perform rituals to aid concentration or invite the influences of beneficial forces. Therefore, be established in samadhi.

47. **Of all these practitioners of yoga [who regularly experience refined superconscious states], that devotee who has merged the inner Self in me, who, full of faith, reverences me, is the most steadfast in me.**

Of all devotees of God who experience samadhi, that one who has dissolved all sense of individuality in Pure Consciousness and who is surrendered completely in it, is fully established in God.

In the Upanishad of the Bhagavad Gita, the science of the Absolute, the scripture of Yoga and the dialogue between Sri Krishna and Arjuna, thus ends the sixth chapter entitled Dhyana Yoga: The Yoga of Meditation

CHAPTER SEVEN

The Yoga of Discernment and Realization

Because every person is a soul expressing through a mind and personality, at the innermost level of their being they want to know the truth of themselves and the complete reality of God. What is not generally understood, or accepted, is that it is actually possible to awaken to this knowledge and fully actualize it in everyday circumstances and relationships. The final solution to all human problems which puts an end to confusion and misfortune, is conscious knowledge of ourselves as spiritual beings in relationship to God that is allowed to be expressively influential. In this chapter, discernment of the truth about God and the importance of realizing God directly is emphasized.

Krishna said:

1. **Hear this, how by practicing yoga with the mind absorbed in me, taking refuge in me, you shall know me completely. There is no doubt about this.**

   Listen carefully, how by practicing samadhi with awareness merged in the reality of God, you shall completely apprehend and experience God as God is. This is definitely true.

   The aspiration of the heart (soul) is to not merely to know about God but to directly realize what God is. For this, thinking, and even intellectual endeavor must be transcended. When all barriers are removed by practice of superconscious states and the cleansing actions of grace, the truth of God is unfailingly revealed.

2. **I will explain to you this knowledge along with realization, which, when understood, nothing further remains to be known in this world.**

   Knowledge of the reality of God will be self-revealed, along with clear comprehension because of direct experience, which, when fully real-

ized, provides complete understanding of God and of the processes of life.

The reality of God which includes everything is that, which, when known and actually experienced or realized, makes possible knowledge of all else that needs to be known. So long as we are not Self- and God-realized, subtle and fine aspects of life cannot be apprehended. This knowledge along with realization cannot be ours so long as delusions and illusions prevail in the mind and awareness. Our successful endeavors to rid the mind and awareness of restricting influences enables us to experience the truth of ourselves and to know the reality of God. When the mind is illumined by soul light and awareness is clear, innate knowledge of God is spontaneously self-revealed.

3. **Among thousands of beings, scarcely one strives for perfection; and even among those who strive, and among those who are accomplished, scarcely one knows me as I am.**

   Among thousands of souls, very few resolutely aspire and steadfastly endeavor to awaken to full illumination of consciousness; and among those who experience samadhi states, very few are completely God-realized.

Most people do not sincerely desire to know God as God is, because their awareness is overly identified with mental and physical circumstances. Being egocentric, they are not aware of their soul nature. Because they do not really know what their potential is, they do not aspire to unfold it. Even among those who become somewhat accomplished or perfected, few among them completely know the reality of God. Many are still in a "divine condition," a state of incomplete Self-knowledge which is more satisfying than former self-conscious states but is still a stage of soul unfoldment that must eventually blossom into accomplished or complete enlightenment.

Why is this fact of God not always readily acknowledged and more obviously demonstrated? Why, if we are supposed to awaken to knowledge and experience of God, do not more people do it? And, if we want to do it, how can it be done in the most efficient way? Some of the causes of lack of God-knowledge and experience, and ways to eliminate them, are:

- *Unawareness of the Existence of God.* Many people do not know that the all-pervading Reality of God exists as the Being, Life, Power, and Substance of all that is. They are relatively unconscious even though marginally functional. They are able to survive and to manage their self-centered, though unfulfilled, lives without awareness of their relationship with the omnipresent Reality in which they live and upon which they are unknowingly dependent for their well-being. If they want to know, their desire to do so will awaken soul awareness and attract learning opportunities. If they do not have the desire to know, in the course of time the innate urge of the soul to have awareness restored to wholeness will result in progressive spiritual awakening. Everyone eventually awakens to soul-awareness and God-knowledge.
- *Disinterest in Knowing About God.* Many people are either so self-centered or unaware of higher possibilities that they have no interest in knowing about God. Interest in spiritual matters will increase as self-centeredness decreases.
- *Insufficient Knowledge of God.* Even when interested, many people do not have sufficient knowledge of God to successfully comprehend what God is in relationship to themselves and the realm of nature. What is needed is for them to desire to know God, pray for guidance, search for valid (true) information about God, and to be satisfied only with complete knowledge.
- *Preoccupation with Personal Concerns.* One may know that it is important to know God but be so preoccupied with personal problems, needs, projects, relationships, or activities that God-knowledge and experience is considered to be of minor importance. What is needed is to rationally determine life's priorities to choose what is most important and give more attention to it. Constant outward flowing of attention and energies confuses the mind and depletes vital forces. There should be a balance of worthwhile, constructive activity and regularly scheduled interludes of rest for the purpose of philosophical reflection and meditative contemplation.
- *Belief that God Cannot (or Should Not) Be Known.* Even with desire to know God, there may be the prevailing beliefs that: (1) God cannot be known; (2) God should not be known. In the former instance, one may not understand that the soul is an individualized Field of God's Consciousness and that this fact can be apprehended and directly experienced or realized. In the latter instance, one may erroneously believe that God is supposed to remain a mystery to human beings — that God purposely created us to be ignorant of the truth, that there will always be a gap (an open space or distance) between God and souls. If these beliefs based on misunderstanding exist, they should be

immediately renounced in favor of right understanding. It is best not to debate or discuss the matter with others who are similarly confused. The more useful approach to knowledge is to follow the guidance of the heart (the soul) and use intelligence and intuition to discern the truth. Complete knowledge of God is innate to soul consciousness and needs but to be awakened and unfolded. We should consider the discovery of the reality of God to be a fascinating adventure and the solution to all problems.

- *Desire to Know God Restricted by Psychological Disorders.* If desire to know God is hindered by emotional unrest, mental restlessness or confusion, addictive tendencies, or self-defeating attitudes and drives, one can calm the turmoil and peacefully, competently facilitate psychological wellness and spiritual growth by choosing attitudes and behaviors which are entirely constructive and life-enhancing. This is the knowledgeable, intentional right-action way to effectively remove all obstacles to soul unfoldment which allows God-realization.

4. **Earth, fire, water, air, ether, mind, intellect, and egoism— these are the eight divisions of my nature in manifestation.**

The five physical elements; the capacity to think; power of intellectual discernment; and the illusional sense of independent existence, are the eight categories of Consciousness manifesting in the objective field of nature.

The five physical elements are earth (density), water (fluidity), fire (transformative characteristics), air (gaseous aspect), and ether (space with cosmic particles with potential to express). These are produced from five corresponding subtle element essences which are products of interactions of the gunas, the primary constituent qualities of nature. The subtle essences interact to produce the physical elements, each comprised of one-half of the dominant subtle essence and one-eighth portion of each of the other four. The earth element is tamasic. The water element is tamasic and rajasic. The fire element is rajasic. The air element is rajasic and sattvic. The ether element is sattvic.

When an impulse to project a universe arises in the Field of God Consciousness at the beginning of a new universal cycle of manifestation, a portion of God's awareness partially identifies with the field of primordial nature (God's creative force—Om, the vibrating sound current—self-manifested as time, space, and cosmic particles with potential to express). Reflected Consciousness (Bhishma) is produced so that cosmic individuality can make possible the further manifestation of: (1) Universal or Cosmic Mind pervaded by intelligence; (2) causal, astral, and physical realms. From the realm of Reflected Consciousness outward, the realms or fields of fine, subtle, and gross matters and all actions occurring in them are made possible by the interactions of the triple qualities of nature (sattva, rajas, and tamas gunas). The seven realms or fields are defined as:

- *Realm of God* beyond all relative or manifested realms.
- *Realm of the influential Spirit of God*, the life and light that enlivens and illumines, which, when reflected from the field of primordial matter, individualizes as souls.
- *Realm of spiritual reflection* produced when the Spirit of God shines on the field of primordial nature. Souls here, although almost fully enlightened, retain a mistaken or illusional sense of independent existence.
- *Realm of primordial nature*, Om self-referring and manifesting as space, time, and cosmic particles. Soul awareness influenced by the knowledge-veiling and form-producing characteristics because of identification with this realm or field, become attached to matter, experience delusion, and have attention turned outward to further involvement with fine, subtle, and gross manifestations of nature.
- *Realm of electricities and magnetic auras*, the causal sphere with fine element essences that make possible further subtle and gross universal manifestation. Souls dwelling here are enveloped in a sheath or covering of causal matters and can use intellectual and mental capacities.
- *Realm of vital life forces*, the astral sphere. Souls dwelling here are further enveloped in an astral sheath of life forces.
- *Realm of gross matter*, the physical universe comprised of the objectified qualities of the essences of the five elements governed by the influences of the gunas.

Not only is the soul "made in the image and likeness of God" because it is an individualized unit of God's Consciousness, all of the other primary characteristics which mark us as members of the human race are also those which are characteristic of God's cosmic body, the universe. When the egocentric or self-conscious soul becomes involved with matter, sattvic influences of soul consciousness produce a field of individualized mind comprised of characteristics identical to those of Universal or Cosmic Mind. The mind receives and processes information. It connects soul awareness with the objective realm. The subconscious level of the mind is the storehouse of impressions (samskaras). At the level of mind-identification the soul has access to Universal or Cosmic Mind. Mental states, thoughts, desires, and imaged intentions influence Universal Mind to respond, resulting in circumstances being attracted which correspond to our mental states and processes. When the mind is pure, only sattvic impulses, thoughts, desires, and imagery arise in it. When the mind is clouded, conditioned, and conflicted, impulses that arise in it are influenced by rajas guna which causes restlessness when the mind is passive, and passionate or forceful actions when the mind is expressive. Tamasic influences cause apathy when the mind is passive, and destructive moods and thoughts when the mind is active.

The discerning aspect of the mental field, the intellect, makes possible determination of what is true. A devotee of God should cultivate intellectual skill to know the difference between what is important and what is not, and what is temporal and what is permanent. A purified intellect enables one to understand the reality, aspects, and actions of Consciousness. The eighth century philosopher-seer Shankara, in his treatise *Atmabode* (Self-Knowledge), defined *soul* as the light of Consciousness reflected in the organ of intelligence. The soul's identification with mind and matter is said to be its first intellectual error, from which arises all other misconceptions and their resulting delusions.

The five sheaths or soul coverings are:

- *Bliss sheath*, produced when the light of the Spirit of God individualizes as a soul. With awareness of its spiritual essence somewhat modified by a weak sense of independent existence, the soul can experience the sheer joy of being. The Sanskrit name is *anandamaya kosha* (*ananda*, bliss; *maya*, primordial nature; *kosha*, covering).
- *Knowledge sheath*, of fine causal substance by which the partially deluded soul is able to intelligently discern. The Sanskrit name is *jnanamaya kosha* (*jnana*, knowledge).
- *Mind sheath*, of fine causal substance by which the soul can process information, or think. The Sanskrit name is *manomaya kosha* (*manas*, to think).

- *Vital force sheath*, the astral body with the chakras. The Sanskrit name is *pranamaya kosha* (*prana*, life force).
- *Physical sheath*, the body of gross elements nourished by food. The Sanskrit name is *annamaya kosha* (*anna*, food).

When the cosmic forces and fine element essences of the universe are fully projected or emanated, the attraction-influence innate to Supreme Consciousness causes the element essences to manifest corresponding gross, liquid, fiery, gaseous, and ethereal aspects in the physical realm, completing the outward flow of nature's manifesting actions. The field of manifested nature is now prepared for what is yet to occur in the course of many millions of solar years:

- Where conditions are suitable for living things to exist, the continuing actions of the attraction-influence of Supreme Consciousness pervading the universe partially unveils the sheath of matter to allow vital forces to express so that vegetation can emerge.
- When the sheath of vital force is partially unveiled to allow mental capacities to be utilized, simple organisms and animal forms emerge.
- When the mental sheath is unveiled to allow intelligence to express, human beings with powers of rational thinking emerge.
- When the intelligence sheath is unveiled or transcended to allow spiritual qualities to be apprehended, the soul awakens to Self-knowledge and can remove awareness from delusions and illusions.
- When the finest sheath is unveiled or transcended, the soul awakens from all influences of primordial nature and is liberated.

The illusory self-perception of independent existence (egoism) is the root cause of delusion. When it is purified, the soul can function in relationship to the phenomenal realm while knowing that its mild sense of individuality is but a viewpoint which enables it to relate to the field of nature while remaining soul-aware. A spiritually awake person never thinks, "I am a mind-body being." Such a one always knows, "I am an individualized unit of omnipresent, omniscient, omnipotent Consciousness, a ray of God's life forever anchored in the Absolute."

5. **This is my inferior [lower, outer] nature. Know it to be different from my highest nature, the Godhead or Oversoul by which this universe is maintained.**

This is the objective manifestation of Consciousness. Know it to be different from the Field of God by which the field of manifest nature is maintained.

The superior (higher) nature of God emanates the universe and individualizes units of itself as souls. Although the universe is contained within the Field of God, God is not confined by or restricted to the manifest realms.

6.   Understand that all beings have origins in this [the highest nature]. I am the origin and dissolution of the universe.

Comprehend the fact that all souls have their origins in God. God originates the universe, and contains its fine essences when matter is dissolved at the end of a cycle of manifestation.

While all souls originate in the Field of God's Being, as do the universes, we cannot accurately say that souls are produced and universes are emanated because of God's desire to make this happen. When we project our ideas of personhood upon God, it then follows that we are likely to also presume that God thinks, feels, and acts very much as human beings with conditioned minds think, feel, and act. In many religious traditions, God is portrayed variously, as kind, loving, caring, stern, harsh, judgmental, condemning, requiring of souls their worship and praise, and even their sacrifice to atone for errors. By people lacking knowledge, God is often blamed, criticized, feared, petitioned for forgiveness or for benefits, and blindly worshipped as a substitute parent. The reality of God can be known, and it is our duty (dharma) to acquire God knowledge and to awaken in God.

When the universes are dissolved at the end of a cycle of manifestation, cosmic forces return to their origin—to the field of unmanifest primordial nature—where they remain dormant until another universe is projected within a new field of space and time. It is likely that many universes are undergoing the processes of manifestation, evolution, and dissolution in space-time fields other than the one in which our universe is presently expressing. If so, all of them have their origins in God.

7.   Nothing transcends me. The entire universe is strung on me like pearls on a string.

Nothing exists beyond Consciousness. All aspects of the universe are maintained and organized by Supreme Consciousness.

8. **I am the essence and wetness of water, I am the radiance of the moon and sun. I am the sacred syllable [Om] referred to in scripture. I am the sound in air and the vitality of life.**
All-pervading Consciousness is the essence of the manifested elements, the reflected and radiant light, and of Om, the primordial sound current. It exists in the sound frequencies conveyed by air and is the vitality that enlivens.

9. **I am the pure fragrance in earth, the brilliance in fire, the life of all beings, and the austerity of ascetics.**

All-pervading Consciousness is the essence of fragrances, the luminosity of transformative actions, the life force and consciousness of all souls, and the purifying actions of those who engage in disciplined practices for self-mastery.

10. **Know me to be the primary cause of all creatures. I am the intelligence of the intelligent; the splendor of the splendid, am I.**

Know that Supreme Consciousness causes all creatures to manifest. It is also the discernment when intelligence prevails and the brilliance of that which shines.

11. **I am the might of the strong who are devoid of base passion, and I am that desire in beings which is righteous.**

Supreme Consciousness is the power of those who demonstrate their strength without passion, and the desire arising in souls which is in accord with righteousness.

Pure or sattvic characteristics of Supreme Consciousness are more obvious and effective when strength is demonstrated by rational choice and clear intention. Desire arising as an impulse to be fulfilled to accomplish purposes which support evolution also indicate that the desire originates at the innermost core of the soul.

12. **And those states of being which are sattvic, rajasic, and tamasic—know them to proceed from me. But I am not in**

them; they are in me.

Know that the various states [of nature] which are pure, energetic, and lethargic, are emanated from Supreme Consciousness. Supreme Consciousness is not contained by them; they are in Consciousness.

Nature's various states are effects of influences of the three constituent qualities or gunas which have origins in the Field of God. These are emanated from God and become expressive in the field of primordial nature and nature's further objective projections as the universe. They exist within the all-pervading Field of Consciousness.

13. **This entire world, deluded by these three states of being composed of the qualities [of nature], does not recognize me because I transcend them and am eternal.**

Embodied souls, their awareness clouded by the influences of the actions of the gunas, do not apprehend all-pervading, timeless Consciousness which is beyond the gunas.

14. **Divine indeed is this illusory universe of mine—the constituents of which are the three qualities [of nature], and difficult to penetrate [perceive beyond]. Only those who take refuge in me alone transcend it.**

God's creative energy is expressing as the universe which is manifested by the interactions of the gunas. It is not easy for one who is overly identified with the illusory characteristics of nature to perceive that which is their cause, but it can be done by focused contemplation and awakening to knowledge of the Absolute.

A problem cannot be solved by the same states of consciousness and actions which produced and maintain it. The problem of delusion cannot be solved by states of consciousness or actions which are its cause. Because the universe can be perceived, it is not an illusion; our misperceptions about what we see and sense, cause us to consider the field of nature to be illusory.

15. **Unrighteous, spiritually unaware people, confused and deluded, and attached to their self-serving existence, do not seek me [Supreme Consciousness].**

An unrighteous person is one whose actions are intentionally or unintentionally in conflict with purposeful, evolutionary processes because of being spiritually unawake, confused, deluded, and attached to egocentric interests. Being self-centered, there is no conscious desire to acquire higher knowledge. The soul urge to awaken will eventually prevail.

16. Four types of virtuous people worship me [Supreme Consciousness]: those who are distressed, those who desire material wealth [of various kinds], those who desire [higher] knowledge, and the wisdom-impelled devotee.

Virtuous people desiring a well-ordered, fulfilled life approach God according to their needs or as their understanding determines. Some seek a relationship with God because they have suffered loss, are ill, or want to experience improvement of well-being. Others seek rewards, such as material gain. Still others desire insightful knowledge of God and of their relationship with God and the world. A few are impelled by aspiration to awaken to enlightenment, to comprehensive knowledge of God and of life processes that liberate the soul. So long as one's aspiration is sincere and constant, the initial motivation for seeking God-knowledge is not important. As one persists with an open mind and a surrendered heart, spiritual growth will progressively occur and the inner light will illumine one's path.

17. Of these, the wise devotee, ever devoted to the Divine, is distinguished. I am exceedingly dear to that devotee and that devotee is dear to me.

Of all who desire self-improvement and higher knowledge, the wisdom-impelled devotee who is steadfastly devoted to the ideal of God-realization is exceptional. That devotee's devotion increasingly attracts the influences of the redemptive actions of grace.

Spiritual growth is usually most rapid for the devotee who fervently yearns to quickly awaken in God and who chooses to live righteously (in harmony with the laws of life that support evolution), who improves intellectual abilities, engages in entirely constructive actions while being unattached to their results, and surrenders self-consciousness in favor of God-realization.

The key to spiritual fulfillment is to remain steadfast on the path known to be the highest and most useful for the devotee. Many begin with strong resolve, only to give up too soon and fall back into former, self-defeating ways of thinking and behavior. Others repeatedly start with enthusiasm and stop when results are not forthcoming, or they become distracted, lazy, or disinterested. The ideal devotee—and the outcome of persistent discipleship—are described in the following verse.

18. **All of these [four types of seekers] are indeed noble, but the devotee of wisdom I consider as my own Self. That one whose devotion is steadfast abides in me, the supreme attainment.**

Whatever the motive, all who seek to grow spiritually are responding to their innate urge to unfold soul qualities. The one who is devoted to actualizing knowledge-wisdom that liberates is demonstrating the pure impulse of the heart [soul]. That one whose devotion persists awakens to God-realization, the ultimate state.

19. **At the end of many incarnations, the devotee of wisdom resorts to me, knowing the wholeness of Consciousness. Such a great [God-realized] soul is difficult to find.**

After numerous embodiments in the field of nature, the devotee intent upon knowledge that liberates, aspiring to complete God-realization above all else, awakens in God. Souls completely awake in God are rare [in this world].

So long as the soul is deluded, it tends to identify with the field of nature, thus the sequential episodes of reincarnation. When sufficiently Self-realized, the soul discerns that it is other than a mind or body and apprehends the reality of God. If a residue of karma remains, the soul can be steadfast in God-realization while the karmic conditions are exhausted by necessary actions and experiences or dissolved by the superior influences of superconscious states.

20. **Those bereft of knowledge, their minds distracted by desires, resort to other gods and engage in various religious rites, constrained by their own [conditioned] natures.**

The "other gods" one may blindly worship can be as diverse as fame, name, power, success, material things for their own sake, the forces of nature, imaginary gods and goddesses or angels, imaginary enlightened beings, extraordinary but still limited abilities (siddhis) so long as egoism rules their use, ecstatic states, preliminary superconscious states, and conditions other than full illumination. So long as a person is sincerely endeavoring to apprehend what is true, even if understanding of God is minimal, some spiritual growth will be experienced. All worship (turning to God in humility and reverence) elevates the spirit and can only be helpful. A direct approach to spiritual growth is to seek sources of valid knowledge to acquire as much factual information as possible and put it into practice. If one is fortunate enough to have a guru (teacher) who is intelligent and wise, and will commit to a program of learning and right living and practice, progress can be rapid.

21. Whatever form [of God] a devotee sincerely believes in and worships, to that devotee I bestow steadfast faith.

However God is imagined [or known] to be, sincere devotion awakens soul qualities and attracts to the devotee influential support from the all-pervading Field of God.

The direct way to knowledge of God is to contemplate (ponder, analyze, meditate upon) the aspect of God which seems most valid, while being receptive to unfoldments of insights that allow clear perception of the reality of God. If at first the devotee feels more comfortable seeking a relationship with God as a caring Being, this relationship can be contemplated. Or God can be contemplated as the omnipresent Field of Consciousness, a cosmic Presence, light, sound (Om), or as the Absolute Reality. Shankara, in his treatise on *Self-Knowledge*, wrote:

> Realize individualized Supreme Consciousness [soul] to be distinct from the body, sense organs, mind, intelligence, and nondifferentiated primordial nature; it is the witness of their functions and the ruler of them. As the moon appears to be moving when clouds move in the sky, so also, to the nondiscriminating, individualized Supreme Consciousness [soul] appears to be active when in reality only the senses are active. As the movement that belongs to water is [sometimes] attributed, because

of lack of knowledge, to the moon which is reflected in it, so also enjoyment and other limitations which belong to the mind are falsely attributed to Supreme Consciousness. The nature of Supreme Consciousness is eternity, purity, reality, awareness, and bliss, just as luminosity is the nature of the sun, coolness of water, and heat of fire.

Any sincere endeavor to experience the Presence of God brings the devotee's awareness into a relationship with it and attracts the blessing-grace which spontaneously flows.

22. Whatever the devotee with that faith desires or asks for, is provided as decreed by me.

Whatever a devotee with steadfast faith desires or requests, is provided because it is characteristic of Consciousness to be spontaneously responsive to wants and needs.

When we are established in soul contentment and are aware of our relationship with the Infinite, it is easy to have firm faith in God. We live in God at all levels of life. At the soul level, we are rays of God's Consciousness. At the mental level we are in relationship to Universal Mind, God's Mind. At the physical level we live in a universe which is a continuum, one manifestation of nature's forces with various aspects. When we are in harmony with the rhythms of life, our wants are satisfied and our needs are met because the processes of life are inclined toward fulfillment of purposes. Just as this creative process can and will satisfy every life-enhancing desire and need we have, so it ensures our success on the spiritual path and our spiritual growth and illumination. With soul awakening, we see through the illusion of separateness, knowing that we live in a spiritual universe.

23. The fruit [result] of those with small understanding is temporary. The worshipers of gods go to the gods; my devotees come to me.

The effects of desire with limited knowledge [of how to desire with intention and of how the law of causation operates] are of minor consequence and soon fade. Those who desire temporary relationships with various aspects and forces of nature can have them; God-surrendered devotees awaken in God.

We identify with (and attract to ourselves) that to which we give our attention. If we are primarily interested in superficial matters, we can have them, but they will neither satisfy the heart nor endure. If we desire a relationship with souls on the astral plane or with beings whom we presume to be enlightened, we can fantasize about them and remain deluded. If we desire to relate only to the cosmic forces, we can do so and still remain oblivious to ultimate truth. One who sincerely aspires to Self-knowledge and God-realization should disregard everything that is impermanent and surrender self-consciousness in order to experience oneness.

24. Though I am unmanifest, the unintelligent think of me as being manifested, not knowing my transcendent nature which is eternal and supreme above all else.

Though the Absolute remains ever what it is, devotees without full knowledge of the truth think of the Absolute—the transcendent, changeless Reality—as being manifested. The universe is a projection of cosmic forces with origins in the Field of Pure Being.

25. Veiled by my maya [manifestation of primordial nature] I am not perceived by all. The deluded people of the world do not know me as the unborn eternal Reality.

Obscured by the actions of cosmic forces [gunas, qualities of nature] the Absolute is not known to those who cannot apprehend it. Those whose awareness is clouded do not know that the Absolute is forever transcendent.

26. I know the beings that are past, that are present, and that are yet to come [in the future]; but no one [who is spiritually unawake] knows me.
The Absolute is self-aware of expressions of itself as souls past, present, and yet to be expressed; but deluded souls are not yet aware of the true nature of the Absolute.

27. All beings fall into delusion at birth because of intellectual errors which arise from desire and dislike.

All souls identify with self-conscious awareness when embodied because of perceptual errors resulting from unconscious identification with mind and matter.

The soul's initial involvement with matter can be considered to be its first "birth" or embodiment. Because of a false sense of independent existence, it identified with the mind and, later, was born into a physical body. The important involvement to understand and awaken from is that of the soul's relationship with mind and matter. Other "births" and "deaths" are relatively insignificant as they have only to do with transitions between physical and astral realms for souls involved with these levels, and astral and causal realms for more spiritually aware souls, which tend to continue so long as the soul is unenlightened. An exception is when enlightened souls incarnate for the purpose of playing a role as a participant in evolutionary processes. Even these souls, however, usually demonstrate symptoms of partial delusion—which usually fades as they grow to adulthood and begin to fulfill their destined mission.

28. But those devotees whose deeds are pure and whose errors have ceased, liberated from the delusion of opposites they acknowledge me with steadfast commitment.

But those devotees who live in accord with their innate inclinations to be in harmony with life-enhancing circumstances and who no longer err in thought or act, their awareness removed from erroneous beliefs, honor all that is divine with their total dedication to right thinking, right behavior, and surrender of self-consciousness in favor of God-realization.

29. Those who turn to me, aspiring to be released from old age and death, know the Absolute and the Supreme Self in all actions.

Devotees who seek to know God and practice yoga [samadhi], aspiring to awaken from episodes of aging, death, and other troublesome conditions incidental to self-conscious, embodied existence, awaken to realization of the transcendent reality of God, and of God expressive in all actions in all realms.

30. Those who know me as that which governs material and divine realms, and all holy offerings, they truly know me with unwavering contemplation even at the hour of departure [from the body].

Devotees who know God to be the determining factor in all that occurs in physical and subtle realms, and to be the agent of all enlivening and nurturing actions, maintain their knowledge when they experience transition from the body.

To the spiritually awake soul, God is clearly known as the transcendent Being, and the animating life, influential power, manifesting substance, and transformative actions (holy offerings) of the universe. Knowing this, the devotee lives peacefully and freely in the world. At the time of transition, withdrawing attention from external circumstances, and from body and mind, the soul experiences transcendent perceptions or awakens completely to realization of oneness.

In the Upanishad of the Bhagavad Gita, the science of the Absolute, the scripture of Yoga and the dialogue between Sri Krishna and Arjuna, thus ends the seventh chapter entitled Vijnana Yoga: The Yoga of Discernment and Realization

CHAPTER EIGHT

The Yoga of the Absolute Reality

The permanent, self-existing aspect of Consciousness is known as the Absolute because there is nothing beyond it. It cannot be comprehended by the mind because the mind is produced by the gunas or qualities of nature. Its reality can be intuitively apprehended and directly experienced.

Arjuna inquires:

1. **What is Brahman [the Absolute Reality]? What is the Supreme Self? What is karma? What are the domains and characteristics of the elements of the worlds and of the gods?**

   What is the Absolute, all-pervading infinite Consciousness? What is the presiding Spirit, and what causes effects? What are the realms and characteristics of the elements of the worlds and their presiding deities or controlling influences?

2. **What is the basis of sacrifice in this body? How are you to be known by the self-controlled at the time of transition?**

   What is the agent of holy offerings that result in transformation? How do devotees established in Self-knowledge awaken in God at the time of leaving their bodies?

   The rush of questions is characteristic of a person who is new on the spiritual path. Now the devotee, respectful of the teacher and willing to learn, asks the right questions.

Krishna answers:

3. **The Absolute Reality is the imperishable Eternal. It is the inherent nature of the Supreme Self, that which manifests and pervades the worlds and individualizes as the essential being of creatures. Karma is the influential agent that causes universal manifestation, and souls to be individualized and**

embodied in various circumstances.

Changeless Pure Consciousness without attributes is the Absolute. It is referred to as the Supreme Self or Being. It pervades the universe from the Field of God through all levels of manifestation. Souls are individualized units of the Supreme Self which have identified with mind and matter. The force of originating causes produces effects. Souls first become involved with mind and matter when influenced by the outflowing creative force (Om) emanating from God which causes universal manifestation. Deluded or spiritually unaware souls are ever being acted upon by cosmic forces, environmental forces, and the forces of their desires until they awaken to levels of soul awareness which remove them from these influences. The "gods" or presiding deities are the influential forces produced by the interplay of gunas which regulate nature's actions.

4. **The basis of all manifest forms and actions are the guna influences in the field of nature; the agent of transformation is the Spirit of God; the basis of sacrifice here in this body, is myself.**

    The basis of all manifest forms and actions is the combination of tendencies of the gunas or qualities in the field of nature; that which causes transformation of all kinds is the enlivening life of God; the basis of holy offerings or self-giving in the universe and in the body is the indwelling true Self.

A devotee sacrifices by offering thoughts, moods, and actions to God. This is our holy offering to life, freely given without desire for personal reward. The actions of the universe are freely flowing to support evolutionary processes. To be God-attuned our actions should be like this.

5. **At the time of leaving the body, that devotee who departs contemplating me alone, attains my state of being; there is no doubt about this.**

    At the time of transition, by contemplating the transcendent Field of Pure Consciousness, the soul naturally awakens to the stage of knowledge-realization. This certainly happens.

6. **Whatever state of being one contemplates when departing the body, one experiences that state.**

Our perceptions and experiences during and immediately after transition are determined by our states of consciousness and mental and emotional states. If one's awareness is not clear and calm at the time of transition from the body, subtle mental impulses (vasanas) can disturb the mental field and cause confusion, as may happen during ordinary meditation when attention is internalized but not yet concentrated on the object of contemplation. At the time of transition, it is best to be calm and meditative, secluded from distracting circumstances and from people who are confused or emotionally disturbed.

7. **Therefore, at all times meditate on me, with mind and intelligence fixed on me. You shall then surely come to me.**

Because this is so [because the state of being one contemplates when departing the body determines what will be experienced afterward], at all times contemplate your relationship with the Infinite, with your attention and powers of discernment focused on it. By doing this, you will surely awaken in God.

8. **That devotee, disciplined by yoga practice, who meditates on the Absolute, awakens to that transcendent state.**

The devotee who has accomplished self-mastery by the practice of samadhi and who flows attention without interruption to the Field of Pure Consciousness, realizes it.

9. **The devotee who meditates on that which is omniscient, which is subtler than the subtle, the supporter of all, whose form cannot be imagined, who is effulgent like the sun, beyond darkness;**
10. **At the time of departure from the body, with steady concentration, endowed with devotion and with the power of yoga [samadhi], having directed the vital force between the eyebrows, that one awakens in God.**

The radiant light of Consciousness ever shines behind the veils of gross and subtle matter. That light of Consciousness should be perceived and merged with during transition from the body.

Devotees who have habitually perceived this light during meditation can easily see it and merge with it at will. Every meditator who withdraws attention from objective circumstances and
from sensory organs and mental processes "dies to the world" to
experience samadhi. Final merging in the light of Consciousness
is called *mahasamadhi* or "great oneness." Directing life force to
flow upward through the chakras and into the spiritual eye is a
preliminary procedure. With perception of the inner light, one
can contemplate it and merge awareness in it.

11. **I shall briefly explain that which the knowers of the scrip-
    ture call the imperishable, which desire-free ascetics enter,
    and because of their desire for it choose a life of self-control
    [brahmacharya].**

An ascetic lifestyle is one of voluntary simplicity. One need
not be reclusive to live like this. All that is needed is to choose to
give attention to life's essentials. *Brahmacharya* (*Brahma*, God;
and *charya*, going) means inwardness—living established in
soul awareness, not letting thoughts be unregulated or energies
be depleted in nonessential outward involvements. This can be
perfected while living a natural, fully functional, productive life.

12. **Closing off the senses, confining awareness to the innermost
    core of being, having placed the vital force in the higher
    chakras, established in meditative contemplation;**
13. **Uttering the single-syllable Om [which has origins in God],
    the devotee who renounces the body and goes forth, awakens
    to the highest realization.**

Yogis may practice meditation procedures which enable
them to consciously regulate flows of life force for the purpose of
mastering physical and mental processes and adjusting states of
consciousness at will. One procedure is that of bringing attention
and life force upward through the spinal pathway to the higher
chakras, spiritual eye, and top of the head. As the soul's life force
descends into the body from the medulla oblongata at the base of
the brain, so the yogi reverses the flow to send life force back to the
brain centers. This effectively internalizes attention and focuses
concentration at the spiritual eye. One then has but to listen to Om
and merge in it and the all-radiant light of Consciousness. If Om

is heard spontaneously, there is no need to verbally or mentally chant the mantra. Otherwise, verbal or mental chanting of Om can precede contemplation of it and inner light. This procedure can be practiced as a meditation routine until proficiency is acquired; it will then be easy to use at the time of final departure from the body.

14. That devotee who constantly meditates on me only, by that practitioner of yoga I am easily realized.

The devotee who always remains absorbed in contemplation of God, by that practitioner of samadhi God is easily realized.

15. Coming near to me, those mahatmas [great souls] who are accomplished in yoga do not reincarnate in the realm of imperfection.

Awakening to transcendent states of consciousness, highly Self-realized souls do not return to gross material realms where disharmony often occurs.

16. From the realm of God outward, all manifest realms are places of rebirth; one who awakens in me does not return.

The realms of primordial nature and the causal, astral, and physical realms are those to which deluded souls return, but one who awakens completely in God does not return to them.

17. Those who know that the day of God extends for a thousand yugas and that the night of God is also a thousand yugas, they are the knowers of the day and night.

Those who know that the duration of universal manifestation is a thousand cosmic cycles and that the night of God is the same, they are knowers of the day and night.

Vedic seers taught that universal processes occur in time-segments or yugas of approximately 400 billion years duration. With one thousand such cycles estimated as a day of objective manifestation, the duration of a universe could be estimated to be approximately 400 trillion years. With current estimates indicating the age of our universe to be twelve to twenty billion years, it is still in its infancy. Sri Yukteswar's calculations regarding a

24,000 year cycle, with 12,000 years ascending and 12,000 years descending, is in reference to Planet Earth and our solar system's movement through the galaxy.

18. At the coming of the day, all manifestations emerge from the unmanifest field, and at the coming of the night they dissolve into the same unmanifest field.

At the beginning of a new cycle of universal manifestation, aspects of nature emerge from the unmanifest field of primordial nature; as the cycle of universal manifestation begins to end the cosmic forces return and merge into the same unmanifest field of primordial nature.

During the night of God, the gunas are in a state of equilibrium in the field of primordial nature. When an impulse to manifest arises from within the Field of God and disturbs this condition of balance, the field of primordial nature becomes distorted and the manifestation process begins again.

19. This multitude of existences that again and again come into manifestation, inevitably dissolve with the coming of the night, and emerge again at the coming of the day.

The field of primordial nature is as eternal as Consciousness which emanated and maintains it. A universe is not ever created or destroyed; it is produced out of the field of primordial nature and dissolves into it. Its objective manifestation continues until the gunas begin to be restored to a condition of equilibrium, then a return to the unmanifest state begins. The dissolution of our universe is many trillions of solar years in the future.

Just as universes and their varied phenomena are produced by the impulse within the realm of God because of the existence of their primary causes—the inherent qualities or gunas—so do the impulses of our individualized field of awareness produce mental phenomena when our attention is inclined to flow outward. We can experience tranquil, thoughtless states of samadhi during which mental impressions are dormant, only to have thoughts again emerge when we return awareness to objective states. The practitioner of samadhi should have as the ultimate aim the realized state of pure consciousness which effectively removes soul awareness from attachments to mental states and sensory experiences. One can then live in this or any world while inwardly established in enlightened understanding.

While talking with Paramahansa Yogananda during my first year of discipleship training with him, he invited my questions. I inquired about some of the saints he had written about, wondering whether or not they were fully liberated. He said, "Not many [of them] are liberated. Many saints are content to enjoy the ecstasy of God-communion, sometimes for millions of years, before awakening completely in God." After a quiet pause, he said, "But you must go all the way!"

20. But transcending this unmanifest field is another unmanifest field which is superior to it, which does not perish with the dissolution of the manifested realms.

Transcending the unmanifest field of primordial nature is the unmanifest Field of God which is superior to it, and which does not cease to exist when the universe dissolves into its source.

The Godhead, being the origin of the field of primordial nature, is superior to it, and continues to persist when the universes are dissolved at the end of a cycle of manifestation.

21. This unmanifest field [the Absolute] is indestructible and eternal, the most transcendent level, realizing which, devotees do not return. This is my supreme domain.

This [the unmanifest Field of God] is indestructible and eternal. It is the transcendent level, which, when devotees realize it, they do not return to the realms of nature. This is the timeless Field of Absolute Existence-Being.

The true goal of yoga (samadhi) practice is to awaken from helpless relationship to nature's primary cosmic forces (the gunas) by restoring awareness permanently to the wholeness of the most transcendent state of God-realization. When flawless realization is permanent, the soul does not again become blindly involved with nature's actions.

22. Realizable by steadfast devotion, this is the supreme state in which all existences abide and by which this universe is pervaded.

This transcendent state can be realized by unwavering devotion. Pervading the universe, it is that in which all souls [and all manifested things] dwell.

The unwavering devotion that makes possible realization of this pure state of consciousness, is aspiration demonstrated by our necessary constructive actions along with surrender of self-conscious states so that spontaneous unfoldments of soul qualities can occur. This pure state is not a destination, a place to which to go; it exists where we are, at the core of our being.

23. Now I will explain that which determines whether or not practitioners of yoga reincarnate.

Now the influential factors that determine whether or not devotees who practice samadhi reincarnate will be revealed.

When soul awareness is unconsciously (or by conscious choice or agreement) identified with the field of nature, its relationship with the forces of nature and occurring circumstances continues until awareness is removed from involvement. Unconscious souls at the mercy of circumstances have no more choice in determining their fated (karmic) experiences than ordinary people have in choosing their dreams when they sleep. Souls which are partially awake, and have some understanding, can somewhat choose their circumstances and have moderate control over their thoughts and states of consciousness. Fully awake souls can choose to intelligently, freely live in relationship to nature's processes or can withdraw from them at will.

24. Fire, light, day, the two weeks of the new moon, the six months of the northern phase of the sun—those who depart the body knowing the Absolute awaken fully to it.

This verse has several code words which have meaning to devotees who practice samadhi. While some yogis do plan their departure from the body during the first two weeks of a waxing moon, in the spring of the year, and when other astronomical aspects are considered to be favorable, more important is knowledge of how to have the support of subtle processes. *Fire* and *light* are qualities of vitality and luminosity characteristic of *day*, of being spiritually awake. *Moon* is symbolic of the reflected light of consciousness which provides some knowledge of observed circumstances. During the new moon or waxing phase the reflected light increases, allowing improved perception of observed circumstances. The *northern phase of the sun* is symbolic of its return to its brightest state. Yogis refer to the front part of the body as east, the region of sense perceptions and their enjoyments ruled by the mind. The back part of the body, with the spinal pathway and chakras, is referred to as west, the place where one goes to retire from sense perceptions and enjoyment of them. The lower region of the spinal pathway is referred to as south, ruled by the three lower chakras, related to illusory perceptions and subjective enjoyments. The upper region of the spinal pathway is referred to as north, ruled by the higher chakras, related to clear perceptions and transcendent realizations. Therefore, the most favorable time to depart the body is when the *sun*, the inner light of consciousness, is moving northward (upward) toward the spiritual eye and crown chakra. Departing the body under these favorable conditions, the soul can experience the removal of awareness from sensory and mental conditions and awaken to liberation.

25. Smoke, night, the two weeks of the waning moon, the six months of the southern phase of the sun—then departing under the lunar influence the devotee is reincarnated.

Smoke: hazy or unclear perceptions. The *two weeks of the waning moon*: perceptions due to reflected light of consciousness are becoming increasingly obscured. The *southern phase of the sun*: the inner light of consciousness is moving downward toward increasing involvement with lower chakra influences which contribute to illusions and attachments to enjoyable sensations. Departing the body under these unfavorable conditions, the soul tends to remain involved with delusions and illusions and attached to perceptions and enjoyment of sensations; thus, the inclination to return to physical embodiment. There is always the possibility, however, that spiritual awakening can continue in the astral and causal realms without the soul having to return to the material realm.

**26. These two paths of light and dark are thought to be perpetu-
ally influential. By one, the devotee does not return to this
realm; by the other, the devotee again returns.**

The path of light (of the sun) leads to ultimate revelation. The
path of darkness leads to continued involvement with delusion
and illusion. At the time of departure from the body, because of
proficiency acquired by prior practice, an accomplished devotee
is able to consciously withdraw attention from externals to the
spinal pathway and bring awareness and life forces up through
the chakras. Doing this dissolves gross attachments at the base
chakra, subtle attachments at the sacral chakra, attachments
to mental phenomena at the lumbar chakra, attachments to
self-sense at the dorsal chakra, attachments to enjoyment of
knowledge of subjective phenomena at the cervical chakra, and
attachment to bliss and other fine perceptions at the spiritual eye,
to effectively experience release in the inner light. As life force as-
cends toward the spiritual eye and crown chakra, the brilliance of
the inner light replaces the light of reflected consciousness which
provides perception and knowledge of relative circumstances.

The devotee should then surrender to the brilliant inner light,
ignoring visions and other transitory perceptions. One may see a
tunnel of light in the spiritual eye. If golden light is experienced
along with awareness of Om, one should merge in light and sound,
remaining alert with aspiration to transcend both. One may then
experience freedom in vast blue light and infinite space, but this
is not the final stage. Beyond that is brilliant white light which
beckons the soul to realize Pure Being.

**27. The practitioner of yoga who knows these two paths is never
confused. Therefore, at all times, be steadfast in yoga.**

*Knowing these two paths, the devotee who practices samadhi remains
possessed of understanding. Therefore, at all times, be steadfast in
samadhi.*

Preliminary samadhi states can be attended by continued
mental activity, and illusions can be present. Knowing the higher
way, one who practices samadhi will direct attention upward,
aspiring to transcend sensory and mental involvements. To be

steadfast in samadhi is to be established in Self-knowledge, intent upon realizing pure states of consciousness and awakening to absolute realization.

28. The yogi, knowing this, transcending the effects of good deeds associated with study of scripture, holy offerings, austerities, and acts of charity, awakens to the supreme, original state of Absolute Being.

The awareness of the devoted practitioner of samadhi is removed from involvements with the karmic influences of mental impressions (samskaras) and their effects as described in various scriptures, and from all other compulsive involvements and actions related to the phenomenal realms. This occurs because of awakening to full God-realization.

> *In the Upanishad of the Bhagavad Gita, the science of the
> Absolute, the scripture of Yoga and the dialogue between
> Sri Krishna and Arjuna, thus ends the eighth chapter
> entitled Akshara Brahma Yoga: The Yoga of the
> Absolute Reality*

CHAPTER NINE

The Yoga of Royal Wisdom and Royal Mystery

The theme of the previous chapter is continued, with insightful explanation of higher realities and how the awakening soul can more fully know and realize them.

Krishna spoke:

1. **To you who do not dispute this teaching, I will declare this most secret knowledge combined with realization, which, by knowing, you shall be released from all error.**

   To you who do not disbelieve the truth and who do not argue or debate when being taught it, innate knowledge will be self-revealed along with experience, which, by knowing, you will be freed from all intellectual error and illusion.

   While personal perceptions and revealed information should always be examined in the light of intelligence, when valid knowledge is discerned, it should be immediately accepted. Honest questioning is helpful; petty arguments only serve to perpetuate ignorance.

2. **This is royal, secret knowledge, a supreme purifier, in accord with the way of righteousness, easy to practice, and eternal.**

   What is revealed is higher knowledge, which, to one whose powers of perception are minimal, must remain a mystery. When understood, it cleanses the mind of delusions (erroneous beliefs) and illusions (misperceptions). It is entirely compatible with the processes of evolution which nurture growth and unfoldment and is easy to practice when understood and applied. It is the everlasting facilitator of spiritual growth and liberation of consciousness.

3. **People who have no faith in this knowledge, who do not experience God-realization, return to mortal existence.**

This revealed knowledge of the true nature of Consciousness should be accepted without allowing doubts to confuse the mind. If it is not fully apprehended and experienced as a transformative influence, one will remain in the self-conscious state, fated to experience transient conditions which correspond to that deluded state.

4. **This entire universe is pervaded by my unmanifest aspect. All beings abide in me; I do not abide in them.**

This entire universe is pervaded by God's Consciousness. All souls abide in God's omnipresent Consciousness, but God's Consciousness is not confined in them.

5. **And yet beings do not [actually] abide in me. Behold my divine yoga-power! I cause beings to manifest, sustaining them though not dwelling in them.**

Even though all souls abide in God's Consciousness, the physical and mental characteristics do not. Behold the effects of the truth-veiling power of maya [primordial nature] which causes delusions and illusions! God's reflected light individualizes as souls, sustaining them, yet not being confined by their personal illusion of independent existence [egoism].

6. **As the mighty flowing wind, moving everywhere, ever abides in space, so all souls abide in me. Reflect upon this!**

As air exists in space, so all souls dwell in the omnipresent Consciousness of God. Souls are individualized (not independent or separately existing) units of God's Consciousness, like bubbles in a boundless ocean of Infinite Life. This fact can be analyzed until intellectually understood, then reflected upon and contemplated until experienced as true.

7. **All [unenlightened] beings go into the field of primordial nature at the end of a yuga [of universal manifestation]; and at the beginning of the next yuga I send them forth.**

All [unenlightened] souls go into the field of primordial nature at the end of a cycle of manifestation; when the next cycle of cosmic manifestation begins, the impulse from within the Field of God's Being that impels the process sends them forth.

We can only relate to that to which our knowledge and awareness corresponds. When the cosmic forces (gunas) are returned to the field of primordial nature at the conclusion of a duration of universal manifestation, souls which are still identified with nature's forces remain involved with them. They remain unconscious until the next cycle of universal manifestation unfolds on the screen of space and time, then flow into outer involvement once more. Only when souls awaken from deluded involvement with nature do they transcend its influences.

8. **Interacting with primordial nature, again and again I send forth this multitude of beings, which, influenced by primordial nature, are powerless to resist.**

Interacting with primordial nature, which is produced from Om, again and again cyclic impulses toward universal manifestation send souls which are powerless to resist [because of their deluded state] into involvement with nature's transformative actions.

Unenlightened souls are powerless to resist nature's actions because they are unconsciously identified with them. The way to freedom from blind involvement with time, space, and karma (cause and effect) is to improve understanding of God and life's processes, and to cultivate authentic spiritual growth. Spiritual growth is only authentic when it is demonstrated as knowledgeable, functional freedom.

9. **These actions do not bind me. To them I remain indifferent and unattached.**

These actions of cosmic manifestation do not restrict God's Being, which remains self-complete and detached.

The universe exists in God's omnipresent Consciousness as an idea exists in our field of awareness. Since the universe is a manifestation of primordial nature, which is God's self-referring creative force (Om) expressive as space, time, and cosmic forces which produce cosmic particles and all aspects of objective nature, it is inferior to God. Just as we can be conscious of, yet indifferent to, the contents of our field of awareness, so Supreme Consciousness is neutral in respect to the universe and its actions and contents.

10. Influenced by my intention, primordial nature produces all animate and inanimate things. The universe then proceeds.

Impelled by an impulse to express that arises in the Field of God's Being, the field of primordial nature produces all aspects of the universe out of itself. The impulse to manifest is primary cause; all else that happens are effects of the original impulse.

11. Embodied, deluded people, not knowing my higher nature as the cause of beings, do not regard me with esteem.

Incarnated souls who are unaware of the existence [and causative influences] of God can neither acknowledge nor appreciate the reality of Supreme Consciousness.

12. Those of vain hopes and actions, who lack knowledge, cling to their confused, self-serving, mean-spirited condition.

Their thoughts and actions, self-serving because of egoism, souls devoid of knowledge tend to remain tenaciously attached to confused, self-satisfying, ill-tempered, deluded states of consciousness.

The minds and bodies of souls that are overly identified with the gross matter side of nature, influenced by tamas guna, tend to be tenaciously attached to illusions of independent existence (egoism) to the degree of being defensive of it. Unable (or unwilling) to reflect upon and comprehend a higher order of reality, they cling to personal viewpoints and persist in self-serving behaviors until awareness-cleansing spiritual awakening occurs.

13. But those awakened souls established in their divine nature, knowing me as the imperishable origin of all beings, single-mindedly reverence me.

Spiritually awake souls, knowing God to be the eternal origin of souls, not allowing anything to distract their attention, humbly acknowledge God.

14. Always acknowledging me, endeavoring with firm resolve, and with devotion to me ever steadfast, they reverence me.

Ever absorbed in awareness of the Presence of God, steadfastly committed to right living and spiritual practice, spiritually awake souls remain devoted to God.

15. **Others make sacrifices to me as the Absolute and as the various manifestations [in the field of nature], knowing me as diversely manifesting, omnipresent, and omniscient.**

Other devotees, with insightful knowledge, offer their actions to God as the one, eternal Being, and as the all-pervading, all-knowing reality of all aspects of nature.

16. **I am the ritual action, I am the sacrifice, I am the medicinal herb, the sacred text, the clarified butter, the fire, and the holy offering itself.**

Because God alone exists, God is the performance of intentional actions, the acts of self-giving, the herbs which nurture health, the truth of revealed scriptures, self-discipline and other positive characteristics supportive of spiritual practice, the transformative actions of kundalini energies, and the self-giving process.

During the performance of formal religious ritual, various ceremonial actions may be performed; symbolic items may be used; and selections from sacred texts may be spoken for the purpose of improving one's awareness of the Presence of God, purifying the sanctuary, or inviting transformative energies into the environment. A devotee performs the inner ritual of meditation practice, offering life force to the chakras and dissolving egoism in superconsciousness to realize God.

17. **I am the father of the universe, the mother, the one who arranges all things, the grandfather, the object of knowledge, that which cleanses or purifies, the sacred syllable Om, and the Veda [revealed knowledge].**

God is the cause of the universe, the field of primordial nature [from which the universe is produced — the mother], the determining, intelligently directed influence that regulates universal actions, the Absolute Field of Consciousness beyond the Godhead, that in which all knowledge exists, the cleansing or redemptive power, the flowing creative force [Om], and the knowledge that is self-revealed.

18. **I am the goal, that which upholds, the ruling influence, the abode, the refuge, the friend, the origin, the ground of creation and the dissolution, the treasure house, and the imperishable seed [source].**

God is that which is to be realized by souls aspiring to liberation, that which supports all manifestation, the determining or regulating influence, that in which everything exists, that to which souls turn for comfort and fulfillment, the nurturing Presence, the origin of everything, the basis of the manifestation and dissolution of universes, the realm of all that is of real value, and the forever existing origin of the manifested aspect of itself.

19. I radiate heat, I withhold and send forth rain, and I am both immortality and death, being and nonbeing.

Consciousness is the ultimate source of heat [and all phenomena], regulates [by natural processes] weather patterns, is immortal, is [the appearance of] death [of mortals], and though self-expressed as individualized beings remains transcendent.

20. Those who know the three Vedas, who drink the sacred nectar, whose errors are cleansed, reverence me with holy offerings and seek a way to heaven. They go to the pure realm of the lord of gods and enjoy there the pleasures of the gods.

Those devotees to whom knowledge has been self-revealed, who are nourished by the tranquility of God-communion in samadhi, whose delusions are cleansed by knowledge and the redemptive actions of superconscious influences, are devoted to realizing God because they aspire to divine status. They experience what they desire and enjoy the results of their actions.

When advanced superconscious states unfold and soul tranquility is experienced, a fine, rejuvenating essence is produced in the brain that vitalizes and strengthens the entire physiology, and refines the nervous system and brain. In ancient yoga scriptures this is referred to as nectar or *soma*, the food of the gods. At this stage of soul unfoldment the physical body is increasingly sustained by the soul's life forces.

Many religious traditions teach that righteous souls go to a glorious light realm inhabited by celestial beings when they die to the material world. Because of the mental law of correspondences—the causative principle that determines that we tend to experience what we imaginatively desire—many souls will experience astral conditions that reflect their states of consciousness and expectations, just as their earth-life experiences are presently reflecting their assumptions. For a devotee to aspire to liberation, any conditioned state of consciousness or flawed perception is a limitation to be transcended.

21. Having enjoyed the vast realm of heaven, when the force of their constructive karma is exhausted, desirous of pleasures, they enter [return to] the realm of mortals to continued cycles of physical births and deaths.

After a duration of enjoyment, when the supporting causes which resulted in their pleasant state are neutralized, still craving ego-desired satisfaction, they reincarnate to continue their experiences as determined by their degree of understanding and the influences of their karmic condition.

22. But those who meditate with devotion on me alone, for them who thus persevere, I provide what they lack and preserve what they already have.

Those souls which are devotedly surrendered entirely in God are provided by God's grace with all they need for fulfillment, and what they have already attained they never lose.

God's grace is the result of supportive inclinations of life to maintain order. Because all-pervading Consciousness is outside of the field of time, the actions of grace are ever-present and immediately expressive to the degree that nature and souls are responsive to them. Devotees who remain absorbed in God have their needs provided by grace. Redemptive actions of grace contribute to physical regeneration, psychological transformation, and spiritual unfoldment. Nurturing actions of grace unfold supportive events and circumstances for the well-being and affluence of individuals. Life as wholeness is self-referring. When we are in harmony with its actions we are included in its processes. The actions of grace are impersonally impartial; they are expressive when and where they find an outlet.

23. Even those who worship other gods with faith, also worship me, though they do so without understanding.

Even people who sincerely reverence their concepts of God because they lack knowledge of God's real nature, are aspiring Godward.

Because only God exists, "other gods" are but imaginal ideas of devotees who are unable to comprehend what God is, or who prefer to honor a form or aspect of divinity which comforts the mind or seems to them more personal and attainable. If devotion is honest and aspiration is sufficient to allow one to progressively unfold, what is true will ultimately be self-revealed.

24. **For I am the enjoyer and the lord of all holy offerings. But because they [those whose understanding of God is limited] do not recognize me in truth, they fall.**

God expresses as and through all who sincerely worship. But because the knowledge of egocentric devotees is minimal, after an interlude of reverent meditation they return to their former, restricted states of consciousness.

25. **Devotees of the gods go to the gods; devotees of ancestors go to the ancestors; devotees of the spirits go to the spirits; those who are devoted to me come to me.**

Those who worship their concepts of God or various aspects of cosmic forces are inclined to identify with and experience them; those who yearn to commune with souls in a family relationship may do so [or at least remain in that state of dependency]; those who desire to dwell in astral realms with souls awaiting reincarnation tend to have their desire fulfilled; devotees who aspire to God-realization awaken in God.

Until we are completely awake to the truth, we may tend to cling to our beliefs and considerations about what God is—to what we have been taught, to what is believed by others whom we know, or to what has been partially revealed to us. At this level, because we are still involved with mental phenomena, the possibilities of continued illusional perceptions are almost endless. Some devotees desire only to be reunited with members of their family, or with compatible souls which are also working out their salvation. Souls devoted to knowledge and realization of the full reality of God can awaken completely to it.

26. **Whoever offers to me with devotion and a pure heart, a leaf, a flower, a fruit, or water, that offering of devotion I accept.**

However the pure-hearted devotee's offering to God is presented, that devotion establishes a relationship with God.

Whatever token offering is presented to the Infinite during ritual worship is acceptable as a gesture of devotion. Although the ritual act does not influence God, it can help to remove egoism or self-sense from the awareness of the devotee so that an increased awareness of the Presence of God can be apprehended.

27. **Whatever you do, whatever you eat, whatever you offer, whatever you give, whatever austerities you practice, do that as a holy offering to me.**

Whatever you intentionally do, eat, offer, or give, whatever self- disciplined practices you perform, do everything as a sacred act of offering to God.

Whatever we consciously do should be considered as essential to our relationship to the Infinite. In this way, every moment is devoted to spiritual practice, to being in harmonious relationship with the rhythms of life and established in Self-knowledge and God-awareness.

28. **You will certainly be freed from the effects of constructive and destructive actions. Liberated, with your mind disciplined by the yoga of renunciation, you will come to me.**

You will certainly be freed from karma. Liberated, your mind disciplined by this practice of renunciation, you will awaken to complete God-realization.

29. **I am the same to all beings. There is none disliked by me or who is dear to me. But they who worship me with devotion are in me and I am in them.**

God has the same relationship to all souls because God's Consciousness is expressing as every soul. Because God is the reality of every soul, God is incapable of disapproval or favoritism. But devotees who surrender in God with complete devotion experience themselves in God and God in and as them.

30. **Even if one who is prone to error worships me with single-pointed devotion, that one is to be considered as righteous because rightly resolved.**

Even if a person whose behaviors are not perfect surrenders to God with complete devotion, that one should be considered as righteous because of being rightly resolved.

Until we are flawlessly skillful in the performance of our duties and chosen actions, so long as we do our best we are on the right course in life. Our behaviors will not be error-free until we are living knowledgeably and spontaneously as the result of being Self-realized. We are only asked to live up to the highest potential of which we are presently capable.

31. Quickly that one becomes virtuous and experiences everlasting peace. Know for certain, no devotee of mine ever perishes.

Quickly that one unfolds virtuous soul qualities and experiences everlasting peace. Know for certain, no devotee ceases to exist.

Intentional behavioral modification enables us to remove unwanted habits and function effectively. Soul-restricting inclinations and habits can be replaced by right endeavor, as explained in the *Yoga Sutras* 2:33,34:

> To overcome and neutralize destructive, instinctual drives and tendencies, one should cultivate opposite qualities and habits.
> Instinctual drives and tendencies may be mild, moderate, or intense. Because they can cause pain and suffering, they should be removed by cultivating the virtues.

32. They who take refuge in me, even if they are born in vile or low circumstances, regardless of who they are, also awaken to their highest good.

Devotees who turn to God, regardless of the conditions of their birth or their present status, also awaken to Self-realization.

If we are intent upon spiritual growth and liberation of consciousness, our personal history is of no importance. Nothing we have experienced in the past need interfere with our aspiration and dedicated endeavors to awaken to Self-knowledge and to live effectively. Soul unfoldment is not determined by gender, racial or cultural circumstances, or our experiences prior to our choosing to know God. What is essential to soul unfoldment is sincere resolve, constructive living, and effective spiritual practice.

33. How much easier, then, is this awakening for the pure in heart and the devoted saints! Having come into this realm—a place of sorrow for many—devote yourself to me.

If devotees of ordinary circumstances can awaken in God, how much easier it is for those devoted ones whose hearts are already pure and whose soul qualities are somewhat unfolded! While you are in this physical world, which for many is a realm of sadness, devote yourself to realizing God.

34. Concentrated on me, be devoted to me; making holy offerings to me, worship me. Thus steadfast, with me as your supreme aim, you will come to me.

Ever attentive to being aware of the Presence of God, remain thus devoted. Engaged in self-giving to God, surrender in God. Thus steadfast, with God-realization your highest aspiration, you will awaken in God.

Inconsistent endeavor to facilitate spiritual growth is of minor value to its unfoldment; devoted endeavor to live constructively and to nurture awareness of the Presence of God results in rapid soul unfoldment.

In the Upanishad of the Bhagavad Gita, the science of the Absolute, the scripture of Yoga and the dialogue between Sri Krishna and Arjuna, thus ends the ninth chapter entitled Rajavidya Rajaguhya Yoga: The Yoga of Royal Wisdom and Royal Mystery

CHAPTER TEN

The Yoga of Divine Manifestations

More information about Supreme Consciousness and its various aspects and manifestations is now revealed to the soul as meditative contemplation continues.

I have paraphrased the italicized paragraphs so that when compared to the original verse the themes and inner meanings of Sanskrit names and concepts can be understood. If the verses with several Sanskrit words represent a major challenge to the reader, the italicized versions only can be perused.

Krishna spoke:

1. **Again, hear my supreme word. To you who now delight in my words, I will tell it to you.**

   Be attentive to the inner revelation of the highest truth. To you who are now happy to have these revelations, more will be revealed from the essence of your innermost true Self.

2. **Neither the multitude of gods nor the great seers and sages know my origin for I am the source of them.**

   Neither those who have achieved temporary divine status nor highly realized but not yet fully enlightened souls know the origin of the Godhead, for the Godhead is their origin.

In this story, nearly illumined souls, whether dwelling on earth or in subtle realms, are referred to as "gods" (*devas*, shining ones). Sages are souls wise with knowledge. Unless enlightenment is complete, total knowledge of Consciousness is not possible. To pierce the veil of unknowing, meditative contemplation should be practiced by a devotee as described in the *Yoga Sutras* 3:1-6:

> An undisturbed flow of attention is concentration.
> Unwavering, internalized concentration is meditation.
> When the object concentrated upon is transcended and its

reality is experienced, this is samadhi.

When concentration, meditation, and superconscious perception are simultaneous, this is perfect contemplation.

As a result of mastery of perfect contemplation, the light of direct knowledge dawns in one's field of awareness.

Perfect contemplation should be practiced progressively to experience higher states of consciousness.

3. **That one who knows me, the unborn, without beginning, the ruling influence of the worlds, is among mortals undeluded and liberated from all misfortune.**

    That devotee who knows God as self-existent, beginningless, the intelligently directed power that regulates universal actions, is of all embodied souls free from ignorance and liberated from the effects of prior actions and from episodes of misfortune.

4. **Understanding, knowledge, freedom from delusion, patience, truth, self-restraint, tranquility, pleasure, pain, birth, death, and both fear and fearlessness,**
5. **Harmlessness, impartiality, contentment, austerity, benevolence, fame, disrepute—all of the conditions and states of varied beings—arise from me [the Field of Divine Consciousness] alone.**

    The drama of life occurs in Consciousness which is omnipresent and expresses according to the influences present at various levels of manifestation. Because Consciousness alone exists, nothing can occur independent of it.

6. **The seven great seers of old, and the four ancestors of the human race emanated from me, and born of my mind are all these beings of the world.**

    The seven aspects of God that regulate universal processes and the four aspects of Om [its pervading force, cosmic particles, space, and time] were produced from God's Being, and produced from God's Cosmic Individuality are all embodied beings.

By now the reader is aware of the intent of the author of the *Gita* to reiterate certain key points for the purpose of emphasis and to encourage a more insightful examination of them. The author is not merely telling an interesting story for the purpose of entertainment: an overview of philosophical principles and recommendations for lifestyle choices and spiritual practices that can liberate the spirit is being presented.

7. That one who knows this truth of my reality and my power and its manifestations, is without doubt united with me.

The devotee who knows the truth about God's power to express and its manifestations, is truly established in God-realization.

One who is fully enlightened—who truly knows the facts of Consciousness and its processes of self-expression, is established in samadhi (oneness, wholeness) whether absorbed in meditative contemplation or not.

8. I am the origin of all. From me all creation is emanated. Knowing this, wise devotees, endowed with devotion, constantly contemplate me.

God is the origin of beings and things. From God the universe is emanated. Knowing this, wise devotees, endowed with devotion, reverently acknowledge the reality of God and meditate with attention flowing to God.

Although meditation practice is recommended for the purpose of undistracted contemplation, we should train ourselves to always be aware of our relationship to the Infinite. Forgetfulness of ourselves as spiritual beings is a primary cause of difficulties and unhappiness.

9. Those who think of me, who are surrendered in me, enlightening each other and speaking of me, are soul-satisfied.

Those whose thoughts are of God, whose lives are surrendered in God, who speak only words of truth and encouragement to others, are spiritually fulfilled.

It is not that thinking of God, cultivating an attitude of God-surrender, and relating to others in entirely constructive ways immediately results in spiritual fulfillment—although these are beneficial behaviors to be nurtured. When we are soul-content, we naturally behave like this.

10. To those who are constantly steadfast and who worship me with love, I bestow the yoga of discrimination by which they come to me.

To those devotees who are unwavering in right living and spiritual practices and who are wholeheartedly devoted to God, grace unfolds powers of discernment which provide them insight and realization of God.

Soul unfoldment and improvement of powers of discernment may occur rapidly or it may occur more slowly but progressively. If awakening is rapid, we can consider ourselves to be fortunate and be thankful for our blessings. If awakening is slower but progressive, we can likewise be thankful. What is to be avoided is frustration that contributes to unhappiness and despair. The key is to remain steadfast with the flame of devotion brightly burning. Our spiritual fulfillment is certain.

11. Remaining as I am, out of compassion for them [souls devoted to spiritual practices] I remove the darkness born of ignorance with the luminous lamp of knowledge.

While God remains ever the same, because of the devotee's devotion, the actions of God's grace remove darkness born of delusion with the shining light of direct knowledge.

With the dawning of revealed knowledge, all restrictions to soul awareness cease. The ego-fixated soul cannot liberate itself, although attentive right living and meditative contemplation will effectively remove some of the physical and mental obstacles to Self-knowledge. The final unveiling of soul awareness is accomplished by grace. When only a mild degree of egoism exists, complete soul-surrender in God results in realization of oneness.

Arjuna said:

12. You are the Supreme Reality, the supreme abode, the supreme purifier, the eternal divine Spirit, the primordial God, unborn and all-pervading.
13. All the seers and sages declare this to be so, and now you yourself say it.
14. All that you tell me, I believe to be true. Indeed, neither the

gods nor the unenlightened souls know your manifestation.

15. **Supreme One, you know yourself by yourself; the source and ruler of all beings, God of the gods, and ruler of the universe.**

16. **Please fully describe how, by self-manifestation, you pervade the worlds and abide in them.**

17. **How may I, by constant meditation, know you? And what various aspects of your being am I to contemplate?**

18. **Explain to me in further detail your power and manifestation. I am never fully satisfied with hearing your words which are like nectar.**

After preliminary insight, the soul, now alert and happy, meditatively contemplates with renewed interest for the purpose of discovering more about the reality of Consciousness and how to fully comprehend it. The behavior of the aspiring soul now represents a complete conversion from that vividly described in the early chapters of this story.

Krishna replied:

19. **Listen! I shall explain to you my self-manifestations, but only those most prominent ones, for their extent is endless.**

   Be attentive! Some revelations about more obvious self-manifesta-tions—which are really endless in number—will now be unfolded from within you.

To "listen" is to be attentive, to look, to be receptive to the truth. Meditative contemplation should be an act of conscious intention so that awareness remains clear, free from mental and emotional influences and from the subtle influences of rajas and tamas gunas. The soul is now prepared to have access to partial knowledge of the reality of God.

20. **I am the Self [the true Being] abiding in the heart of all beings. I am the beginning of beings, the middle, and the very end as well.**

   God is the reality of every soul. Because everything, including time, is included in God's Being, the reality of God is evident in all aspects of occurring events.

Cosmic perceptions unfold in the field of the meditator's awareness. The Spirit of God is apprehended as the essence of souls, the all-pervading Reality which includes all souls, and the field of Great Time which contains the universe.

21. Of the supreme gods, I am the preserver [Vishnu]; of the self-shining lights, I am the radiant sun; I am the chief among the gods of storms that water the earth; in the sky at night I am the moon.

Of the controlling aspects of nature, God is the preserver. God is the sun, the ruling influence of prevailing winds that cause rain to fall, and the moon that reflects the light of the sun.

As soul awareness expands, with thoughts and mental imagery yet influential, the meditating devotee may begin to relate perceptions of omnipresent Consciousness to philosophical concepts and natural phenomena. Because Consciousness is the single Reality, all manifestations are its expressions. The process of relating Consciousness to mental concepts and various aspects of nature is described in the following verses.

22. Of the Vedas, I am the Sama Veda; of the gods I am Indra; of the senses I am the mind, and I am the intelligence of beings.

Of unfolded revelations, Supreme Consciousness expresses as tranquility; of the controlling influences, Consciousness regulates the fluctuations occurring in individualized fields of awareness of souls; of the faculties of sense perception, Consciousness manifests as the mind; and Consciousness produces the faculty of discriminative intelligence used by embodied souls.

23. Of the Rudras I am Shankara. I am the lord of wealth of varied kinds of beings. I am fire of the gods and the Meru of mountains.

Of the radiant forces, Consciousness is supreme. Consciousness expresses abundantly, is the purifying influence of the vitalizing energies, and is sovereign over all phenomenal expressions.

24. Of the sources of knowledge honored in houses I am Brihaspati, the first among them; of commanders of armies I am the Skanda; of bodies of water I am the ocean.

Of the sources of knowledge, Supreme Consciousness is primary; of virtuous influences, God is the power that makes possible success in all undertakings; of fields of consciousness, God alone is omnipresent and unbounded.

25. Of the great seers I am Bhrigu; of words I am the single syllable Om; of holy offerings I am the silent chanting of mantra; of immovable things, the Himalayas.

Of souls with keen powers of intuition, Consciousness is the revealer; Consciousness manifests as the creative force, Om; is the spontaneous reverberation of Om in the meditator's field of awareness; and is permanent and supreme above all.

26. Of the trees I am the sacred ashvattha; of the divine seers, I am Narada; of the gandharvas [celestial singers] I am Chitraratha [whose chariot is bright]; of the perfected I am the sage Kapila.

Consciousness expresses as the immortal tree of life; the processes of cosmic manifestation and the return of soul awareness to wholeness; the radiance perceived in the spiritual eye by the meditator; and the revealer of knowledge of categories of cosmic manifestation.

27. Know that I am Ucchaishravas of horses, born of nectar; of princely elephants I am Airavata; and of men, the king.

Know that Consciousness produces the life force that animates forms and returns a devotee's life forces through the sushumna to the higher chakras; is the revealer of wisdom; and is the ruler of the devotee's senses and states of consciousness.

28. I am the thunderbolt of weapons; the wish-fulfilling cow; the progenitor Kandarpa [god of desire, god of love]; and of serpents I am Vasuki [king].

Consciousness manifests as the light and sound of Om that produces the primordial field of nature; as the blessing-grace that redeems soul awareness; as the attraction-influence that causes souls to individualize and living things to reproduce; and as kundalini power that pervades the universe, which is dormant in spiritually unawake people and dynamically active in spiritually awakened devotees of God.

29. I am Ananta of the Nagas; Varuna of the water creatures, Aryaman of the ancestors; and among those who maintain law and order I am Yama [god of death].

Consciousness manifests the field of primordial nature that causes nature-identified souls to experience temporary delusion; as the ocean of cosmic manifestation in which souls dwell; and as a devotee's self-mastery that enables one to awaken from the delusion of mortality to realization of immortality.

30. I am Prahlada of the demons; of the calculators I am time; I am the lion, king of beasts; and of birds I am Garuda.

Consciousness expresses as joyous aspiration that overcomes all aspects of varied obstacles to Self-knowledge; as the divisions of time analyzed by those who endeavor to determine cycles of cosmic actions; as omnipotence that is supreme among varied, phenomenal powers; and as the devotee's expansion of awareness that dissolves delusions and illusions.

31. Of purifiers, I am the wind; Rama of the warriors; Makara of the creatures of the sea; and of the rivers I am the Ganges.

Of purifying influences, Consciousness is the life-breath or prana that enlivens; the righteousness that prevails in the face of disorder; samadhi perceptions that remove restrictions from the devotee's field of awareness; and the self-revealed, redemptive wisdom that freely flows when soul unfoldment is spontaneous.

32. I am the beginnings, the middle, and the endings of creation; of all knowledge I am the knowledge of the Supreme Self, and the logic of those who debate.

Omnipresent Consciousness includes past, present, and future time; is Self-knowing; and is the knowledge that is revealed to those who intelligently inquire about it.

33. Of letters I am [the letter] A, and the unifying connection between compound words; I alone am Infinite Time; I am omniscient and arrange all things.

Supreme Consciousness is the first among all aspects of itself that later manifest; that which exists between categories of manifested phenomena and which unifies; is beginningless and endless Great

Time that remains removed from relative space-time; and is the all-knowing, regulating influence in the field of nature.

34. I am all-destroying death and the origin of things that are yet to be. Among the qualities born of nature I am fame, prosperity, speech, memory, wisdom, firmness, and patience.

Supreme Consciousness dissolves and emanates universes. Among the qualities born of nature, Consciousness makes possible expressions of Self-manifestation, influences that support well-being, vibratory sound frequencies, impressions in fields of awareness that retain information about relative occurrences, valid knowledge, firm stability in intuitively perceived truth, and as soul-tranquility which enables the devotee to be patient in all circumstances.

35. Of chants and hymns I am Brihatsaman; of meters I am Gayatri; of the months I am Marga-shirsha, and of seasons I am the flower-abounding spring.

Of sacred mantras Supreme Consciousness is the liberating influence; of mantras which are faithfully recited, the knowledge innate to Consciousness unfolds as mind-illuminating wisdom; during occasions for devotional meditation, ever-present Supreme Consciousness is immediately accessible; and of the times for devotees to have awareness restored to wholeness, the prevailing existence of Supreme Consciousness allows instantaneous enlightenment.

36. I am the gambling of the dishonest, the splendor of the splendid; I am victory, endeavor, and the goodness of the good.

Supreme Consciousness veiled by its own self-emanated field of primordial nature allows deluded souls to behave and have experiences in accord with their states of consciousness. The empowering qualities of Consciousness are expressed as victory over obstacles, resolved endeavor, and as pure sattvic characteristics.

37. Of the Vrishnis I am Vasudeva; of the sons of Pandu I am Arjuna; of the sages I am Vyasa, and of poets I am Ushana.

Of the various aspects of Supreme Consciousness, all-pervading Spirit as affluent splendor is but one; of the chakras, Supreme Consciousness expresses as fiery self-control and aspiration to God-knowledge; of the self-revealing aspects of Supreme Consciousness, two of them are wisdom-knowledge and inspired devotion.

38. Of disciplinarians I am the scepter, and the guidance of those desirous of victory; of secrets I am silence and the knowledge of the wise.

The principle of cause and effect disciplines behaviors of souls which are not yet wise in the performance of duties and actions. The "secret place" where knowledge unfolds is the silence that prevails when restless tendencies [vasanas] are quieted and mental fluctuations [vrittis] cease.

39. I am also the seed of all creatures; there is nothing moving or unmoving that could exist without me.

Consciousness is that from which all souls and aspects of nature are projected into manifestation; there is nothing that exists that could be in manifestation without Supreme Consciousness as its cause and innermost essence.

40. My divine manifestations are endless. What I have declared to you is only a partial description of the extent of them.

The self-manifestations of Supreme Consciousness cannot be numbered because they are many and the process is continuous. This soul-revelation is only a glimpse of the cosmic panorama.

41. Whatever is manifested, gloriously endowed with grace and vitality, understand it to have originated from but a portion of my splendor.

Whatever is in manifestation that is splendidly endowed with life-enhancing qualities, know that to have emanated from but a small portion of the radiance of Consciousness.

42. But what need do you have for this detailed knowledge? I pervade and support this entire universe with but a portion of myself.

But why do you need to know these details? Supreme Consciousness pervades and maintains the entire universe with but a minute part of its wholeness.

Knowing some of the details about how Consciousness expresses is helpful in enabling us to live effectively on earth and in subtle astral and fine causal realms. However, when the soul is attentively engaged in meditative contemplation for the purpose of realizing the Absolute beyond all manifested aspects of Consciousness, knowledge of relative matters is not necessary.

In the Upanishad of the Bhagavad Gita, the science of the Absolute, the scripture of Yoga and the dialogue between Sri Krishna and Arjuna, thus ends the tenth chapter entitled Vibhuti Yoga: The Yoga of Divine Manifestations

CHAPTER ELEVEN

The Yoga of Universal Revelation

The aspiring soul has been informed about the reality of the Absolute without name or form and is convinced of its supremacy. Now, not content with memories of partial cosmic conscious realizations as described in the preceding chapter, the soul yearns to know the many aspects of the one Being, Life, Power, and manifesting Substance of God.

Arjuna said:

1. **The highest knowledge of the Supreme Self you have given to me by your grace has banished my confusion.**
2. **Your explanation of the origin and dissolution of things and of your imperishable reality has been heard by me.**
3. **Thus you have described yourself; I now desire to truly see your divine form [the diverse manifestations and expressions of Consciousness].**

Knowledge about God has been progressively unfolding. The next stage of revelation will provide direct experience of what has so far only been intellectually grasped.

4. **If you consider it is possible for me to see it, show me the fullness of your eternal Self.**

Desire to know God by personal realization is helpful. The next stage of soul unfoldment is possible when the devotee, prepared by disciplined practice and having acquired essential knowledge, is receptive to revelation and asks to know the allness of God. Although spontaneous soul unfoldments occur to the degree that we are receptive to them, we can also ask (inquire, desire to know) for revelation that will blossom from the innermost core of our being.

Krishna said:

5. **Behold my multiplied hundreds and thousands of forms of various kinds, divine, and of various colors and shapes.**

    See the many and varied manifestations of Consciousness.

6. **Behold the Adityas, the Vasus, the Rudras, the two Asvins, the Maruts too, and many wonders never before seen.**

    See the celestial deities, the beneficent gods, the forces that herald the dawn and promote healing, and the cosmic forces that determine nature's processes; and many wonderful things you have never before seen.

While the core message of the *Gita* transcends religious and cultural conditions, because the author of this story was communicating to people familiar with Vedic religious traditions, the symbolism of gods, goddesses, and various organizing and influential aspects of cosmic forces is portrayed in language meaningful to them.

To have a sense of what a devotee experiences as cosmic perceptions unfold, it can be helpful to read the following verses without pausing. Then, read them again more carefully.

7. **Behold now the entire universe, with everything moving and not moving unified in my body, and whatever else you desire to see.**

    Look upon the entire universe, with everything animate and inanimate unified in Consciousness, and whatever else you desire to see.

8. **Because you cannot see me with your own eyes, I will give you divine sight; behold my majestic power!**

    Because you cannot see the wholeness of Consciousness with your limited powers of sense perception, intuition will awaken from within you; behold the superior power of Consciousness in manifestation!

Sanjaya said:

9. **Having thus declared, the great Lord of yoga revealed to Arjuna his supreme form.**

Inner knowledge having thus intimated what is to occur, Consciousness self-revealed the truth of its manifest aspects.

10. **Of many mouths and eyes, wondrous aspects, divine ornaments, and uplifted weapons.**

Of many cosmic energy-absorbing characteristics and viewpoints, wondrous aspects, arrayed with grace-endowing qualities and with powers to fulfill intended purposes.

11. **Wearing divine garlands and apparel, with divine fragrances, of marvels comprised, the resplendent Reality, without beginning or end, facing in all directions.**

Adorned with appropriate coverings or sheaths at various levels of Self-manifestation, with fragrances of the vibratory frequencies of pranas or life forces, marvelously interacting, the resplendent truth of Consciousness, beginningless and endless, omnipresent.

12. **If a thousand suns should at once arise in the sky, such brilliance might faintly resemble the splendor of that great Being.**
13. **There, Arjuna beheld the entire universe with its diverse expressions and aspects in oneness, of many categories in the body of the God of gods.**

Remaining where it was, the soul apprehended the entire universe as a continuum — as one manifestation of Consciousness with a series of connected aspects and functions — as wholeness in which diverse empowering influences are expressive.

Arjuna spoke:

14. **Then Arjuna, overwhelmed with amazement, bowing his head to the Lord, said:**
15. **In your body, O God, I see the gods and the various kinds of beings assembled; Brahma on his lotus seat, and all the sages and divine serpents.**

The soul, awed by its experience, endeavoring to rid itself of any residue of egoism, further inquires:
    In the field of manifested Consciousness I see the empowering influences that regulate cosmic processes and their various kinds of influential agents of action; The Creator aspect of Supreme Con-

sciousness, and all the enlightened souls and expressive aspects of kundalini [the dynamic creative energy of Consciousness].

16. **I see you everywhere, your form as infinite, with many arms, bodies, faces, and eyes; but not the end, middle, or the beginning of you do I see, O Lord, whose form is endless.**

I intuitively perceive the self-manifestations of Consciousness throughout its entire field of expression as boundless; but I do not perceive the full extent of the endless processes of Consciousness.

17. **You, who are difficult to behold, I see crowned, with club and discus, a mass of light, shining everywhere, with incomparable radiance as of the sun and blazing fire.**

I perceive the reality of manifested Consciousness with its varied aspects of controlling power; I perceive an all-pervading, intensely shining light whose radiance is unique.

18. **I believe you are the unchanging, the Supreme to be realized, the ultimate resting place of all; you are the everlasting protector of the eternal law, the primeval Spirit.**

I acknowledge Consciousness to be permanent, the superior Reality to be realized, the ultimate to be experienced; Consciousness is the forever guardian of the principles which uphold the order of the universe, the originating, life-giving Reality.

19. **I see you with infinite power, beginningless, endless, without a middle; with countless arms, the moon and sun are your eyes, the blazing fire of your mouth illuminating the universe with your radiance.**

I perceive Consciousness to have infinite powers, as untouched by time and universal processes; with numberless aspects and agencies of action, the planets and stars in space are to me like the eyes of invisible Consciousness looking upon the worlds, and the energetic powers flowing from the source of cosmic manifestation illumines the universe with its radiance.

20. **The space between heaven and earth is pervaded by you alone. Seeing your formidable form, the three worlds tremble, O great Being.**

The connecting gaps between subtle and gross realms are pervaded by Consciousness. Being subject to the awesome cosmic manifestations and actions of Consciousness, the processes of causal, astral, and physical realms are responsive to it.

21. **The throngs of gods enter you; some, in fear, praise you with their salutations; the perfected ones acknowledge you with abundant signs of recognition.**

Multitudes of nearly enlightened souls approach the final stages to the realization of the reality of Consciousness; some, uncertain, acknowledge God with reverent gestures and spiritual practices; the seers, the enlightened souls, acknowledge God with rejoicing.

22. **The Rudras, Adityas, Vasus, and Sadhyas; the Vishvedevas, the two Ashvins, the Maruts, and the Ushma pas; the throngs of gandharvas, Yakshas, Asuras, and perfected ones, beholding you, are astonished.**

All of the agencies by which the expressive powers of manifesting Consciousness are influential, are subject to the impulses of the intelligently directed purposes of Consciousness.

23. **Seeing your great form, with many mouths, eyes, arms, thighs, feet, and mouths gaping with many tusks, the worlds tremble and so do I.**

Perceiving the fully manifested form of Consciousness and its diverse aspects and actions, [it seems to me that] the worlds [must] know their relationship to Supreme Consciousness, as I do.

24. **Seeing you touching the sky, blazing with many colors, open-mouthed and with enormous glowing eyes, I tremble indeed, and I find neither courage nor tranquility.**

Perceiving the varied aspects of universal manifestation of Consciousness, I am in awe, and lack courage and tranquility.

25. **Seeing your open mouths with their tusks, glowing like the flames that consume time and all things, I lose my sense of direction and do not find comfort or refuge, O Lord of gods, abode of the universe.**

Perceiving the processes of transformation and dissolution of cosmic forces, my powers of meditative concentration are impaired and I am not able to experience mental peace or samadhi.

26. **Entering into you are all the sons of Dhritarashtra, together with the throngs of kings: Bhishma, Drona, and Karna, the son of the charioteer along with our chief warriors.**

Now being dissolved in Supreme Consciousness are the destructive tendencies of the undiscerning mind, together with many other awareness-restricting influences: the delusion of independent selfhood, the influential potencies of mental impressions [samskaras], and mental resistance to soul unfoldment along with the other disturbing tendencies and habits.

27. **Quickly they enter your open mouths with many tusks; the heads of some are seen between your teeth, their heads pulverized.**

Quickly they are dissolved in Supreme Consciousness; some of them are perceived to be voraciously consumed.

28. **As the many fast-moving currents of the rivers flow to the ocean, so those heroes of the world enter into your flaming mouths.**

As the many fast-moving currents of the rivers flow to the ocean, so those characteristics, tendencies, and habits of the deluded mind are dissolving in the brilliant light of Consciousness.

29. **As moths swiftly enter a blazing flame to perish there, these creatures speedily enter your mouths and perish.**

As moths swiftly enter a fire to perish, so these aspects of the deluded mind speedily become absorbed in the light of Consciousness and are eliminated.

30. **Filling the universe with fiery splendor, your fierce rays blaze forth, swallowing all the worlds.**

Filling the universe with fiery splendor, the transformative influences of Consciousness are all-inclusive.

31. **Tell me who you are, with form so awesome. Salutations to you, O Great God; have mercy! I wish to understand you, primal One, for I do not comprehend your actions.**

Reveal to me the truth of Consciousness, with manifestations so awesome. I reverently acknowledge Consciousness in manifestation; I ask for grace! I desire to fully realize the allness of Consciousness, for [at the moment] I do not yet comprehend it.

Krishna said:

32. I am Time, the mighty cause of dissolution, come forth to annihilate the worlds. Even without any action of yours, all these warriors arrayed against you shall cease to exist.

An expressive aspect of the field of primordial nature produced by Om flowing from God's Consciousness is time that determines cycles of universal manifestation and dissolution. Even without any personal endeavor by the samadhi-absorbed soul, all obstacles to Self-realization will be eliminated by God's grace.

33. Therefore, arise and gain glory! Having conquered the enemy, enjoy the prosperous kingship. They have [already] been slain. You should be only the agent.

Therefore, be alert and awaken to Self-knowledge and realization of God! Having overcome all obstacles to enlightenment, enjoy the results of unfolded soul qualities. The obstacles have already been overcome by superconscious influences. You should only be the agent of right actions.

34. Drona, Bhishma, Jayadratha, also Karna, and others who are warrior heros, have [already] been slain by me. Do not hesitate! Fight! You shall conquer the enemy in battle.

The mental conditionings [samskaras] which support self-defeating habits and addictive tendencies, the deluded sense of independent selfhood, attachment to mortal existence, the mind's resistance to accept constructive change, and other dominant subconscious characteristics which cause problems, have already been rendered helpless by samadhi influences. Confront the opportunity before you! You are destined to be victorious in your spiritual practices.

Sanjaya speaks:

35. Having heard these words, Arjuna, trembling with terror, folded his hands and bowed, prostrating himself, and in great fear spoke in a faltering voice:

Having had this revelation, the soul, anxious and uncertain, sur-rendered egoism to superconsciousness and continued to engage in attentive meditative contemplation, then acknowledged:

36. Rightly does the universe rejoice and is grateful to you. The demons flee in terror in all directions and all the throngs of perfected ones in adoration salute you.

It is proper that all beings in the universe rejoice and be thankful that Supreme Consciousness is unfailingly influential in cosmic and personal affairs. The forces in opposition to orderly unfoldments of consciousness are banished and multitudes of enlightened souls acknowledge Supreme Consciousness with unwavering devotion.

37. And why should they not reverently acknowledge you, O great One, who are the original Creator, greater even than Brahma! Infinite Lord of gods, you are the abode of the universe, the imperishable, the existent, the nonexistent, and that which is beyond both.

And why should they not acknowledge Supreme Consciousness in this way, that which is the primary cause of universal manifesta-tion, superior even to the aspect of God that is influential in causing nature to emanate the worlds! The Infinite Ruler of cosmic forces that empower and transform the field of nature contains the uni-verse. Supreme Consciousness is imperishable, is said to exist when manifesting the worlds, is said not to exist in relationship to nature-produced phenomena because of its transcendent aspect, and in fact is indescribable.

38. You are the primordial God, ancient Spirit, and supreme resting place of the universe. You are the knower, the object of knowledge, and the supreme state [to be realized]. The entire universe is pervaded by you, O One of infinite forms.

Being is the primary aspect of Consciousness, the timeless, active agent of cosmic processes, and the source and abode of the universe. It is the knower, the object of knowledge, and the supreme knowledge to be known or realized. The universe is pervaded by Consciousness and is self-manifesting as numberless forms and aspects.

39. You are Vayu, Yama, Agni, Varuna, the moon, the Lord of creatures and the great grandfather. A thousand salutations

to you, and again salutations, salutations!

Consciousness expresses as vital forces in nature and in the body of the meditating devotee, and as self-control, that which sustains all things in the universe, all things that reflect its light, the intelligently determining influence that is all-pervading, and the cause of individualization of souls and of world manifestation. The soul continues to reverently acknowledge Supreme Consciousness.

40. **I bow to you from in front and behind, I bow to you on all sides. Of infinite power and boundless might, because you pervade all, you are all.**

The soul, overflowing with love and gratitude, acknowledges omnipresent, omnipotent, unlimited Supreme Consciousness.

41. **O Krishna, whatever I have impetuously said as if in ordinary friendship, in ignorance of your greatness, because of my negligence or even because of my affection,**
42. **And if disrespect was shown to you even in a lighthearted, humorous way, while at play, or while seated or taking meals, or in the presence of others, O immeasurable One, I ask your forgiveness.**

O Supreme Consciousness, my own indwelling Reality and the Reality of all, for whatever I have said or done in the past because of not knowing the truth, may I be forgiven.

43. **You are the father of the world, of the moving and the motionless, you are to be revered by this world. You are to be venerated. There is nothing like you in the three worlds. How could there be another greater than you, O great Being who are of incomparable glory?**

Supreme Consciousness is now known to be the cause of world manifestation and is reverently acknowledged as such.

44. **Bowing down, prostrating before you, I ask your forgiveness, O Lord. Be kind to me as a father to a son, a friend to a friend, a lover to a beloved.**

The soul is impelled to surrender remnants of limited self-consciousness for the purpose of remaining established in cosmic consciousness, and is now receptive to the influences and actions of a supportive universe which is a manifestation of impulses originating in the Field of Supreme Consciousness.

45. Having seen what has never before been seen, I rejoice, yet my mind trembles with fear. Show me your previous form and be gracious, O Lord of gods, the abode of the universe.

The soul, with a sense of independent selfhood and still mildly uncertain about what is yet to unfold, desires to have awareness restored to the condition in which it can again relate to God on more personal, familiar terms.

46. I desire to see you as before, wearing a crown, holding a scepter, holding a discus in your hand; you who have all forms, become that form again.

The devotee desires to perceive the aspects of God as apprehended before the cosmic conscious experience, with the familiar characteristics and attributes which comfort the mind.

Krishna speaks:

47. By my grace, by my own power, this supreme form has been shown to you; my form of splendor, which is universal, infinite, and primal, which has never before been seen by anyone but you.

By the actions of grace, this supreme manifestation of God has been revealed to the receptive soul. Because of conditioned mental states, degree of ability to comprehend, and the influences of the gunas, each soul's unfoldment experiences are unique. Therefore, it is stated that no other soul has ever perceived the manifestations of Consciousness exactly as this soul has perceived them.

48. Neither by ceremony, scriptural recitation, ritual offerings, gifts, nor by austerities, can I be seen in such form in this realm by any other than you.

Neither by routine ceremonial gestures, quoting from scriptures, mechanical performance of lifestyle routines and meditation practices, the giving of gifts with expectation of reward of some kind, nor by arduous practices can a revelation such as this be experienced by anyone other than you.

49. Do not be afraid or confused because of having seen this awesome form of mine. Be again free from fear and be cheerful. Behold my previous form!

Do not be afraid or confused because of having experienced this revelation of Supreme Consciousness. Be again free from fear and be cheerful. Now perceive the aspects of Consciousness with which you are more familiar.

Sanjaya speaks:

50. Having thus spoken to Arjuna, Krishna again revealed his previous form. Having resumed his gentle, gracious appearance, he calmed the terrified Arjuna.

Having thus been revealed to the soul, Supreme Consciousness was again perceived with modifying attributes. This calmed the devotee's mind and removed anxiety.

Arjuna said:

51. Seeing your gentle form again, O Krishna, I am now composed and my mind is restored to its normal condition.

Perceiving the familiar aspect of God which comforts the mind, the devotee feels more secure and self-confident.

Krishna said:
52. This form of mine which you beheld is difficult to see. Even the gods constantly yearn to behold it.

This self-revealed cosmic aspect of Consciousness is difficult to realize by the ordinary devotee. Even the nearly enlightened souls yearn to experience it.

53. This form of mine you have beheld cannot be seen by the study of scripture, the practice of austerities, the giving of gifts, or by ceremonial ritual.

This self-revealed cosmic aspect of Consciousness cannot be realized by mere scripture study, various disciplines practiced for psychologi-

cal transformation, by charitable giving, or by exoteric ceremonial practices.

54. **Arjuna, this form can only be known, seen, and entered into by steadfast devotion.**

This cosmic aspect of Consciousness can only be known, seen, and completely realized by steadfast devotion.

55. **That devotee who performs all actions for me, who knows me as the Supreme [Reality], is devoted to me, abandons all attachment, and who is free from ill will toward any being, comes to me.**

That devotee who performs all actions as an offering to evolution, who knows the Absolute as the Supreme Reality, who is sincerely devoted to realizing God, who relinquishes all attachments, and is devoid of ill will toward any other soul, awakens to the truth.

The emotionalism and mental instability of the devotee as described in these verses indicates that the cosmic conscious experience is still only partial; there is insight along with mental imagery and self-conscious endeavors to relate the universal vision to traditional ideas. However, the experience is sufficient to inspire the devotee to further right practice.

In the Upanishad of the Bhagavad Gita, the science of the Absolute, the scripture of Yoga and the dialogue between Sri Krishna and Arjuna, thus ends the eleventh chapter entitled Visvarupa Darsana Yoga: The Yoga of Universal Revelation

CHAPTER TWELVE

The Yoga of Devotion

The awakened soul, now informed of basic philosophical principles and having had a glimpse of the boundless reality of God, further inquires about the most suitable approach to unfold innate potential and realize the Absolute Truth.

Arjuna asked:

1. **Of the devotees who worship you with constant devotion, and who worship the Absolute, which has better knowledge of yoga?**

   Of the devotees who engage in spiritual practices with constant devotion to God, and of those who contemplate the Field of Pure Consciousness, which has superior knowledge of spiritual growth processes and samadhi states?

Krishna answered:

2. **I consider them to be the most devoted to me who, endowed with supreme faith and firm concentration, worship me with unwavering devotion.**

   Those who wholeheartedly aspire to know God, engage in spiritual practices and surrender self-consciousness to experience God-consciousness, are acknowledged as true devotees of God.

It is possible to realize God by devotion alone. For this, the devotee needs to yearn to know God and surrender (renounce) all erroneous beliefs and illusions about God so that spiritual growth can spontaneously occur. To love God from a distance— remaining in a self-conscious state, thinking of God as removed from the soul—is not sufficient to cause adjustments of states of consciousness that allow authentic spiritual growth. There must be complete surrender of self-sense so that realization along with knowledge of God can unfold from the innermost core of one's being. Spiritual growth is faster when devotion to God is supplemented by intentional practices for the purpose of purifying the mind and facilitating unfoldments of superconscious states.

3. **But those who reverence the imperishable, indefinable, unmanifest, all-pervading Reality which is beyond thoughts and is unchanging, immovable, and eternal,**
4. **Who control the senses, are dispassionate, and rejoice in the welfare of all creatures, also attain me.**

But those who aspire to know the Field of Absolute Pure Consciousness, who have mastered the senses, who are even-minded, and joyfully wish all beings the highest good, also realize God.

It is as possible to be devoted to realizing the Absolute as it is to be devoted to God's various aspects. Our approach to God-realization is a matter of psychological temperament and capacity to discern the truth. A balanced approach is to simultaneously be devoted to God—as God is presently comprehended—and to aspire to knowledge and realization of the most refined aspect of God. Surrendered devotion, and insightful reflection on the core reality of God supported by constructive living and spiritual practices, quickly restores soul awareness to wholeness.

5. **Those who contemplate the Absolute have more difficulty, for it is not easy to realize by embodied beings.**

Self-conscious souls—influenced by the illusion that they are independent beings in relationship to God—usually experience difficulty in comprehending the Field of Pure Being without attributes or qualities. For most devotees, it can be more easily known and experienced when devotion and yoga practice reinforce intellectual and intuitive inquiry. Truth seekers whose approach to knowledge is devoid of devotion sometimes lack the drive of aspiration that is necessary to maintain their resolve to know God. Or they may acquire a portion of knowledge of God and erroneously think they have it all. Without complete understanding, pride of having acquired partial knowledge may cause them to become self-righteous or arrogant.

The direct way to apprehension and experience of Absolute Reality is to contemplate "Who (what) am I?" and "Who (what) is

God?" Whatever one thinks oneself to be, is not what one truly is. Whatever one thinks God to be, is not what God truly is. Every belief must be allowed to drop away so that Self-knowledge and God-knowledge can be experienced. This process cannot be forced; it is to be engaged in as a gentle, alert examination of the truth until knowledge is Self-revealed from within.

6.   **But of those who renounce all actions in me, and regarding me as the supreme object of worship, meditate on me with undistracted yoga practice,**
7.   **Whose contemplation is absorbed in me, I soon deliver from the ocean of death and reincarnation.**

Those who surrender all actions in God, who engage in meditative contemplation of God that results in unwavering samadhi, soon experience liberation by God's grace.

The "ocean of death and reincarnation" is the manifest field of nature in which spiritually unawake souls dwell. Not clearly knowing subtle and fine realms, they must relate to and function in the realms where their understanding consigns them. It is by constantly aspiring to higher knowledge, practicing disciplines for Self-mastery, and becoming proficient in repeated practice of superconscious states that one awakens from the "dream of mortality" because of direct realization of God.

8.   **Meditate on me alone, reflect upon and contemplate me. Thus you shall live in me thereafter; of this there is no doubt.**

Be engaged exclusively in meditative contemplation of God. You will then realize that you are living always in God. This is true.

Novice meditators may meditate upon any object or theme that enables them to acquire proficiency in concentration. When sufficient skill has been acquired by practice, attention should be directed to God alone. Preliminary practices may include prayer, mantra, pranayama, and listening to Om. Then one should contemplate the highest aspect of God of which one is capable, inquiring, "What is it like to experience God?" and "What is it like to experience the Absolute beyond all attributes?" When not meditating, the devotee should always think of God, reflect upon one's relationship with God, and ponder the true nature of God. Spiritual growth will then be steady, when meditating and when not meditating. Awareness of the Presence of God will be constant. Insights will surface in the devotee's field of awareness. One then knows that living consciously in God is sufficient.

9. **If you are unable to remain absorbed in me, endeavor to realize me by constant practice of yoga.**

   If you are unable to remain absorbed in samadhi, endeavor to awaken to realization of God supported by spiritual practices and repeated samadhi experiences.

If it is not immediately possible to experience unbroken awareness of God, the devotee should live constructively, engage in self-analysis, study about God and the spiritual path, and continue regular practice of meditation and samadhi states. Resolve to know God should be steadfast, confirmed by right living and dedicated spiritual practice. Of utmost importance is willingness to become emotionally mature: self-responsible for thoughts, feelings, and behaviors, and agreeable to looking directly into the heart of life in order to know the truth about God.

10. **If you are incapable even of yoga practice, then you shall attain perfection by service to me, performing all actions for my sake.**

    If you are unable to practice samadhi, you can awaken to knowledge by service, by performing actions which support evolution.

If superconscious states are not immediately experienced, dedication to the spiritual path can be confirmed by right living that supports orderly thinking, and circumstances. We do not have to be enlightened to live constructively. When we have been informed of the right way to live, doing so is but a matter of choice. Psychological transformation is then facilitated, mental and physical restrictions to soul unfoldment are removed, and we learn to live consciously. For this, our every thought, desire, emotional state, relationship, routine behavior, and action should be thought of as our offering to the well-being of others and the universe. Everything should be done without self-centered motive. We need not think of being rewarded for our good works; the ever-present blessing is that, by living in the right way, we are in harmony with *the eternal way of righteousness.*

11. If you are unable to do this, resort to devotion to me; be self-disciplined, abandoning the results of all actions.

If you cannot do this, be devoted to God [in accord with your understanding]; live a well-ordered, disciplined life without being attached to the results of what you do.

If unable to immediately perform productive, constructive actions, the devotee should cultivate devotion to God, live in accord with what is known to be highest and best, and observe regular routines of activity and spiritual practice without anxiety about the outcome. Progressive spiritual growth will occur naturally when conditions are ideal for it to happen. Simple faith and surrendered living has produced many saints—devotees through whom divine qualities are expressed. One should always honestly endeavor to live up to the highest level of knowledge and functional ability of which one is capable. In this way, spiritual growth is encouraged.

12. Knowledge is better than practice, meditation is superior to knowledge, renunciation of the results of action is better than meditation for peace soon follows renunciation.

Having partial knowledge of God is better than having to engage in spiritual practices to acquire it; meditation practice that provides direct experience of God is superior to having partial knowledge; renunciation [not clinging to perceptions] of the results of spiritual practice is best of all for it results in soul peace or tranquility.

Knowledge of God can be acquired by study and astute application of what is learned and unfolded by contemplating the true nature of God. To unfold realized (actual, complete) knowledge of God, meditation practice is helpful. When meditation practice has resulted in tranquil realization, personal endeavors can cease because further unfoldments will be spontaneous. There should be no attempt to hold fast to perceptions as they unfold; one should observe and experience progressive realizations as they unfold from gross to subtle and from subtle to fine levels.

13. **That practitioner of yoga who has no ill will toward anyone, who is friendly and compassionate, free from attachments to possessions, free from egotism [arrogance], indifferent to both unpleasant and pleasurable experience, and patient,**

This verse describes the psychological and spiritual condition of one who is established in understanding and Self-mastery that results from attentive nurturing of the virtues, right living, and of dedicated practice of yogic procedures.

14. **Who is always contented and even-minded, who is self-controlled, has firm conviction, whose mind and intellect is fixed on me, and who is devoted to me, is dear to me.**

That practitioner of samadhi, who is always tranquil and dispassionate, who is self-controlled, has firm conviction, whose attention and powers of discernment are focused on God, and who is devoted to God, vividly experiences the Presence of God.

Being established in realization of wholeness, having thoughts and intellect directed Godward while being devoted to knowing and experiencing God, purifies the devotee's awareness and results in an intimate relationship with the Infinite. The term "dear to me" is not meant to imply that God can be influenced by our actions; only that our right actions can result in increased awareness of God. At such moments it seems to us that God is caring, supportive, and altogether good. The next few verses continue this theme.

15. **That one who neither causes distress nor is distressed by others [or circumstances], who is free from attachment to pleasure, impatience, fear, and agitation, is dear to me.**

That devotee who neither causes conflict nor is disturbed because of what others do or what circumstances are, who is no longer attached to pleasure, and who is devoid of impatience, fear, and psychological conflict, more easily awakens in God.

When we are at peace within ourselves we are neither inclined to cause discomfort for others or to create circumstantial conflict, nor do the behaviors of others and transient circumstances and events disturb our peace of mind and soul. This ideal state of being results from attentive practice of the first requirements for success in yoga practice: being harmless, truthful, honest, using vital forces only for constructive purposes, and living without attachments of any kind.

16. That one who is free from cravings and anxiety, who is pure, capable, impartial, and who, having renounced all self-serving motives, is devoted to me, is dear to me.

That devotee who is not addicted to anything and who has renounced restless expectation for results of spiritual practice, who is pure-minded, competent, impartial, and no longer driven by egocentric motives, is devoted to God-realization, is responsive to God's grace.

All of the life-enhancing qualities can be unfolded quickly by remembering our relationship with the Infinite and by living so that we can always be in harmony with it. The attitudes and behaviors to renounce are those which are characteristic of self-conscious awareness. When we adjust our viewpoint from being egocentric to being soul-aware, attitudes and behaviors which restrict spiritual growth are immediately replaced by those which are entirely supportive of it.

17. That one who does not rejoice, hate, grieve, or have insatiable desire, who has renounced ideas of what is personally agreeable or disagreeable, and who overflows with devotion, is dear to me.

That devotee who does not become excited because of transitory happenings, who is devoid of aversion, sorrow, and never-satisfied desire, who is not opinionated, and whose devotion is ardent, is easily absorbed in God.

The key here is "who overflows with devotion" to God. When soul-surrendered devotion to God flows powerfully, the characteristics of the egocentric self-conscious state are removed.

18. That one who behaves equally to friend and enemy, honor and disgrace, cold and heat, pleasure and discomfort, free from attachments,

That devotee who remains calmly soul-centered and behaves appropriately in all circumstances,

Some indications of the Self-realized state are that one treats all people with equal respect, is unmoved by the opinions of others, even-minded during occasions of temporary discomfort, and while being prudent in the use of resources is not possessive or dependent.

19. Indifferent to blame or praise, silent, content, homeless, even-minded, and full of devotion; that one is dear to me.

That devotee who is indifferent to what others say, whose speech is controlled, who is content with what is provided according to personal actions and acts of providence, who is not attached to any place, who is even-minded and spontaneously devotional, is easily attuned to the Infinite.

20. Those who, with faith, are devoted to me as the highest object of contemplation, who honor this eternal law, are exceedingly dear to me.

Those devotees who are devoted to God above all else, and live in accord with supportive principles of the eternal way of righteousness, are easily harmonized with the Divine will.

Two supportive actions are mentioned in the final verse of this chapter: (1) being devoted to God above all else; (2) demonstrating devotion by right living. These actions comprise the essence of the spiritual life. We may assert that we love God but be unwilling to conform our lives to the soul's impulses or to nature's laws. We may endeavor to live constructively while neglecting to understand what God is or to be devoted to realizing God. When our devotion to God-realization is demonstrated by our actions, we are on the right course.

In the Upanishad of the Bhagavad Gita, the science of the Absolute, the scripture of Yoga and the dialogue between Sri Krishna and Arjuna, thus ends the twelfth chapter entitled Bhakti Yoga: The Yoga of Devotion

CHAPTER THIRTEEN

The Yoga of Discernment of the Field of Actions and the Knower of the Field

The first verse in this chapter is not numbered because it does not appear in all versions of the *Gita*.

Arjuna spoke:

• **I wish to know about material nature and God, the field and the knower of the field, knowledge and the knower of knowledge.**

Krishna replied:

1. **This body is said to be the field. Those who are wise in such matters say that one who knows this is a knower of the field.**

   The physical body is declared to be the field [where the devotee accomplishes salvation]. People who are knowledgeable in such matters declare that one who comprehends this is a knower of the field.

   In chapter one, the first verse announces that self-serving mental characteristics and tendencies are confronted by soul qualities and virtuous tendencies on "the field of righteousness-the field of unrighteousness." Now, in chapter thirteen, the first words attributed to Krishna, the indwelling Spirit of God of every person, describe the body to be the field where spiritual growth occurs. In the physical realm, the body includes the astral and causal bodies, and the mind. Since spiritual growth can continue in astral and causal realms after the soul's transition from the physical body, there, the astral or causal bodies would be designated as the field in which transformative processes and illumination of consciousness can occur.

2. **Understand that I am the knower of the field in all fields. True knowledge is considered by me to be that of knowledge of the field and of the knower of the field.**

Understand that God is the knower [because all-pervading] of all fields in which events occur. The knowledge which liberates is that which includes comprehension of the field where events occur and of Consciousness which is the observer and knower of what occurs.

All-pervading Consciousness knows itself and the realm or field in which it expresses. When one is fully enlightened, one is knowledgeable about Consciousness in its various aspects and expressions and of the processes of cosmic manifestation. One is then said to know the truth that liberates the soul from delusions. So long as any degree of unknowing persists, enlightenment is not complete.

3. **Now, hear briefly from me what the field is, its characteristics and modifications, from whence [and how] it comes into manifestation, who the knower of the field is, and what are its powers.**

   Now, be receptive to the revelation that is unfolding regarding the nature of the field of the body, its characteristics and modifications, where it comes from and how it manifests, and the identity and powers of the knower of this field of the body.

4. **Sages have distinctly sung of it in many ways in various hymns and with well-reasoned comments on the Absolute.**

   Enlightened souls have clearly described their revelations about matter and spirit along with their rational statements concerning the Supreme Reality.

The wise words of others who have experienced self-revealed knowledge of Consciousness and its varied expressions, can be helpful to us by providing information which lights our path and serves to encourage us to our own self-discovery. What others have known, we can know. If we are to be Self-realized and enlightened we must awaken to knowledge of God for ourselves. The knowledge others have liberates them; only the knowledge we have liberates us.

5. **The [five] elements, egoism, intellect, the unmanifest [witness], the ten senses, the mind, and the objects of the senses,**

This verse mentions the twenty-four principle aspects of cosmic manifestation as the basis of the field of the body.

The *five elements* include the five fine essences of ether (space with cosmic forces), air (prana or life forces), fire (transformative essence), water (liquid), and earth (solids).

Egoism is the illusory sense of independent existence.

Intellect is the faculty of determination or discernment.

The *unmanifest witness* is the soul in relationship to all other aspects of body-mind. In relationship to cosmic manifestation the unmanifest witness is all-pervading Consciousness.

What are referred to as the *ten senses* include the capacity to perceive by seeing, hearing, tasting, smelling, and touching, and to be active by speaking, exercising manual dexterity, walking, eliminating waste matters, and procreating.

The *mind* processes information.

The *objects of the senses* are the objectified element essences manifesting as matter that can be seen, heard, tasted, smelled, and touched.

6. **Desire, aversion, pleasure, pain, the physical form, the exercise of intelligence, and steadfastness, are brief descriptions of the field [of the body] with its modifications.**

Mental characteristics are included in the field of the body because they are objects which can be known. We are aware of desire, aversion, pleasure, and pain. We are aware with intention when we exercise our faculty of intelligence and when we are steadfast in our resolves. We are spirit-mind-body beings. The spirit, the soul, is the witness or observer of physical and mental processes. When not established in Self-awareness the soul is inclined to be identified with the body and with mental contents. A helpful first stage of spiritual growth is actualized when we are able to discern the difference between ourselves as spiritual beings and the body and mind we use. This cannot be done so long as we are egocentric and mistakenly believe that we are creatures independent of God.

7. **Absence of pride, freedom from hypocrisy, nonviolence, patience, honesty, serving the teacher, purity, constancy, self-restraint,**

Characteristics of soul-inspired attitudes and behaviors are now described.

There can be *no pride* when egoism is absent.

There can be *no hypocrisy* when truthfulness is normal.

Harmlessness is characteristic of our behavior when understanding is awakened.

Patience is easy when we are soul-content.

Honesty is spontaneous in the presence of knowledge.

To *serve the teacher* means to listen to instruction and abide by it, whether instruction is transmitted through the written or spoken word, or revealed from within.

Purity is the prevailing state when restricting influences are absent from the mind and body.

Constancy is unwavering, persistent flowing of attention to God, and dutiful practice of procedures and routines helpful to total well-being and spiritual growth.

Self-restraint is remaining settled in soul awareness.

8. **Indifference to the objects of the senses, absence of egoism, remaining mindful of the misfortunes of birth and death and of old age, disease, and pain;**

To be *indifferent to sense objects* (sights, sounds, things, and circumstances which are perceived) is to observe and relate to them with detached objectivity.

To be *devoid of egoism* is to clearly know ourselves to be rays of God's light; that, of ourselves, we are neither unique nor deserving of special consideration.

Remaining mindful of the misfortunes of physical birth, death of the body, the debilitating circumstances that sometimes attend the aging process, and the inconvenience and discomfort of disease and various kinds of pain, should inspire us to learn how to remove ourselves from these conditions by eliminating their causes and awakening to our higher potential.

9. **Nonattachment, absence of clinging to family members, or to one's dwelling place, and constant even-mindedness toward desired and undesired events;**

Nonattachment is easy when we have right understanding

and are established in awareness of soul. We can then have, and even enjoy, relationships and can relate to all aspects of life freely and appropriately.

Not clinging to family members is easy when we are no longer in a dependent or controlling mode of behavior; when we can have affectionate, supportive relationships while allowing others freedom to grow, express, and fulfill their own destiny.

While we may feel comfortable *in our house or in the community* where we live, we are advised to remember that, as spiritual beings, locations in space are temporary and that we ever dwell in God.

To be *even-minded* toward events and circumstances frees us to make wise choices and be unaffected by external conditions.

10. Unswerving devotion to me with concentrated yoga, frequenting secluded places, dislike for crowded places,

Unwavering devotion to God in meditative contemplation and experience of samadhi, remaining inwardly soul-content at all times, not needing the false support of superficial social interaction or the presence or opinions of others,

When we put important matters first, all else that we do will be supportive of us. Of primary importance is to be devoted to knowing and realizing God by being regularly absorbed in meditative contemplation and superconsciousness.

The *secluded place* in which we should dwell is the sanctuary of the soul—by learning to enjoy deep meditation and by being soul-centered when otherwise active or in relationships.

Thus soul-content, we will not desire the company of gatherings of people who assemble for the purpose of nourishing their ego-needs or gratifying their addictive desires for companionship and sense stimulation.

11. Constancy in knowledge of the Absolute—insight into the end of knowledge which is truth; this is declared to be valid knowledge. Its opposite is ignorance.

The devotee's apprehension of the existence and real nature of the Field of unmodified Pure Consciousness should be constant. The consummation of unfoldment of innate soul knowledge is clear comprehension of what is so—the facts, the final truth—and is evidence of the fully enlightened state. Flawed understanding is defective, and is untruth.

12. I will declare that which has to be known, which, by knowing, immortality is realized. It is the Absolute, which is declared to be neither existent nor nonexistent.

Innate intelligence of the soul will reveal that which has to be known, which, by knowing, the soul realizes its immortality. That is the timeless, unmodified Field of Absolute Pure Consciousness which enlightened teachers declare to be impossible to describe.

Although the Absolute Field of Consciousness cannot be described, because it is the core reality of the soul it can be directly experienced. When thoughts and feelings are quieted and attention is returned to the innermost center of our being, and we remain alert and aware, all that remains is experience of our reality as pure consciousness. This realization cannot be created or attained; it can only be acknowledged and experienced. As our essential reality, it is never other than what we are at the innermost level of our being.

13. With hands, feet, eyes, heads, faces, and ears everywhere, the Absolute remains ever what it is, including every manifest thing.

Omnipresent, unbounded, the Field of Absolute Pure Consciousness pervades and includes within itself the entire universe.

Pure Consciousness exists beneath the finest aspect of manifested nature. We do not have to go anywhere to search for it. Anything we do to facilitate our awareness of it is for the purpose of purifying the body and mind so that physical and psychological characteristics which restrict soul awareness are removed. The constructive things we do to nurture our total wellness and spiritual growth are intentional actions or kriyas. To the degree that physical and mental obstacles to clear perception of Reality are removed, we can flawlessly know what is true and experience it. Such knowing along with experience is realization.

14. It appears to have the characteristics of the senses yet is free from the senses, unattached yet maintaining all, free from the qualities of nature yet experiencing them;

When relating to manifest things, Supreme Consciousness appears to have characteristics of that which it enlivens yet it is unattached to anything, including the gunas, while making possible their actions.

The gunas belong to the field of primordial nature. They do not exist in the Field of Pure Consciousness. Only because the Field of the Godhead emerged from the Field of Pure Consciousness and issued forth the flowing Om current, do the gunas, the qualities of nature, exist.

15. Because it is subtle, it is outside and inside of moving and unmoving beings, though not comprehended. It is simultaneously far and near.

Because Supreme Consciousness is subtle, it is around and within all beings, but is not comprehended by them. It is omnipresent.

16. It is undivided yet appears to be divided, the sustainer of all beings and that which dissolves and produces them anew.

Supreme Consciousness is ever whole regardless of the various outer appearances in the field of nature. It sustains all souls [of people and creatures] and absorbs them and produces new ones.

Souls may eventually remove awareness from the illusory sense of individualized existence. Then, only the ego ceases to exist; the Absolute remains. The process of individualization of Consciousness as souls and the dissolving of the sense of individuality is constant. In our universe, and others, there are multitudes of souls.

17. It is the Light of Lights that is beyond darkness; the knowledge, the object of knowledge, and that which is to be realized by knowledge. It is seated in the hearts of all.

Supreme Consciousness is the true light that transcends the field of primordial nature; it is perfect knowledge, the source of all knowledge, and that which is to be comprehended and experienced by self-revealed knowledge. It is innate to every soul.

18. **Thus the field, knowledge, and the object of knowledge have been briefly described. My devotee who understands this, enters into my state of being.**

Thus the body as the field of knowledge, knowledge itself, and the source of knowledge have been briefly revealed. The devotee of God who truly comprehends this revealed truth, awakens fully in God.

19. **Know that primordial nature and Spirit are beginningless. Know also that modifications and qualities of the field of nature, arise from primordial nature.**

The substances of the universe and the enlivening Spirit of God are eternal. All modifications of the field of primordial nature occur when the gunas interact. When interactions of the qualities of nature are pronounced, a universe is manifested.

20. **Primordial nature is the basis of causation. The Spirit is the basis of experiences of pleasure and pain.**

All manifested aspects and forms of nature emerge from the field of primordial nature. It is the enlivening Spirit of God that is conscious, enabling souls to experience sensation described as pleasant or unpleasant. Pleasure and pain can be identified as being physical, mental, or spiritual. Physical sensations identified as pleasurable or painful are common to everyone. There can also be mental happiness or depression and anguish, and soul elation or frustration. It is the soul, the indwelling life, that experiences sensations at various levels. The indwelling essence of creatures, vegetation, and all else that has life, can respond to pleasure-causing conditions and react to conditions which threaten or cause discomfort.

21. **The Spirit, abiding in nature, experiences the qualities born of nature. Attachment to the qualities of nature is the cause of the soul's diverse incarnations.**

The soul experiences nature's qualities because of identification with them. Addictive attachment to the gunas and their actions and effects is the cause of the soul's bondage to cycles of reincarnation. Spiritual growth occurs when: (1) kundalini energies awaken spontaneously, causing gradual or instantaneous adjustments of states of consciousness and the unfoldment of innate soul knowledge; (2) by self-disciplined practices and superconscious meditation physical and mental restrictions are removed, allowing soul awareness to be liberated from attachments. The stages of spiritual growth through which one can progressively awaken are:

- *Unconsciousness.* Mental dullness, apathy, and boredom are common. Awareness of spiritual matters is almost entirely absent. If religious, one usually directs prayer to a conceptualized aspect or form of deity. Normal activities and relationships are routine, as necessary or as one is inclined by desire or whim. Intellectual powers are limited. Memories, habits, and learned or acquired behaviors dominate lifestyle. Small-mindedness and self-righteousness may be dramatized. Tamas guna is powerfully influential. *Base chakra awareness.*
- *Dysfunctional Self-Consciousness.* Mental confusion and conflicted emotional states are normal. Egocentric behaviors prevail. Meditation may be practiced in the hope that a degree of inner peace might result, or to facilitate visions, ecstatic states, and various phenomena. Illusions are common, as are attachments, dependency, addictions, and self-defeating behaviors. Actions are irrational. Behaviors are unpredictable. Neurotic needs, complaints, blaming, and irresponsibility are common—as are fantasies about everyday matters and higher realities. Subconscious influences dominate mental and emotional states. Rajas guna with strong tamasic influences prevail. *Second chakra awareness.*
- *Functional Self-Consciousness.* Healthy-minded, superior human conscious condition. When meditating, the major purpose may be to elicit relaxation and experience psychological and physiological benefits only, with little aspiration to higher understanding or spiritual growth. One may tend to cling to pleasurable meditative states as one habitually clings to pleasurable mundane experiences and circumstances. Normal activities and relationships are rational, nurturing choices. Actions are performed skillfully. Some intellectual understanding of God may be present. Rajas guna influenced by sattva guna prevails. *Third chakra awareness.*
- *Superconsciousness.* The level of awareness at which committed discipleship is easier. Partial or complete Self-knowledge, depending on the degree of spiritual wakefulness. Knowledge that one is a ray of God's light. When meditating, superconscious states easily unfold, allowing clear perceptions of God and higher realities. Ego-sense diminishes with increasing Self-realization. Normal activities and

relationships are chosen and experienced without compulsion. Sattva guna with some rajas guna influences prevails. Influences of tamas guna may linger. *Fourth chakra awareness.*

- *Cosmic Consciousness.* Partial or complete knowledge-awareness of universal processes and realization that the universe is a play of cosmic forces. When meditating, perceptions and realizations are transcendent. Comprehension of primordial nature (as Om, cosmic forces and particles, space, and time). Normal activities and relationships are enjoyed with higher understanding. Sattvic influences prevail. *Fifth chakra awareness.*

- *God-Consciousness.* Partial or complete knowledge and realization of God with transcendent realizations common. Even if some mental restrictions (samskaras) persist, their influences are weakened and dissolved. Insightful actions prevent accumulation of further mental conditionings. With more realizations yet to unfold, the soul is liberated from delusions and illusions. Only minor guna influences are present and are barely influential. *Sixth chakra awareness.*

- *Full Enlightenment.* Complete knowledge-realization of God and of universal processes. When meditating, realizations are transcendent. When relating to mundane realms, full enlightenment remains undiminished and all actions are appropriately spontaneous. Beyond the influences of the gunas. No compelling residue of karma remains. *Seventh chakra awareness.*

22. The Spirit [soul] in relationship to the body is called the witness, that which gives consent, the supporter, the experiencer, the ruler of the mind and senses, and the Supreme Self.

In relationship to the cosmic body (the universe) God as the Oversoul is the witness of all that transpires and plays various roles. It is the Reality that is supreme above all manifested aspects of nature. The soul is the witness, the consenter, the supporter, the experiencer, and ruler of mind and senses in the body because it is individualized Spirit. Even when we are intent upon right living endeavors and spiritual growth practices, inwardly we should know, "I am pure consciousness." This statement is not to be repeated for the purpose of causing the mind to believe it; it is to be acknowledged as the truth and awakened to in fact.

The spiritually unawake person's major problem is that of incorrect self-identification; thinking and feeling oneself to be a limited, conditioned, human being instead of recognizing the truth that the soul, the real being, is a ray of God's light.

23. One who knows Spirit and [the modes of] nature in this way, regardless of the present life-condition, is not born again.

When we know the truth about God and nature, because of our enlightenment there is no necessity to reincarnate. If spiritual awakening is fairly recent, it may be that some effects of karmic or genetic influences have yet to be overcome, but these do not diminish our realization. When liberated, although the soul is not compelled by karma to be reincarnated, it may agree to do so to serve evolution or for the enjoyment of expressing.

24. Some devotees perceive the reality of the Self by meditation; others do so by the discipline of knowledge; and still others by the yoga of action.
Some devotees perceive God in samadhi when meditating; others do so by superior intellectual and intuitive means; and others by the yoga of action [that remove obstacles to Self-knowledge].

25. Others, not knowing these ways, devoted to what they have been taught by others, also transcend death.

Devotees who do not know the ways of samadhi, direct insight, or specific yoga practices, may learn from knowledgeable teachers and also experience spiritual growth that results in God-realization.

Knowledge of spiritual growth processes is not limited to saints and sages who have awakened to enlightenment by yogic methods, or to any region of the world or to any religious tradition. So long as an enlightenment teaching is authentic, it can be the means of facilitating soul unfoldment for devotees who are prepared to experience it. A learning experience that can quicken a devotee's spiritual growth is to have a spiritually intimate relationship with a God-realized guru or teacher who can instruct, encourage, and share accurate knowledge of God and of how to facilitate soul unfoldment.

26. Know, Arjuna, that any being that is born, whether animate or inanimate, arises from the union of the field and the knower of the field.

Know that all souls which are individualized, whether they are conscious or unconscious, undergo the experience because Spirit [the knower] interacts with the field of primordial nature.

Souls are born into a body according to conscious or unconscious desire or because of karmic necessity. In relationship to the processes of mind and matter involvement, what is true for one soul is true for all. The way to awaken from unconscious involvement with mind and matter is also the same for all souls.

27. One who sees Supreme Consciousness existing in all beings, not perishing when they perish, truly sees.

When we are established in flawless understanding of God and of the processes of life, we know that the all-pervading Consciousness of God is imperishable. We also know that our eternal well-being is assured when we are Self-knowledgeable and God-conscious.

28. Because of seeing the one Supreme Consciousness existing everywhere, and not hindering the Self by the self, the devotee attains the highest state.

Because of seeing the one Supreme Consciousness as omnipresent, and not restricting soul awareness by unwise self-conscious behaviors, the devotee awakens to the highest state.

Although the soul cannot be harmed, its awareness can be clouded by intellectual errors, misperceptions, an accumulation of mental and emotional conflict and trauma, and too much outward flowing of attention. A devotee is advised to acknowledge the reality of God and to live a wholesome, moral, constructive life so that soul awareness can remain clear and insightful. Whatever mental or emotional state, behavior, or relationship that inhibits soul awareness, should be renounced in favor of supportive mental and emotional states, behaviors, and relationships.

29. That one who knows that all actions are performed exclusively by the qualities of nature and that the Self is not the doer, truly knows.

The gunas, by manifesting mental and physical characteristics in nature (including our minds and bodies), make all actions possible. While using the mind and body, and efficiently implementing causes for desired corresponding effects, we can remain established in soul awareness. We can live without being forgetful of ourselves as immortal beings in God.

30. **When the devotee perceives the various states of being as resting in the One, and from That alone emanating outward, the final state [the Absolute] is realized.**

When we ponder the reality of souls and the realms of nature we should spontaneously be reminded that they reside in the omnipresent Reality of God. Souls as rays of God's light and nature as the product of God's flowing, creative energy (Om) are not creations; they are emanations from their common source. The only difference between God and souls is that God is unbounded and souls are temporarily restricted by their sense of individuality. The only difference between primordial nature and manifested nature is that in manifested nature the forces inherent in primordial nature are more outwardly projected. Clear knowing of the reality of Supreme Consciousness and the actions of nature is present with full enlightenment.

31. **This imperishable Supreme Self is beginningless and devoid of qualities; even though abiding in the body, it does not act and is not contaminated.**
32. **Just as, because it is subtle, all-pervading ether is not tainted, so the Self abiding in the body is not tainted.**

Supreme Consciousness, individualized and expressing through a mind and body, is not the performer of actions and is not marred by any perception or experience. It, in truth, is never born and never dies: it only identifies with mind and body and separates from them in the course of time. Regardless of what a self-conscious, spiritually unawake person thinks, does, perceives, or experiences, the innate soul nature remains untouched. At the innermost level, the soul, being a ray of God's light, is omnipresent. Only its identification with mind and body creates the false sense of localized awareness.

33. As the sun alone illumines this entire solar system, so the Lord of the field illumines the entire field.

The "lord" or ruling influence of any field of manifestation is Consciousness which enlivens it. All-pervading Consciousness enlivens the universe, and individualized Consciousness, as the soul, energizes the mind and enlivens the body.

34. They who, with the eye of knowledge, clearly know the distinction between the field and the knower of the field, and of the process of liberation of beings from matter, attain the supreme state.

It is forthrightly declared that enlightenment unfolds soul-liberating knowledge, illumines the mind, and assures the devotee of conscious freedom because of realized transcendence. The message is clear: neither fainthearted faith, feeble attempts to be good, lazy performance of spiritual practices, nor sentimental devotion, will suffice for one who aspires to spiritual fulfillment.

In the Upanishad of the Bhagavad Gita, the science of the Absolute, the scripture of Yoga and the dialogue between Sri Krishna and Arjuna, thus ends the thirteenth chapter entitled Kshetra Kshetrajna Vibhaga Yoga: The Yoga of Discernment of the Field of Nature and the Knower of the Field

CHAPTER FOURTEEN

The Yoga of Discernment of the Qualities of Nature

It has already been explained that interactions of Spirit and nature cause individualization of souls and produce the universe. More specific details are now revealed to describe how the constituent qualities of nature regulate cosmic forces and influence soul awareness, personal behaviors, and circumstances. What are the gunas? How do they affect mental processes and states of consciousness? How does one become free from nature's influences? What are some of the characteristics of a liberated soul? These questions are answered in this chapter.

Krishna said:

1. **I will again declare that highest and best knowledge, which by having known, all the sages have gone to supreme perfection.**

   Innate knowledge that is superior above all, will again be unfolded from within you. Having this knowledge, all enlightened souls have awakened to spiritual fulfillment.

   The "going" of enlightened souls to spiritual fulfillment occurs as an awakening from self-conscious states to superconscious states; from a condition of limited understanding to the freedom of self-revealed comprehension of the reality of Consciousness and its processes.

2. **Relying on this knowledge and having become established in me, they are not born into the realm of nature at the time of manifestation of the worlds, nor are they disturbed at the time of dissolution of the worlds.**

   Relying on this knowledge and having become established in God-realization, fully enlightened souls are not born into the realm of nature when a new universe is manifested, nor are they disturbed when the universe dissolves.

3. **Great Brahma is my womb; in that I put my seed and from it all beings originate.**

The manifesting aspect of God in relationship to the field of primordial nature is where Spirit originates the processes of universal manifestation; it is responsive to the creative impulse that spontaneously arises from within the Field of the Godhead.

Because we cannot presume the Field of Pure Consciousness to be motivated by need or desire, we can only declare the processes of universal manifestation and dissolution to be driven by motiveless necessity: that it is characteristic of Consciousness to express as it does. Because this cannot be comprehended by the intellect, it must be intuitively apprehended by the soul.

4. **Whatever forms are produced in any womb, Brahma is their womb, and I am the father who casts the seed.**

Whatever is born of nature, the aspect of God that makes possible all manifestation is the real source, and an impulse of Supreme Consciousness makes possible the production of forms.

From the emanation of universes, to chemical changes, energy transformations, and biological processes, it is the same Spirit of God that makes them possible. Without energy, life, and innate intelligence, the processes of nature could not occur. The origin and support of all manifest things is Consciousness.

5. **Sattva, rajas, tamas—the three qualities born of nature—bind the imperishable dweller in the body.**

The three gunas are the qualities or attributes within the field of nature that regulate cosmic forces. They are the attributes of the polarized Field of God's manifesting Consciousness: sattva from the positive pole; tamas from the negative pole; and rajas as the neutralizing actions occurring between them. Their influences can be observed throughout the universe, in the far reaches of space and near at hand. Acting within the field of nature, their influences only indirectly relate to souls. When souls are strongly identified with mind and body, the actions of the gunas within mind and body which affect mental and physical states, can result in either clouding or clearing of awareness. How the influences of the gunas can bind "the imperishable dweller"—the soul—to the body is explained in the following verses.

6. **Of these, sattva, being pure, is illuminating and health-giving. It binds by attaching the soul to happiness and to knowledge.**

Sattva guna (*sat*, that which is: truth, reality) is the attribute of the positive polarity of the Field of God's manifesting Consciousness and possesses a dominant power of attraction. It attracts the two other attributes to itself to result in stillness. Its actions are cooling, enlivening, purifying, and redemptive. It illumines the mind. Its influences on the body contribute to lightness, health, and improved functional abilities.

Its binding or restricting influence on the mind is due to the soul's fascination by and attachment to: (1) happiness of all kinds, even that of subtle elation because of spiritual progress experienced or the awe of discovery; (2) knowledge of life's processes and of God. When attachments to even subtle perceptions are renounced, complete soul awakening easily occurs.

7. **Rajas is of the nature of passion arising from craving and attachment. This restricts by attachment to action.**

Rajas guna is the neutralizing mode. It enables actions to bring together the embodied soul's powers of sense perception with the objects of their desires, thus resulting in temporary satisfaction of desire. This quality has value in enabling us to accomplish purposes and to survive. Its actions are energizing, heating, and stimulating. When desires are unregulated, or when restlessness is allowed to prevail, rajas guna promotes purposeless physical activity, and random thought processes and emotional instability when physical actions are repressed or subdued.

8. **Tamas is born of ignorance which confuses all embodied beings. This binds with negligence, indolence, and unconsciousness.**

Tamas guna is the attribute of the negative polarity of God's manifesting Consciousness. It possesses the quality of repulsion and contributes to inertia or heaviness. Its actions contribute to slowness, dullness, and unconsciousness: conditions which cloud awareness, darken the mind, weaken powers of perception, and diminish intellectual powers.

9. Sattva causes attachment to happiness; rajas causes attachment to action; tamas obscures knowledge and causes attachment to negligence.

To enjoy living and to be happy is compatible with spiritual growth so long as we do not become fixated on the cause of enjoyment or the experience itself. To be creatively functional and effective in accomplishing purposes is useful so long as we are not under any compulsion. We are wise, however, to regulate rajasic influences and to weaken and remove tamasic influences.

10. When the influence of sattva is dominant, it prevails over rajas and tamas; when the influence of rajas is dominant, it prevails over sattva and tamas; when the influence of tamas is dominant it prevails over sattva and rajas.

All three guna influences are as omnipresent as God's all-pervading Consciousness because they are products of the polarity of that Consciousness. When one guna influence is dominant, the influences of the other two are weak or nondetermining. When two guna influences are blended, the third guna influence is weak or nondetermining. It is recommended that devotees on the spiritual path overcome tamasic influences by implementing inspired (sattvic), constructive actions (rajasic).

11. When the light of knowledge shines through all gates of the body, then it should be known that sattva is dominant.

Because sattva guna contributes to illumination and lightness, its characteristics can be observed in the actions of the mind, behaviors, choice of lifestyle and companions, habits, and the normal state of well-being, including the skin's radiance of health and the light in the eyes.

12. **When the influence of rajas is dominant, greed, ego-driven endeavors, restlessness, and desires become pronounced.**

Pure rajas influence is characterized by a drive to satisfy ego-impelled desires and physical urges when active, and by restlessness and dissatisfaction when inactive. Rajas influences mixed with influences of tamas guna impel a person to base, sensual pursuits and to immoral and unethical behaviors.

13. **When the influence of tamas is dominant, darkness, inertia, heedlessness, and confusion become pronounced.**

Tamasic influences contribute to inertia and to perceptual errors. Tamasic influences can be weakened and replaced by sattvic influences by adopting healthful lifestyle routines, aspiring to spiritual awakening and growth, nurturing mental and functional skills, feeding the mind and consciousness with positive ideas, and by association with people who are alert and skillfully functional. The constructive way to overcome mental and physical laziness is to intentionally do what one knows is best to do, disregarding thoughts or feelings of likes or dislikes. If inertia is a reaction to confusion or to inability to decide upon a course of action, nonessentials should be eliminated so that only essential actions are in the forefront of one's agenda. Helpful information can be acquired, prayer for guidance can be supportive, and possibility-thinking can be effective in adjusting one's point of view and attracting desired circumstances.

14. **When the embodied soul makes its transition under the dominance of sattva, it attains the pure realms of those who know the highest.**

Sattvic influences can contribute to higher states of consciousness which enable one to apprehend the reality and actions of Consciousness at subtle levels. For soul liberation, even sattvic influences have to be transcended because they disturb soul peace and keep one involved with subtle perceptions and sensations.

15. **One who departs the body with rajas dominant is reborn among those who are attached to actions. If departing when tamas is dominant, dullness prevails and one is reborn among**

people who are deluded.

Because of the principle of mental correspondences (as within, so without), rajasic influences on the mind compel the soul into involvements where restlessness and sensation-seeking can be dramatized. Likewise, strong tamasic influences tend to cause the soul to gravitate to circumstances which are compatible with their characteristics. It is true that a soul influenced by sattvic qualities can be born into challenging circumstances. If this occurs, one will soon transform the circumstances or depart from them when free to exercise the choice to do so. Souls influenced by rajasic or tamasic qualities can be born into harmonious sattvic circumstances, and may benefit from them, disrupt them, or leave them for circumstances in which they feel more comfortable when free to exercise their will to do so.

16. The fruit of good action is sattvic, but the fruit of rajasic action is pain, and that of tamasic action is ignorance.

The results of constructive, wholesome actions are elevating and life-enhancing. The results of restless, disorganized actions are unsatisfying or discomforting. The results of actions motivated by delusion contribute to more confusion and ignorance.

17. From sattva, knowledge is born; from rajas, desire is born; and from tamas, negligence and delusion result.

The natural site or abode of sattva guna is the mind. When the mind is orderly and alert, objective knowledge is easily acquired and subjective knowledge spontaneously unfolds. Rajasic influences generate desire and fuel urges for sensation and acquisition of power. Tamasic influences are darkening and life-suppressing.

18. Those who are established in sattva go upward; the rajasic stay in the middle; established in tamas, the lowest quality, they go downward.

Souls strongly influenced by sattvic qualities experience steady mental, emotional, and spiritual growth. Souls strongly influenced by rajasic qualities experience continual involvement with uncontrolled mental states, fluctuating moods, attempts to satisfy restless cravings, and circumstances which support their condition. Souls strongly influenced by tamasic influences tend to go more deeply into their delusions and their soul-restricting circumstances.

19. **The seer who perceives no other agent of action than the gunas, and knows that which is higher than them, attains my state of being.**

   The devotee with insight who discerns that the qualities of nature are alone the agents of action, and who knows the reality of Supreme Consciousness which transcends them, awakens in God.

20. **When the embodied soul transcends these three qualities of nature which originate the body, it is released from birth, death, old age, and pain, and realizes immortality.**

   The actions of the three modes or attributes of nature produce the mind and the physical body. The soul is liberated from all mental and physical involvements when awareness is removed from the influences of nature's characteristics. To this end, the devotee should contemplate the instruction in the previous chapter regarding the distinction between Spirit and matter and the soul and the body, remembering, "I am not mind or body; I am pure Spirit!"

   A question that needs to be answered is: By what means are the gunas able to influence our minds and bodies? Obvious ways they can be influential are by the thoughts we generate, the moods we choose to dramatize, the foods we eat, the environment we choose for our habitual activities, and the everyday circumstances we choose or allow. The influences of the three qualities or attributes of nature are strengthened by the thoughts and moods we generate and are present in the environment and in the foods we consume.

   The guna influences produced the elements of which the universe is formed: ethereal matter in space, gaseous matter, fiery matter, liquids, and solids. The ether-air governing principle is *vata dosha,* which has air as the dominant characteristic and influences movement and circulation. The fire-water governing principle is *pitta dosha*, which has fire as the dominant characteristic and is psychologically and biologically transformative. The water-earth governing principle is *kapha dosha*, which has water as the dominant characteristic and is influential in producing and maintaining the gross aspects of the physical body. When these three governing principles are in a state of balance, psychological and physical health is supported. When they are imbalanced, deficient, or excessive in their influences, psychological and physical functions are disturbed. Understanding the influences of the doshas, and knowing how to choose a lifestyle which contributes to balancing the mind-body constitution, can be helpful to facilitating total wellness and spiritual growth. This approach to healthy, functional living, known as Ayurveda (*ayur*, life; *veda*, knowledge), has been the wellness system of choice for millions of people in Asia for at least three thousand years.

Arjuna asked:

21. By what characteristics is one who has transcended these three qualities recognized? How does that person behave? And how does such a one go beyond these three gunas?

The divinely inspired soul is now asking: What is it like to be liberated? How does a liberated person act? How is spiritual fulfillment accomplished?

Krishna answered:

22. Such a one neither hates nor desires the presence or the absence of light, activity, or delusion.

By now, the answer is predictable: the liberated soul, established in Self-knowledge, is no longer capable of aversion or attachment to any characteristic of the realms of nature. No longer controlled by the gunas, the free soul can appropriately relate to their actions and cooperate with their influences but is not dependent upon them.

23. That one who is unconcerned, and who is not disturbed by the qualities of nature, who knows "the gunas [alone] are expressive," and who remains steady without wavering,
24. To whom discomfort and pleasure are the same, who abides in the Self, to whom a clump of earth, a stone, and gold are the

same, to whom that which is dear or pleasant and that which
is not desirable or pleasant are the same, who is steadfast,
to whom blame and praise are the same,

25. To whom honor and dishonor are equal, who is dispassionate
in relationship to friends and foes and who has renounced
all self-serving initiative for endeavor, is said to have transcended the gunas.

The liberated soul, exhibiting all of the characteristics of its
unfolded qualities moves through the world but is not "of it."
Nothing restricts it in any way, or modifies or dims its awareness
and knowledge of the truth of God and the processes of life.

26. The devotee who has transcended the gunas and who serves
me with the yoga of constant devotion, is prepared for absorption in the Field of Pure Being.

*The devotee who is liberated from the influences of the qualities of
nature and is stable in the samadhi of God-realization, is prepared
for the final, transcendent stage of awakening.*

27. For I am the abode of Brahman, of the immortal and the
imperishable, of the eternal law, the everlasting way of
righteousness, and of absolute bliss.

*For the Absolute is the Field of Supreme Consciousness, of that which
is everlasting and not subject to change, of the principles of actions
which support evolution, and of unqualified, joyous tranquility.*

We awaken to Reality by discovering it as the core of our being. It is omnipresent, the essence of every soul and thing, and
immediately available to be acknowledged and realized.

*In the Upanishad of the Bhagavad Gita, the science of the
Absolute, the scripture of Yoga and the dialogue between
Sri Krishna and Arjuna, thus ends the fourteenth
chapter entitled Gunatraya Vibhaga Yoga: The
Yoga of Discernment of the Qualities of Nature*

CHAPTER FIFTEEN

The Yoga of the Supreme Reality

In this chapter, an explanation is given regarding the persistent, successive, flowing transformations and expressions of life (*samsara*) in the manifested field of nature and how to be removed from their actions. The inner message is that we are not to be passively fixated in conditioned self-conscious states only hoping for salvation; we are to use our powers of intellectual discernment to see through and beyond the surface level of ever-changing appearances and awaken to knowledge and experience of the changeless Reality which is their cause.

Krishna spoke:

1. **They tell of a tree that is eternal, having its roots above and branches below, whose leaves are the sacred hymns of self-revealed knowledge. The one who knows this is a knower of the Vedas.**

    Some people speak of a magical tree that is eternal, having its roots established in higher consciousness and various branches below, with leaves which are the revelations of truth and offerings to evolution which nourish it. The devotee who knows this, is a knower of that Self-revealed knowledge.

    The universe is here compared to a cosmic tree with roots in Supreme Consciousness and branches extending downward (outward), sustained by the freely given offerings of life to nature's evolutionary processes. One who flawlessly comprehends this fact of cosmic manifestation knows the final truth.

2. **Its branches spread below and above, nourished by the gunas, with sense objects as its sprouts; and below its roots stretch forth promoting action in the world of beings.**

    Its branches spread below [outward] into the physical realm and

*above [inward from the gross or physical realm] into the astral and
causal realms, all nourished by the constituent qualities of nature,
with the objects of the senses as its sprouts which grow or produce
attachments; and the lower roots stretch forth to promote actions
[and their reactions] in the physical realm.*

3. **Its form cannot be perceived in this world, nor its end,
   beginning, or its existence. Cutting this tree by the axe of
   nonattachment,**
4. **That abode must be sought from which, having gone, no
   one returns, with the aspiration being "I take refuge in that
   original Spirit from whence the primeval energy streamed
   forth."**

*The reality of world manifestation cannot be perceived by the senses
alone, nor can its processes, or the causes of its manifestation. One
must remove oneself from the influences of involvement with the
manifested realms by calm detachment. Then one must aspire to
realize that Field of Absolute Pure Consciousness, from which, when
established in it, souls do not return to involvement with transient,
phenomenal realms. The liberation-aspiring soul should meditate
in the eternal Source of Om.*

Knowing the difference between formless Consciousness and
its forms and expressions in manifestation, is as important as
knowing the difference between the relationship of the soul and
its mind-body vehicle. For this, it can be helpful to remember
that nature and its processes represent the actions of the subtle
qualities (gunas) which regulate cosmic forces, and these are
emanated from the Field of God as the creative force, Om.

Our bodies are like the cosmic tree of life, with roots above
and branches below. The brain is above; the nerves branch out
below. The crown chakra and spiritual eye are above; the five lower
chakras and their branches or channels (nadis) through which
life forces flow are below. By internalized meditation practice we
can remove awareness from sense-perceived circumstances and
return it to the mind, withdraw life forces to the spinal pathway
and direct it upward to the crown chakra, and contemplate transcendent realities to facilitate awakening to Self-knowledge. This
is the immediate way to enlightenment.

5. **Without arrogance or delusion, with the errors of attachment conquered, dwelling constantly in the Supreme Self, with desires withdrawn, released from the dualities of pleasure and discomfort, undeluded souls go to that imperishable realm.**

Devoid of self-righteous egotism and delusion, with the errors of attachment overcome, established permanently in Self-realization, with the impulse of desires returned to their source, liberated from the conditions of the mundane realm, enlightened souls awaken to the Field of Absolute Pure Consciousness.

6. **Neither the sun, nor moon, nor fire illumines that place to which, having gone, no one returns. That is my supreme abode.**

Nothing of the realms of nature exists in that Field of Pure Consciousness which is permanently experienced. It transcends all outer aspects and expressions.

The Field of Absolute Pure Consciousness is Self-illumined. When we are illumined, we need not look to external sources of knowledge. When stable in complete enlightenment, there is no returning to former states of partial knowledge or to deluded, illusional states of consciousness. We do not have to leave our bodies to be enlightened; we have only to discard mental delusions and see through illusions which obscure perception of what Consciousness is and how it expresses. Any aspect of Consciousness that is expressive is "outer" in relationship to its source. The ideal is to be "inside," permanently established in complete realization of God, looking at life's processes from that point of view instead of being only partially awake looking at the Absolute from the "outside."

7. **A mere fragment of myself, becoming involved as a soul among the living in the realm of nature, attracts to itself the senses, of which the mind is the sixth.**

A mere portion of the Field of Pure Consciousness individualizes as souls in the realm of nature and attracts to itself the five subtle aspects of perception along with a mind.

Just as aura electricities emanate from the field of reflected God Consciousness (Cosmic Individuality, the effect of the light of God shining on the field of primordial nature) to produce Cosmic Mind, the five sense faculties, five instruments of action, five subtle sense objects and their five objective gross element manifestations, so five aura electricities emanate from the soul to produce its mind, sense faculties, instruments of action, subtle sense objects and the physical body. The five aura electricities emanated from the field of reflected God Consciousness comprise the causal realm and the five aura electricities emanated from the soul comprise its causal sheath or body. The sense perceptions make possible observation and connection with objective realms. The cosmic instruments of action comprise the vital or astral realm and the soul's instruments of action comprise its astral body or sheath. The cosmic sense objects objectify as the material universe and the soul's sense objects are objectified when it identifies with a physical body provided by its parents.

8. **When the soul acquires a body, and when departing it, it takes the senses and mind like the wind takes scents from their source.**

    The faculties of sense perception and the mind, used by the soul in subtle realms, are brought with it when it is born into this world and taken with it when it departs.

The soul produces but one mind, and through that mind the sense faculties are produced. Until final transcendence, the same mind is used incarnation after incarnation, in the physical realm and at various levels in astral and causal realms. Memories of perception and experience are impressed upon the mind. These impressions (samskaras) can be pain-producing if life-inhibiting, pleasure-producing if life-enhancing, or neither of these—such as memories useful for knowing our journey through time and space, for accessing acquired knowledge, or for allowing life-supporting habits to enable us to perform routine tasks. The mental conditionings which require a devotee's immediate attention are those which can be pain-producing and which restrict awareness and function. These may include conditionings which contribute to obsessive, addictive, or self-defeating behaviors; cause mental or emotional unrest; or interfere with rational thinking and contribute to misperceptions and illusions.

Pain-producing mental conditionings can be weakened and eliminated by improving overall health and well-being. This can be done by improving personal living circumstances, calm analysis and application of discriminative intelligence, intentional cultivation of opposite or more desirable and life-enhancing qualities and characteristics, willingness to be emotionally mature and Self- (soul)-determined, and the nurturing of spiritual growth. Superconscious (samadhi) states effectively resist, restrain, and dissolve destructive mental conditionings.

9. Using hearing, sight, touch, taste, and smell, the embodied soul enjoys the objects of the senses.

Our sense faculties, which enable us to connect with the natural world, are rooted in the mind which is sometimes referred to as the sixth sense, the cause of the five specialized faculties of sense perception.

10. The soul, acting in relationship to the gunas, is not perceived by those whose awareness is veiled, while those who have the eye of knowledge do perceive it.

People who are not aware of the existence of the soul, or whose attention is fixed on external appearances, do not know that behind the facade of every mind-body being is the immortal soul. Those who have knowledge, easily apprehend their own divinity and the innate divinity of others.

11. Rightly resolved practitioners of yoga perceive the divine nature in the Self; the unintelligent and undisciplined seekers, though striving to perceive the divine nature, do not.

Devotees who are focused on spiritual accomplishment awaken to Self-knowledge; deluded people and undisciplined truth seekers, because their endeavors are faulty, fail [for as long as they remain deluded and undisciplined] to awaken to Self-knowledge.

The spiritual path is for sincere, dedicated, intelligent, fully committed devotees of God. People who are not sincere, dedicated, intelligent, or fully committed, can only have results equal to their actions and capacities. A devotee of God should be extremely curious about what is to be discovered and should be resolved to know the innermost facts of life. Intellectual skills should be refined, and the mantra of empowerment should be, "I am one hundred percent committed to unfolding and actualizing my soul qualities and to knowing the full reality of God!"

12. That brilliance of the sun which illumines the solar system, know that brilliance to be mine.

The inner radiance that makes possible all outer lights is the "self-shining sun" of Consciousness.

Everything in manifestation emerged from Consciousness. Consciousness does not have origins in matter; matter has origins in Consciousness. The finest aspects of manifestation are light frequencies. The narrow band of the light spectrum that we are capable of seeing with our eyes is but a fraction (perhaps a billionth) of the full spectrum, which includes radio waves, gamma rays, and all other rays discernible only by the use of specialized instruments. The universe and everything in it, including our bodies, is light.

13. Entering the earth, I nourish all beings with energy, and having become the watery moon, I nourish all herbs and plants.

Pervading matter, the enlivening aspect of Consciousness nourishes all beings with energy, and the light and gravitational forces of the moon influence the tides and cycles of vegetative growth.

14. Having become the digestive fire, I abide in the bodies of all beings; joining with prana and apana, I transform the various kinds of food.

Consciousness as fiery prana influences the processes of food transformation in the body as apana it eliminates waste products.

According to Ayurvedic texts, the seven stages of food transformation are: (1) plasma (2) blood; (3) muscle; (4) fat; (5) bone; (6) bone marrow; (7) reproductive essences. A final stage is transformation of surplus food essence into subtle energy (*ojas*) which strengthens the body's immune system and contributes to the radiance of total health. Food is transformed by the subtle inner fire element influence produced from rajas guna.

15. **I have entered the hearts of all beings; from me come memory and knowledge, as well as their loss. I alone am that which is to be known in all the Vedas; I am the author of the Vedanta and the knower of the Vedas.**

Consciousness is the essence of all souls; because of its influences all processes incidental to expressive life are made possible. Pure Consciousness is that which is to be known among all revelations [vedas] of truth. Consciousness reveals the final truth [vedanta: the essence of that which has been revealed] of itself and of the processes of life because knowledge of itself is innate to it.

Memory of cosmic processes is the result of impressions of actions made on the Field of Cosmic Mind, just as our memories are the result of impressions of perception and experience on our mind. Knowledge unfolds from Consciousness. Both memory and unfolded knowledge can be obscured by the influences of tamas guna and confused by the influences of rajas guna.

16. **There are two aspects of Consciousness in this world, the perishable and the imperishable. All emanated beings are perishable; the unchanging is called the imperishable.**

There are two aspects of one Being. The perishable aspect is that which is manifested. It is emanated and expressive in the field of space and time and eventually dissolves when its constituent aspects are returned to the field of primordial nature. The imperishable aspect is the enlivening Spirit of God.

17. **But the transcendent Being, the Supreme Self, is other than these, and entering the three worlds as the eternal Lord, supports them.**

The Absolute is the aspect which transcends its self-manifestation as the causative Spirit of God and the emanated causal, astral, and physical realms. It pervades all realms and is their eternal, influential substratum or foundation.

18. Because I transcend the perishable and the imperishable, I am known as the Supreme Spirit.

Because Pure Consciousness transcends the phenomenal realms and the aspect of the causative Spirit of God, it is, in this world, by those who know of it and by those to whom knowledge is revealed, acclaimed as the changeless Reality.

Pure Consciousness, because devoid of qualities and characteristics, has no personality. Some devotional truth seekers imagine Krishna, or some other being, to be a supreme person. Their imaginary concept is their own mental projection motivated by their need, or desire, to personalize that which is impersonal.

19. The one who, without delusion, knows me as the Supreme Spirit, is omniscient, and worships me without reservation.

Enlightened souls which have realized the Absolute, have all knowledge, and remain firmly established in that realization.

When delusions and illusions are absent, the Self-realized soul's innate knowledge of God as God is, is fully unfolded.

20. Thus this most secret doctrine has been taught by me. When, having awakened to this, one becomes wise and fulfills all duties.

Thus this innermost knowledge has been self-revealed from the Field of Pure Consciousness. Having awakened to this, the devotee's knowledge blossoms as wisdom and all necessary actions are fulfilled.

The devotee is established in perfected Self-realization; knowledge matures as wisdom. All that needs to be done has been completed, and what remains to be done is skillfully and effectively accomplished. The struggle is over. Ignorance has been banished. Only the light of realized knowledge remains.

In the Upanishad of the Bhagavad Gita, the science of the Absolute, the scripture of Yoga and the dialogue between Sri Krishna and Arjuna, thus ends the fifteenth chapter entitled Purushottama Yoga: The Yoga of Discernment of the Field of Nature and the Supreme Reality

CHAPTER SIXTEEN

The Yoga of Discernment Between the Higher and Lower Natures

More information about the human condition is now revealed so that the devotee might choose the higher way.

Krishna said:

1. **Fearlessness, purity of heart, abiding in yoga [samadhi] along with knowledge, charitable giving, self-restraint and holy offerings, study of sacred texts, austerity [disciplined practices], and uprightness,**
2. **Nonviolence, truth, absence of anger, renunciation, serenity, freedom from finding fault, compassion for all beings, absence of cravings, gentleness, modesty, steadiness,**
3. **Vigor, forgiveness, fortitude, purity, freedom from malice and from pride; these are the endowments of those born to a divine destiny.**

These behaviors and qualities are sattvic: life-enhancing and elevating. When spontaneously expressed, they indicate spiritual awareness and an abundance of constructive karma (samskaras, mental impressions).

4. **Hypocrisy, arrogance, pride, anger, violence, insolence, and ignorance, are endowments of those born to a lower destiny.**

These behaviors and qualities are rajasic and tamasic, or life-diminishing and awareness-restricting. When spontaneously expressed by an individual, or when uncontrollably demonstrated under duress, they indicate impaired or clouded spiritual awareness and the existence of destructive karma and tendencies.

5. **The divine destiny leads to liberation; the lower destiny leads to bondage. Do not grieve! You are born with a divine destiny.**

The divinely impelled life-path has liberation of consciousness as its outcome; the conditioned, self-conscious life-path, unless changed, results in continued bondage. In this verse the soul is inspired to know that its destiny will surely be consummated in God-realization.

6. **There are two classifications of beings in this world, the divine and the deluded. The divine has been explained at length; now hear from me about the deluded.**

Although all souls are divine, not all are awake to their true nature. Some are awake, and others are unawake or deluded. There are, of course, degrees of wakefulness and of delusion.

7. **Deluded people do not understand when to act and when to refrain from action. Neither purity, good conduct, nor truth is found in them.**

People under the spell of delusion, devoid of intellectual ability, do not know how to behave appropriately and constructively or when not to act. Their minds are impure because conditioned by erroneous ideas and confused by illusions. Their conduct is not constructive. Knowledge of their innate divinity, of the processes of nature, or of God, is not discernible to them at a conscious level.

8. **They say that the universe is without truth, without basis, without God, and was not produced in causal sequence but by the effects of desire alone.**

Deluded people assert the universe to be devoid of meaning, that it has no reality to support it, and that God is nonexistent. They often insist that the universe is formed only of gross matter and that humans and creatures are born only as the effect of desire-driven behaviors of their parents to reproduce.

9. **Holding this view, those lost souls [lacking knowledge of themselves] of limited intelligence and of cruel actions, come forth as enemies of the world.**

Blinded by their delusions and their misunderstanding, confused souls are unable to effectively discern truth from untruth. Their [often] self-centered, destructive behaviors cause them to be in conflict with the actions of evolution.

10. Attached to insatiable desire, full of hypocrisy, arrogance, and pride; having accepted false notions because of delusion, they act with impure resolve.

Because of their lack of spiritual awareness, many people think that life in the world is only for the purpose of satisfying personal desires. If egotistical, they may pretend to be what they are not, express themselves self-righteously and be overly assertive, and honestly but erroneously think and feel that they, as a personality-oriented being, are special or extraordinary. These problems are all due to intellectual error.

11. Obsessed with endless concerns which can only end at death, with gratification of desire as their highest aim, convinced that this is all there is to life,

12. Bound by a hundred snares of hope, devoted to desire and anger, they strive to obtain hoards of wealth by unjust means for the gratification of their desires.

13. They say, this has been obtained by me today; this desire I shall attain; this is mine and this wealth also shall be mine.

14. That enemy has been slain by me, and I shall slay others too; I am a lord, I am the enjoyer, I am successful, powerful, and happy.

15. I am wealthy and high born. Who else is equal to me? I shall make holy offerings, I shall give, I shall rejoice. Thus are they deluded by ignorance.

16. Led astray by many uncontrolled imaginings, enveloped in a net of delusion, attached to the gratification of desires, they fall into impure circumstances.

17. Self-conceited, stubborn, filled with pride and with arrogance of wealth, they make holy offerings only as a gesture, with ostentation and without regard for right procedures.

18. Clinging to egotism, force, insolence, desire, and anger, those malicious people despise me [innate divinity] in their own bodies and in the bodies of others.

It should be remembered that these are but some characteristics of spiritually unawake people because of lack of knowledge, mental conditionings, or some other impairment, and are not characteristics of the soul itself.

19. Those cruel people who despise me, I constantly hurl into

circumstances which correspond to their natures in the cycles of rebirth.

Egocentric, confused souls are driven by the force of their ignorance into circumstances corresponding to their states of consciousness.

20. **After many repeated embodiments, those who, because of delusion do not attain realization of me, go to still lower conditions.**

After successive incarnations, deluded souls that do not awaken to God-knowledge may become even more deluded.

Although some souls experience confused and painful circumstances incarnation after incarnation, to them, their lives are like a disturbed dream from which they will eventually awaken. Without desire for spiritual awakening, the actions of evolution and God's grace will facilitate soul unfoldment.

21. **The doors to destructive circumstances are threefold: desire, anger, and greed. These should be abandoned.**

Desires which are life-enhancing and constructive are not harmful; ignorance-impelled desire and insatiable cravings are definitely destructive. When self-centered desire is thwarted, anger arises because of frustration, clouding awareness and interfering with our reasoning powers. Greed is due to selfishness and feelings of insecurity. Destructive desire, uncontrolled anger, and greed, are to be renounced by the devotee who aspires to spiritual growth and happy, healthy, fulfilled living.

22. **Released from these three doors to darkness, one does what is best for the soul and goes to the highest goal.**

Having completely renounced destructive desire, anger, and greed, the God-surrendered devotee determines behaviors by choosing only those which are spiritually beneficial. By so doing, spiritual progress is rapid and fulfilling.

23. **That one who disregards scriptural guidelines and acts impulsively because of desire, does not attain perfection, happiness, or the highest goal.**

A devotee who ignores how-to-live principles that are supportive of well-being and spiritual growth, and who acts without thinking because of self-centered desires (and conditionings), cannot immediately experience illumination of consciousness and the actualization of soul qualities. Merely hoping for necessary improvement, or reading metaphysical literature without putting into practice what is learned, will not produce satisfying spiritual growth.

24. Therefore, let the scriptures be your authority for determining what to do and what to avoid. Knowing the right way, perform actions in this world.

Enlightened teachers do not insist upon naive adherence to what they say. What is recommended is that what is learned be tested in the fires of personal application so that the devotee has opportunities to verify the teaching by personal experience.

In the Upanishad of the Bhagavad Gita, the science of the Absolute, the scripture of Yoga and the dialogue between Sri Krishna and Arjuna, thus ends the sixteenth chapter entitled Daivasura Sampad Vibhaga Yoga: The Yoga of Discernment Between the Higher and Lower Natures

CHAPTER SEVENTEEN

The Yoga of Discernment of the Three Kinds of Faith

It is helpful to be aware of higher realities and to know how to practice meditation and contemplate the Infinite. It is also of practical value to know how to live effectively. In this chapter, guidelines supportive of total well-being are provided.

Faith, in the chapter title and in some of the verses, refers to respect or deferential regard for, to depend upon or trust, to sincerely believe to be productive of desired results.

Arjuna spoke:

1. **What is the condition of those who do not abide by scriptural guidelines, but with faith make sacrifices? Is it sattvic, rajasic, or tamasic?**

   What is the condition of people who do not abide by recommended procedures for conduct and actions when performing spiritual practices or other rites, but who sincerely believe in the usefulness of their actions? Is it sattvic, rajasic, or tamasic?

The question refers to people who either do not know the most productive way to act or who choose to follow their own instincts— to let their actions be impelled by their conditioned nature. The soul desiring knowledge inquires: Are they influenced by elevating qualities or attributes of nature, by the qualities which nurture passionate desire, or by those which cloud one's awareness?

Krishna said:

2. **The faith of embodied beings is of three kinds: it is sattvic, rajasic, or tamasic. Now hear of this.**

   The deferential regard of human beings is of three kinds: it is either elevating and illuminating, assertively self-serving, or mind-darkening and self-defeating.

3. **Faith is in accord with the basic nature of each person. A person is made of faith. One is what one's faith is.**

   Deferential regard is in accord with the basic mind-body constitution of each person. One's personality and circumstances are the result of preferred attitudes and actions. A person's present state or condition is the result of what is believed and done.

4. **Sattvic people worship the gods; rajasic people worship spirits and demons; tamasic people worship the spirits of those who have died and hordes of nature spirits.**

   People in whom purity and luminosity prevail, honor the aspects of divinity which regulate cosmic processes. People in whom the qualities which contribute to restlessness and desire are strong, honor what they erroneously believe to be benevolent spirits and spirits presumed to be skillful in effecting discord and misfortune. People in whom inertia is dominant and intelligence is obscured, honor the spirits of deceased friends and relatives [and others] and what are mistakenly believed to be spirits which control the elements.

People who are inclined toward spiritual growth but are unable to comprehend the truth about God or about their own innate potential for illumination of consciousness, may endeavor to relate to enlightened, influential beings or forces, hoping to attract their favor or benefit from a sympathetic relationship with them. They may rely on the help of real or imagined saints or other holy personages whose attainment or special powers will assure their well-being or ultimate salvation. While the goodwill and spiritual assistance of enlightened beings can be helpful to a person, and faith in something higher than one's self-conscious state can be elevating, eventually the devotee of God must go beyond all real or imagined intermediate aspects of Consciousness, to the transcendent Reality.

People who are assertively self-centered, motivated by strong desires, and whose philosophical speculations are irrational (not clearly reasoned or determined), may be inclined to imagine the existence of wise, friendly souls in astral realms who are capable of assisting them by telepathic and other means, or even the existence of skillful beings whose influences can be attracted by prayer, affirmation, strong desire, or simple expectation. Such people are also likely to believe in angels, the usefulness of dream messages, visions, various forms of mediumship, spirit guides, and other presumed supernatural phenomena. The word *demon* (Latin *daemon*; Greek *daimon*) used in the above verse refers to imaginary spiritual beings believed to have special abilities and powers. Belief in such entities has persisted through the centuries, in various cultures, because of intellectual and emotional immaturity and the sense of helplessness of the believers.

They are likely to believe in the existence of evil as a distinct entity or force, or a personalized aspect of evil such as the Western concept of a devil or Satan. Not knowing how the universe was produced and what causes various effects, not knowing of the actions and influences of the qualities or attributes of nature, and not knowing themselves to be spiritual beings, deluded people endeavor to create a meaningful theology that will provide them with answers to allow them to have peace of mind. Confused thinking causes some people to mistakenly attribute the cause of pain and misfortune, of themselves and others, to an external, malevolent force or being. People at this level need to learn a higher way to think and live. They need to get out of self-consciousness by awakening to superconscious levels. They need a teacher or a teaching that will provide them with valid information about the reality of Consciousness.

People deficient in intelligence, if religious and inclined to have spiritual support, tend to think of their deceased friends and relatives as being capable of helping them, or may err in thinking that individualized spirit-beings control the forces of nature and can be propitiated and their cooperation negotiated. These people, too, need to be educated, and encouraged to grow to emotional, intellectual, and spiritual maturity.

5. **Egotistical, vain people, impelled by the force of passionate desire, who practice violent austerities which are not ordained by the scriptures,**
6. **Foolishly oppress their physical functions and the indwelling Spirit. Know these to be of deluded resolve.**

Arrogant people who engage in forceful practices in endeavors to fulfill their spiritual aspirations, are unwise in allowing their actions to be determined by their emotions. Their practices restrict their bodily functions as well as the impulse of the soul to experience natural, spontaneous unfoldment. Even if sincere, their approach is unreasonable, impractical, and self-defeating. Such devotees often go to extremes: practicing strenuous exercises; demanding response to prayer instead of surrendering self-consciousness; exerting too much will power when concentrating instead of learning how to quiet the mind and calmly contemplate; depriving themselves of necessary sleep and relaxation; fasting to extremes; and being obsessive or willful instead of maintaining moderate, constructive, life-supportive routines.

7.   **Even the food preferred by all three types is of three kinds, as are their sacrifices, austerities, and gifts. Hear now the distinction between them.**

The food choices of the three mind-body constitutional types reveal their basic condition, as do their religious or spiritual practices, chosen self-disciplines, and offerings to others or for charitable projects. Now learn the clearly defined differences between them.

8.   **Foods which promote life, virtue, strength, health, happiness, and satisfaction, and which are pleasant to the taste, ripe, firm, and agreeable, are preferred by those whose nature is sattvic.**

We consume foods to provide nourishment and energy to the body. The ideal diet comprises clean, natural foods ideally suited to our basic mind-body constitution, in modest but sufficient quantity, which provide needed nutrients and calories, are easy to assimilate, and which have no toxic effect. Such foods are normally chosen by a healthy, educated, clear-thinking, emotionally balanced, spiritually aware person. A simple vegetarian diet is best, with a balance of vegetables, seeds (grains, beans, nuts), and fruits. Ayurvedic texts explain that the first effect of foods is the body's response to their taste. Tastes of food (and other substances) are produced by the actions of the gunas expressing through the five elements. Food tastes, therefore, directly influence the doshas or governing principles of the body: strengthening, weakening, or disturbing their actions. People who are already healthy and functional should choose to remain so, and people who want to be healthy and functional should aspire to be so. A knowledgeable approach to food selection can be helpful to every-one. Devotees of God should not ignore this matter.

9. **Foods which cause discomfort, illness, and sickness, and which are bitter, sour, salty, have excessively hot taste, pungent, dry, and burning, are preferred by those whose nature is rajasic.**

Foods which are pleasantly sweet to the taste and have a sweet post-digestive effect nourish kapha dosha and build and maintain the physical structure of the body. Foods which have bitter, sour, salty, hot, and pungent tastes are appealing to people whose basic mind-body constitution is imbalanced or who are strongly influenced by rajasic qualities (therefore, who are restless, fiery, outgoing, assertive, sense-oriented, and aggressive). Foods which are very dry or very hot to the touch are also appealing to such people. To balance the mind-body constitution, and to maintain balance, all six tastes—sweet, sour, bitter, salty, hot, and pungent—should be included in the daily diet. To strengthen deficient dosha influences, one can increase the tastes which correspond to them; to weaken excessive dosha influences, the tastes which correspond to them can be diminished.

10. **Foods which are stale, tasteless, putrid, and rotting, are preferred by those whose nature is tamasic.**

Such foods are devoid of life force, toxic in their effects, weaken the body's systems, deplete the body of energy, can cause serious illness, and dull the senses. Tamasic people are usually deficient in intellectual powers, have little regard for their personal welfare, and tend to engage in destructive behaviors and self-defeating actions.

11. **Sacrifices dutifully made according to scriptural recommendations, without expectation of reward, is sattvic.**

Religious observances and spiritual practices performed without egocentric motivation are sattvic. They are life-enhancing and spiritually elevating.

Religious observances (private or communal worship, prayer,

pilgrimage to holy places, ceremonial rites) and spiritual practices nurture soul qualities and facilitate the awakening of Self-knowledge. These should be engaged in with clear knowledge of their purpose. Constructive results will naturally follow. Rajasic and tamasic influences will be weakened, sattvic influences strengthened, and samadhi will be stable and pure.

12. Sacrifices made with expectation of reward, and for the purpose of being known to others, is rajasic.

Religious observances and spiritual practices performed with ego-centric motivation or to impress others are rajasic. They result in delusions and illusions.

Even if one has knowledge of how to practice, if one's endeavors are motivated by desire to enhance self-conscious states, or to acquire manipulative powers or status, results will be unsatisfying and delusions and illusions will be increased.

13. Sacrifices which are devoid of faith, performed contrary to scriptural ordinances, without appropriate offerings, are tamasic.

Religious observances and spiritual practices performed without knowledge of procedure, or incorrectly and without self-surrender, are tamasic and devoid of results.

The most beneficial way to engage in spiritual practices is to learn what to do and compliantly adhere to the procedures. The most important venture of our lives is learning how to live effectively and to awaken spiritually. A sincere devotee of God, regardless of the degree of understanding or aptitude for practice when first embarking on the spiritual path, can experience satisfying, authentic soul unfoldment by learning how to practice and persisting with unwavering devotion.

14. Worship of the gods, saints, teachers, and of those who are wise; purity, virtue, inwardness, and nonviolence; these practices are austerities of the body.

Entering into a harmonious relationship with the forces which regulate cosmic and universal actions; attunement with the states of consciousness realized by saintly souls; respect for the teacher [or teaching] and dedicated application of what is learned; emulation of the actions of wise people who can be role models; purity of body, mind, and motives; soul-centeredness; and harmlessness, are disciplines to be perfected by embodied souls.

It is obvious that one who is intentional on the spiritual path is encouraged to give complete attention to every aspect of practice so that soul unfoldment can be accelerated. Casual interest in God-realization may confer a degree of mental peace but will not be transformative. More focused involvement produces satisfying results equal to one's endeavor. Total commitment demonstrated by constructive actions allows superior results.

15. Austerities of speech include using words that are truthful, agreeable, beneficial, and which do not cause distress, and recitation of the scriptures.

Disciplines of speech include speaking truthfully, kindly, appropriately, constructively, and supportively, and speaking the inspired words of enlightened souls.

What we say and how we say it reveals our psychological and spiritual states. We can regulate thoughts, moods, and states of consciousness by choosing to speak precisely, knowledgeably, and purposefully. When our thoughts are disorganized or we are emotionally disturbed, our speech pattern tends to be confused and endeavors to communicate may be ineffectual or even disruptive. Mental and emotional states, and states of consciousness, can be regulated by being intentional when we speak. We can literally talk ourselves into states of confusion or mental clarity, mental and emotional depression or serenity, unhappiness or happiness, fear or confidence, illness or health, depending upon what we choose to talk about and how we talk. We can also influence others in either constructive or nonuseful ways by how we intentionally communicate.

16. Peace of mind, gentleness, silence, self-restraint, and mental purity, are austerities of the mind.

The cultivation of mental peace, gentleness, silence, self-mastery, and mental purity, are the disciplines of the mind.

Mental peace is assured when soul awareness is cultivated and the transformations and fluctuations that ordinarily occur in the mind are allowed to become quieted and stilled.

Gentleness results from being settled in harmlessness.

Mental silence purifies and strengthens the mind. It can be nurtured by cultivating calmness at all times and is induced by superconscious states.

Self-restraint is perfected by selectively choosing to regulate sensory and mental impulses.

Mental purity is experienced by self-restraint, emotional calm, cultivating the virtues of harmlessness, honesty, truthfulness, inwardness (to conserve vital forces), and renunciation; also by repeated superconscious episodes during meditation.

17. Those who practice these three austerities with highest faith, without expectation of reward, are sattvic.

Those who practice these disciplines of the body, speech, and mind with highest deferential regard, without desiring to be rewarded, have a sattvic or pure nature.

18. That austerity which is fraudulently practiced to gain the respect, honor, and reverence of others is rajasic, unstable, and impermanent.

Dishonest, egocentric actions are of no real value. They are superficial because not based on the principles of evolution which uphold and nurture the universe and the matter-related destiny of souls.

19. Austerity [ritual practices] performed with misunderstanding, or for the purpose of harming another, is tamasic.

Incorrect practice of procedures cannot have entirely constructive outcomes. One may pray sincerely but ineffectively. One may meditate regularly without beneficial results. One may exercise faithfully in ways which do more harm than good. A person with an already excessive vata constitution may engage in frantic exercise or a person with an excessive pitta constitution may exercise too competitively.

Any action performed with intention to harm another person

harms the one who performs it. Even the wish to harm another is self-destructive. A devotee should acknowledge the innate divine nature of every person and creature.

20. The gift that is appropriately given to one from whom nothing is expected is sattvic.

Whether we give the gift of good will, our prayers, verbal help or encouragement, assistance of some kind, an object, or money, it should be thoughtful, appropriate, and of value to the recipient, and should be given without desire for personal reward of any kind. The moment we appropriately give is our moment of blessing because we are then in the flow of life's supportive actions. We cannot be small-minded and large-minded at the same time, nor simultaneously spiritually impoverished and spiritually free.

21. The gift that is grudgingly given, with expectation of reward or gain, is rajasic.

Giving is not an investment, it is an opportunity to be of genuine service. When we give freely and appropriately we are open to the flow of life's resources: we are affluent. When we are able to give for the purpose of being helpful and resist doing so, we are blocking the flow of life and withholding from ourselves the blessing-moment of being in that flow. To give a gift with expectation of return is to put ourselves at the level of cause and effect. As devotees of God we should aspire to be removed from the influences of mundane causes.

22. The gift that is given inappropriately or to an unworthy cause, and that is given without respect, or with contempt, is tamasic.

To give inappropriately is to give thoughtlessly, with little regard for meeting the real need of the recipient of the gift, be it a person or a worthy endeavor. To give to an unworthy cause reveals a wasteful attitude. To give without respecting the person or the cause for whom the gift is intended, or with thoughts of contempt, giving only because motivated by feelings of guilt or obligation, may be somewhat helpful to the recipient of the gift but does not improve the personal circumstances of the giver.

A devotee's life should be freely offered to God. This means that we should live in harmony with nature's processes, engage in spiritual practices, awaken from deluded states of consciousness, be agents through which others are blessed, and be responsive to the actions of grace.

23. "Om, Tat, Sat"—this is said to be the threefold designation of the Supreme Reality. By this the brahmins, the Vedas, and the sacrifices were ordained in ancient times.

"Om, That is Real"—this is taught as the threefold indication of the Supreme Reality. By that Reality the practices of the sages with higher knowledge, the revelations of truth, and life's self-giving processes were determined long ago.

Om comprises three sounds—A,U,M—representing absolute supremacy and the beginning and ending of all things. *Tat* (That) is used to refer to the infinite, indescribable, transcendent Reality from which the cosmos emerged into manifestation. *Sat* (truth, that which is) is used to represent Absolute Being or Reality. The mantra is chanted with Om as the preface to "That is Real."

24. Therefore, as prescribed by those who proclaim the Supreme Reality, the performance of sacrifice, giving, and austerity are always preceded by the utterance of Om.

Therefore, as prescribed by the seers of revealed truth, the performance of holy offering of surrendered spiritual practice, self-giving, and self-disciplines are preceded by chanting Om.

For devotees, the inner meaning of this verse is that one should meditate on Om, give the mind to samadhi, and restrain the senses by turning them inward to dissolve one's sense of independent existence in realization of oneness in the Absolute.

25. Uttering "Tat" without expecting rewards, acts of sacrifice, austerity, and various acts of giving are performed by those who aspire to liberation.

Chanting "Tat" without desiring anything in return, the holy offering of spiritual practice, of self-disciplines, and various kinds of giving are performed by those who aspire to liberation.

Without any desire for support of ego-sense, aspiring only to liberation of consciousness, contemplating and surrendering to *That* which is the ultimate Reality, a faithful devotee does everything for the purpose of realizing God.

26. "Sat" is understood to mean Reality and goodness; it is also chanted for an auspicious action.

"Sat" is used to represent Absolute Reality and its rightness; it is also chanted when beginning a significant endeavor.

Contemplating the transcendent Field of Absolute Reality, the faithful devotee dissolves all awareness of independent selfhood into realization of oneness. When beginning to meditate, one should acknowledge the ultimate state to be realized, practice preliminary procedures to facilitate inwardness, rest in the aftereffects tranquility of meditation, and awaken through stages of samadhi to complete illumination of consciousness.

27. Steadfastness in sacrifice, austerity, giving, and actions relating to these practices are also designated as sattvic.

Unwavering participation in spiritual practices, self-disciplined behaviors, giving, and of actions serving these purposes, is also described as being elevating and illuminating.

All of the devotee's meditative practices and supporting actions are preliminary to arriving at that state of being absorbed in contemplation of Om. From there one becomes stable in tranquil Self-knowledge that blossoms into full God-realization.

28. An offering made or a practice performed without faith is called "asat [untruth]," and is as nothing in this world or in the hereafter.

An offering made or a spiritual practice performed without respect or deferential regard is called untruth, and is of no value during the present incarnation or in future circumstances.

In the Upanishad of the Bhagavad Gita, the science of the Absolute, the scripture of Yoga and the dialogue between Sri Krishna and Arjuna, thus ends the seventeenth chapter entitled Sraddhatraya Vibhaga Yoga: The Yoga of Discernment of the Three Kinds of Faith

CHAPTER EIGHTEEN

The Yoga of Liberation
by Surrendered Renunciation

The first chapter of this drama introduced the theme and described the soul's confusion about itself and its relationships and duties. In this final chapter, Arjuna (the now nearly enlightened soul) speaks twice. In the opening verse, inquiry is made about a subtle metaphysical point the soul needs to understand. As the dialogue ends, the soul affirms its now fully self-revealed knowledge and surrenders to its destiny.

Arjuna spoke:

1. **I wish to know the truth about abandonment and of renunciation, and the difference between them.**

    I want to know the facts about nonperformance of actions and of not being attached to the performance of necessary actions.

Krishna replied:

2. **The wise declare abandonment to be relinquishment of actions prompted by desire; they declare renunciation to be relinquishment of attachment to the results of actions.**

    Knowledgeable teachers declare right nonperformance of actions to be the letting go of actions prompted by restlessness, cravings, and the stored-up potency of the samskaras or mental impressions; they declare nonattachment to be the letting go of hopes and expectations of the results of necessary actions.

The basis of relinquishing actions is to know the difference between essential, life-enhancing actions and those which are nonessential and life-diminishing, and to perform only actions to fulfill worthwhile purposes while ignoring others. Essential, life-enhancing actions do not include those which are only for the gratification of the senses, which arise from restlessness and addictive cravings, or are impelled by subconscious conditionings or habit. Suppression of desire results in mental and emotional frustration and physical stress; instead, urges should be regulated, and attention and energies directed to productive purposes.

Only unnecessary actions and involvements are to be relinquished. Life should be lived skillfully: duties should be faithfully performed, worthwhile endeavors should be implemented and completed, and obligations to others should be fulfilled. Doing these things with understanding will not interfere with spiritual growth. To the contrary, right living will enable spiritual qualities and soul abilities to be unfolded and actualized. Right living provides opportunities to verify our knowledge: to demonstrate whether or not our spiritual growth is authentic.

Necessary and worthwhile actions skillfully performed produce predictable results. Living purposefully and doing what is right or appropriate for the moment is the important matter; the effects of our actions will then manifest spontaneously. We need not be anxious about the outcome of what we do, nor should we be mentally or emotionally attached to the results. In this way nonbinding actions are performed and life is enjoyable and free. Devoid of psychological conflicts that attachments produce, awareness remains clear and spiritual growth proceeds easily.

3. **Some learned people declare that action is to be abandoned because it causes pain, while others say that acts of holy offering, giving, and austerity are not to be abandoned.**

Some learned teachers declare that all action is to be relinquished because it causes pain, while others say that spiritual practices, self-giving, and helpful disciplines are not to be relinquished.

Some philosophers who are not yet enlightened declare that actions of any kind bind one to the mundane realm and to cycles of cause and effect. Life-enhancing and spiritual growth practices should be continued with intention until all physical and mental obstacles to functional living and God-realization are removed. When our enlightenment is complete, we no longer have to think about what to do or what to avoid doing; we live freely, spontaneously, and appropriately.

4. Hear my final word about the three kinds of renunciation.

Understand the final revelation of Consciousness regarding the three kinds of renunciation.

5. Acts of holy offerings, giving, and austerity, are not to be abandoned; they are to be performed because they purify the wise.

Spiritual practices, giving of the mind and self-sense to higher consciousness, and necessary disciplines, are not to be abandoned. They are to be performed because they purify the body and mind of devotees who wisely practice them.

Without meditation and other spiritual practices, surrender of self-consciousness in favor of God-consciousness, disciplines for mastery of sense urges and mental states, and the inherited or conditioned obstacles to the free flow of awareness will not be cleansed from body and mind. A devotee is wise to perform those necessary actions which contribute to total well-being and soul unfoldment.

6. These actions are to be performed without attachments to the results. This is my definite and highest understanding.

These intentional actions are to be performed without attachments to results. This is an infallible revelation of truth.

There are two reasons why attachments to results of actions are to be renounced: (1) attachments of any kind support egocentric, self-conscious states; (2) anxiety about the outcome of actions unsettle emotions and cause disordered thought processes.

Our ego or self-sense should be perceived as but a point of view from which to observe and relate to the world while we remain established in soul awareness. We are then said to have a healthy ego. When egoism or self-centeredness prevails, we tend to overly identify with our personality and to be neglectful of soul awareness.

Unsettled emotional states and disordered thought processes strengthen the impulses and tendencies (vasanas) of the mind and keep its movements (vrittis) circulating, clouding intelligence, and keeping soul awareness involved with mental processes.

The result is confusion and restlessness when engaged in routine activities, difficulty in experiencing superconsciousness when meditating, and inability to maintain superconsciousness after meditation practice.

7. Renunciation of obligatory action is not proper; to abandon it because of delusion is tamasic.

To renounce the performance of actions to which one is obligated is inappropriate; to abandon it because of intellectual error will further cloud awareness and restrict soul unfoldment.

If, because of inability to intellectually comprehend the reason for spiritual practice and other activities to which one is obligated by the laws of nature or personal duty, one who desires to experience intellectual, emotional, and spiritual growth, and supportive and orderly circumstances, should heed the advice of knowledgeable people. If, because of temporary ignorance of the facts of life, one is in bondage to various conditions and circumstances, the easiest way to actualize inner growth and overall beneficial improvements is to follow the example of others who are accomplished and functional.

8. That person who abandons actions because they are difficult, or because of physical inconvenience, performs only rajasic renunciation and does not obtain the results of that renunciation.

That person who abandons actions because they are difficult to execute, or because of physical [or other] discomfort, performs only [superficial] renunciation that satisfies the mind and senses and does not realize any spiritually beneficial results.

To fulfill only those duties and obligations that are easy and comfortable is to serve the egocentric sense of selfhood. This behavior is common to millions of people who prefer to live a comfortable self-conscious life and keeps one addicted to habitual behaviors which serve no higher purpose.

9. When action is done as duty, abandoning the results, such renunciation is sattvic.

When essential actions are performed as duty, and attachments to results of actions are relinquished, such actions are life-enhancing and spiritually illuminating.

A devotee of God should want to be in tune with the Infinite, to be an agent of God's will in this world. We can know God's will or impersonal intention by observing the effects of evolution and unfolding our innate knowledge. When we do this, we perceive that the impulse of life that pervades the universe is in the direction of growth and fulfillment of evolutionary purposes or trends. We also acknowledge our soul impulses to awaken, learn, grow, function, and unfold our full potential.

10. The wise renunciate who has no doubts and is filled with goodness, has no aversion to disagreeable actions and is not attached to agreeable actions.

The renunciate devotee who clearly understands this way of life and the reason for it, and who is constantly inspired to right resolve, does not avoid unpleasant but necessary actions and is not attached to those which are pleasant to perform.

A devotee of God should elevate thoughts and awareness above the level of petty, self-serving concerns. The mature approach to duty is to do what needs to be done and move on to whatever else needs to be done. When events and circumstances are unfolding harmoniously about us, most of what we do will be enjoyable. When it is not, when we are confronted by an unpleasant task, we can handle it with dispassionate finesse, and perhaps even learn something worthwhile in the process.

11. Embodied beings cannot abandon actions entirely; the devotee, then, who abandons the results of action is a renunciate.

Embodied souls [in physical, astral, or causal realms] cannot entirely relinquish actions; therefore, the devotee who relinquishes mental and emotional attachments to their results is a renunciate.

No one can relinquish actions entirely, because survival actions have to be implemented to maintain the body and our relationships with nature and society. The necessity to interact with nature will continue until we transcend nature. Until then, we are wise to learn to live effectively where we are. This can be accomplished by doing everything with understanding while remaining free of mental and emotional attachments to the outcomes of actions.

12. After death of the body, the influential effects of actions for those who have not renounced them are threefold: destructive, constructive, and a mixture of these two; there are no effects whatever for those who have renounced them.

The influential effects of actions for those who have not renounced them are threefold: those which restrict soul awareness, those which support its functions, and a mixture of these two. Effects of action are nonexistent for devotees who have renounced mental and emotional attachments to actions and their results.

Unless they awaken to the level of transcendence, souls which depart this realm continue their growth experiences in subtle astral or fine causal realms. Because their mental faculties remain intact, karmic patterns (samskaras, mental impressions) remain with the soul and can be compelling. If pain-causing karmic patterns are influential, the same kinds of difficulties the soul had to confront while physically embodied remain bothersome. If life-enhancing influences are dominant, they are constructively influential. They can be a mixture of these two influences. If karmic patterns are neutralized, when the soul departs the body no compelling influences are carried to the next realm.

Not all actions are physical. Some actions are emotional and some are mental. Our moods and thoughts are actions to which we can be attached or which we can renounce by choice. Attachments to pleasant or unpleasant moods, or to beliefs, illusions, and fantasies can restrict soul awareness. All attachments have to be renounced, by choice or as the result of Self-knowledge and transcendent realizations.

13. Learn from me these five factors for the accomplishment of all actions as declared in the Samkhya doctrine:

Learn from the unfoldment of innate knowledge these five factors for the accomplishment of all actions as expounded in the philosophical system that numbers categories of cosmic manifestation:

14. **The body [the seat of action], the agent of action, the organs involved in action, the various separate actions, and providential influences being the fifth.**

The body is the seat of action. If the soul is physically embodied, all three bodies or soul sheaths are involved because the causal and astral bodies support the physical. Actions occurring in astral spheres involve the astral and causal bodies. In the causal realm, the causal sheath alone is the soul encasement.

The agent of action is the initiative or impulse which originates it. The attributes of nature (gunas) are instrumental agents.

The organs involved are mind, organs of sense perception, and any others according to the action performed.

The various separate, supporting or alternative actions may include breathing and other biological processes, interactions between the mind and the body, and others.

Providence is unplanned good fortune that unfolds because of supportive actions of evolution and grace, the beneficial unfoldments which we may anticipate or which may express in spite of our errors or negligence. Providence is sometimes referred to as spiritual destiny. Knowing this, it can be helpful to perform constructive actions while remaining alert (and responsive) to indications of the actions of providence.

15. **Whatever action a person begins with the body, speech, or mind, whether it is right or wrong, these five are the factors for the accomplishment of all actions.**

Right actions are not in opposition to dharma, the orderly, supportive processes of life. *Wrong actions* are those which are in opposition to the orderly, supportive processes of life.

16. **This being so, one who sees himself as the doer does not truly see, because understanding has not been perfected.**

What has been explained reveals that the true Self is not the performer of actions. To think otherwise is to misunderstand. Egoism, false sense of selfhood, is involved. The true Self of us is ever removed from actions and their effects.

When engaged in spiritual practices, the devotee should know, "I am doing these things to purify body and mind, to restore awareness to knowledge of wholeness. I am not doing these things to improve upon my essential nature as a spiritual being."

17. That one whose mind is free from egoism, and whose intellect is pure, who slays these people, does not really slay and is not bound by actions.

The soul, with the mind liberated from the delusion of independent existence, and with purified intellectual powers, even though it may banish these destructive mental tendencies and inclinations [these people], does not cause their death.

We are reminded of the instruction featured in the second chapter when the soul had to be encouraged to stand against destructive mental tendencies and karmic drives, and remove them by all means possible. The soul was then just beginning its quest for knowledge and was still attached to self-conscious states and characteristics of conditioned human nature. When the soul is sufficiently awake it can resist, weaken, and eliminate all destructive tendencies rooted in the mind by an act of intention, adjustments of mental states and states of consciousness, behavior modification to replace unwanted behaviors with constructive ones, contemplative meditation, and superconscious states. When more fully awake, the soul sees through illusions that once obscured its perceptions of the facts of life and discards delusions. Its superior powers then spontaneously cleanse the mind and body, casting out and dissolving seeds (samskaras, mental impressions) of karma.

18. Knowledge, the object of knowledge, and the knower, comprise the threefold impulse to action. The means, the action, and the agent of action comprise the threefold basis of action.

Knowledge is comprehension or understanding of what is perceived in our field of awareness.

The object of knowledge is that which is observed or experienced. The process of knowing is facilitated by direct perception, inference, induction, deduction, or the testimony of a knowledgeable person. Of these, direct perception provides comprehensive, accurate knowledge.

The knower of knowledge is the soul, the observer and experiencer. When soul awareness is not functioning through the mind and its conditionings, Self-knowledge and knowledge of God and universal processes is immediately present because innate to the soul. Knowledge, an object of knowledge, and a knower of knowledge, impel actions.

So long as there is need for knowledge, the process of knowing, and a knower, the one desiring knowledge is still perceiving from a viewpoint of individualized awareness, observing distinctions between various perceived objects of knowledge.

The means of actions are the instruments which make them possible. The three primary attributes or qualities of nature, the gunas, are instrumental in all actions, as are the various sense organs and organs of actions used by the embodied soul.

The agent of one's actions is self-sense which causes the soul to mistakenly presume, "I am doing this," or "I am the means of this action." In fact, the soul is only the witness to what occurs and is untouched by actions and their outcomes.

19. In the philosophical system in which the categories of cosmic manifestation are categorized and numbered [Samkhya] it is declared that knowledge, action, and the agent of action are of three kinds, distinguished according to the differences in the modes of nature. Hear about this also:

Samkhya philosophy is not considered by masters of yoga to be complete because it does not reveal a total understanding of higher realities. However, its explanations of the actions of the gunas, and other matters having to do with relative knowledge, are considered insightful and reliable.

20. The knowledge by which the imperishable Being in all beings is perceived as undivided, is sattvic.

The knowledge by which Consciousness in all things is perceived as whole even though expressing as souls, is truth-revealing.

When we know that Consciousness alone exists, we know that all souls are rays of God's light, that everything in manifestation is the energy of Consciousness appearing as we see it, and that living things are enlivened by the Spirit of God.

21. That knowledge which perceives multiplicity in all beings because of their separateness, is rajasic.

That knowledge which perceives multiplicity in all beings because of their [seeming] separateness, is distorted and causes mental confusion that results in illusions.

When awareness is unsettled because restlessness and confusion distorts mental processes, misperceptions or illusions occur. One may then falsely presume that a variety of forces and things exist independent of Consciousness. A devotee should be mindful of the truth and acknowledge oneness when thoughts and sense perceptions conflict with what is known to be true.

22. That knowledge which is unreasonably attached to a single, insignificant effect as if it were the whole, without seeing the cause, is small, and is tamasic.

That knowledge which is blindly attached to a single effect as if it represented the complete circumstance, without comprehending the truth, is narrow and indicates inability to comprehend.

When intellectual powers are weak, we may believe that only what is presently available to be sensed is real. Thus we fail to discriminate between what is true and what is only believed to be true. To facilitate spiritual growth, we should accept on faith the teachings of enlightened people even if what is taught cannot immediately be understood. Useful knowledge will then be acquired and continued inquiry will improve comprehension.

23. That action which is obligatory, which is performed without attachment and without desire or aversion, with no wish to obtain a reward, is sattvic.

That necessary action which is performed without attachment, compelling desire, aversion, or expectation of reward, is pure.

When we are grounded in understanding, it is easy to skillfully and cheerfully attend to our duties. Even before understanding is complete, we should endeavor to live as enlightened souls live. Psychological wellness will then become normal and the effects of our rational actions will be constructive.

24. That action which is performed with much effort, impelled by a self-centered wish to fulfill desires, is rajasic.

That action which is performed with extreme effort, impelled by ego-driven urgency to fulfill desires, is impure.

There are times when intentional, energetic actions are necessary. So long as they are wisdom-guided, their outcomes will be beneficial. The key is not to allow actions to be impelled by ego-needs: for self-glorification, satisfaction of sense urges only, or to achieve goals which are of little or no value. When engaged in worthwhile endeavors in harmony with evolutionary trends, we have the full support of the universe and our actions will be almost effortless. When we have to struggle to accomplish purposes, our endeavor may be wrongly chosen, we may lack knowledge of how to facilitate success, or our procedures may be inefficient. Living, accomplishing our basic aims and purposes, and nurturing spiritual growth should be easy and enjoyable.

25. That action which is undertaken because of delusion, disregarding consequences, loss, or injury to others, and without regard to one's capacity to perform it, is tamasic.

That action started under the influence of delusion, disregarding consequences of hardship or pain to another, and without regard to one's ability to perform it, is life-suppressing and destructive.

Most actions performed to satisfy personal needs or inconsequential desires are harmless. When our actions interfere with the rights of others or cause them misfortune or pain, or when our skills are not sufficient to produce worthwhile outcomes, our behaviors are grounded in delusion. They are in opposition to the actions of evolution.

26. When released from attachment, free from egotism, endowed with steadfastness, and unperturbed in success or failure, that person is known to be sattvic.

One who is released from attachment and egotism, is unwavering and purposeful, and is even-minded regardless of the outcomes of actions, is actualizing soul-enlivening, life-enhancing qualities.

When we effortlessly live like this, we are firmly established in soul awareness. We do not then need to endeavor to live in the right way; we do so naturally and spontaneously as impelled by soul-originated impulses and insight.

27. When passionately desirous of the rewards of action, greedy, violent-natured, of impure motives, and subject to joy or sorrow, that person is rajasic.

One who is driven to gratify the urges of the restless mind and out-flowing sense desires, and is greedy, forceful, motivated by impure resolve, and is certain to experience superficial happiness and the anguish of unhappiness, is driven by passion.

When we are self-centered, restless, sense-driven and compulsive, with attention and energies flowing mostly outward, we are inclined to behave unwisely. Then, even the temporary happiness we experience because of our actions, has within it the potential to cause pain of disappointment when it subsides, and the possibility of unhappy circumstances is ever-present.

To overcome strong rajasic influences, constructive lifestyle choices should be implemented.

28. When undisciplined, vulgar, obstinate, cruel, deceitful, lazy, despondent, and procrastinating, that person is tamasic.

One who is undisciplined, uncultured, inflexible because of ignorance, cruel, deceitful, lazy, despondent, and who habitually procrastinates, is blind to truth because of delusions.

When we allow our thoughts, moods, and behaviors to be determined by delusion we perpetuate the problem of ignorance and suffering. It is not always easy for a person who feels heavy and dull-minded to use imagination and powers of self-motivation to improve circumstances. Attachment to existing conditions may support obstinate attitudes which manifest as mental perversity: the self-destructive mental habit of distorting useful information to serve personal, neurotic purposes.

To overcome tamasic influences, wholesome, constructive actions should be implemented, supported by philosophical study and regular spiritual practice routines.

29. Now hear, taught separately and completely, the threefold distinctions of intellect, and of steadfastness, according to the influences of the qualities of nature.

Now discern the clearly revealed truth regarding the threefold distinctions of the ability to understand, and of being firm and unwavering, according to the actions of the attributes of nature.

The importance of a devotee remaining established in clear understanding while being firmly resolved on the spiritual growth path is again emphasized. Until established in Self-knowledge, our awareness is almost always modified by the influences inherent in nature and by our disorganized mental states.

30. That intellect which knows when to act and when not to act, what is to be done and what is to be avoided, and what is to be feared and what is not to be feared, along with understanding of causes of soul bondage and soul liberation, is sattvic.

That discriminative faculty which enables one to know when to act and when to refrain from action, what should be done and what should not be done, what is to be feared and what is not to be feared, and also the causes of the soul's delusions and of its liberation, is truth-revealing.

When the intellect is pure, we can easily know how to live effectively. When we know how and why delusion clouds soul awareness, the solution to the problem can be discerned. When this error is eliminated, the delusions also vanish.

31. That intellect which errs in determination between what is right and what is wrong, and between what is to be done and what is not to be done, is rajasic.

That discriminative faculty which inaccurately determines the distinction between what is in accord with orderly unfoldments [dharmic processes] and what is in opposition to orderly unfoldments, and between what should be done and what should be avoided, is flawed because of confusion.

When intellectual powers are clouded because of restlessness and disordered mental processes, further perceptual errors can occur, causing illusions which produce more confusion. What is then needed is to cultivate emotional and mental calm so that rational thinking can prevail.

32. That intellect which is enveloped in darkness, which erroneously determines wrong to be right, and sees all things in a perverted way, is tamasic.

That discriminative faculty which is covered by darkness, which mistakenly determines actions which are in opposition to orderliness to be correct, and which distorts perceptions, is delusional.

One who is obviously ignorant of the facts of life and whose perceptions are distorted, needs to have role models after which to pattern behavior and energetically aspire to personal improvement until rational thinking is habitual.

33. When practicing yoga, unwavering firmness by which one masters mental process, vital breath, and senses, is sattvic.

When one practices samadhi, the steadfast mastery of mental fluctuations and their influential causes, and of prana flows and sensory impulses, is truth-revealing.

Supportive yoga practices preceding superconscious states are preliminary to experience of yoga as samadhi. With repeated superconscious experiences that culminate in advanced samadhi states, all mental actions are calmed, their influential causes (restlessness and the impulses driven by latent subconscious conditionings) are subdued, the body's life forces are spontaneously regulated, and sensory impulses cease because the devotee is stable in soul awareness.

34. That steadfastness by which one clings to duty, pleasures and wealth, with attachment, and desire for the rewards of actions, is rajasic.

The firm constancy by which one holds on to duty, pleasures and wealth, with mental and emotional attachment and desire for rewards, is encouraged and supported by illusional thinking and the cosmic forces of nature which incite activity.

We need to be attentive to our duties. We should enjoy living. Being responsible for material resources is necessary. What interferes with enjoyable, effective living are mental and emotional attachments and being constantly driven to satisfy egocentric desires, wants, and whims. A devotee of God is not asked to withdraw from life: the sensible approach is to live skillfully and successfully with clear understanding.

35. That steadfastness by which an ignorant person does not abandon [unnecessary] sleep, fear, grief, depression, and conceit, is tamasic.

The persistence by which a person without understanding remains in bondage to excessive sleep, fears of various kinds, mental and emotional depression, and vanity, is evidence of mental dullness, clouded awareness, and delusion.

The tendency to sleep excessively is caused by enjoyment of unconsciousness, an inclination toward nonexistence. Because of having little or no interest in learning how to live effectively, one may prefer to sleep for extended durations of time. Clinging to fears and other psychological states is due to emotional immaturity and obsessive self-centeredness. Mental and emotional depression, while sometimes related to chemical imbalances or disorders of the nervous system, is often due to lack of a clear sense of meaning and purpose for one's life. Attitude adjustment, a healthy lifestyle, and education in how-to-live principles can be helpful to eliminating episodes of mental and emotional depression. Conceit (vanity, an inflated opinion of one's abilities or worth) can be an attempt to compensate for feelings of inferiority or the result of delusional thinking.

36. Now, hear from me of the threefold happiness that is enjoyed because of the practice of yoga, and in which one reaches the end of suffering.

Now, learn from the Self-revealed knowledge that unfolds about the threefold happiness that a person enjoys because of the practice of samadhi, and by which the soul awakens from misfortune.

37. That happiness, born of one's mind, which in the beginning

is like poison but in the end like nectar, is sattvic.

That happiness which arises in one's mind, which may at first be unwanted because it is unlike the kind of happiness that results from stimulation of the senses, but is really regenerative and strengthening, is truth-revealing.

The mind is the abode of sattva guna. When a degree of mental peace prevails, we may at first wonder if we are normal. We may become aware of the fact that with the unfoldment of inner peace our values change because we are no longer dependent upon external circumstances to generate feelings of well-being. Our inwardness may also encourage us to more deeply explore subtle regions of mind and awareness, which may cause mild discomfort as we discover things about ourselves that were heretofore hidden from our conscious awareness. Eventually, when we are stable in soul awareness, our transcendental happiness is nectar-like: it is life-enhancing and soul-empowering.

38. **That happiness derived from contact between the senses and their objects, which in the beginning is like nectar and in the end is like poison, is rajasic.**

    That happiness derived from satisfying desires, which in the beginning seems nourishing and in the end results in disillusionment, is stimulating and of brief duration.

When we base our happiness only upon whether or not our objective desires are satisfied, we put ourselves into a dependent relationship with the world. When circumstances do not unfold agreeably, we are unhappy. When we achieve goals, we are temporarily happy because desire has been satisfied. Without soul peace, we are usually inclined to keep looking outside of ourselves for more projects to complete and more sensory stimulation to provide us with proof that we are alive and vital. Even meditators can be caught up in rajasic endeavors. They may constantly strive for new and different meditative perceptions or for fleeting episodes of ecstasy, revelations about matters other than transcendent realities, and to acquire exceptional abilities because of fascination with them rather than for the purpose of facilitating rapid awakening to refined samadhi states.

39. That happiness arising from [excessive] sleep, indolence, and negligence, which both in the beginning and afterwards, clouds the mind and restricts awareness, is tamasic.

That happiness resulting from excessive sleep, laziness, disinterest, and inattention to important details, which both in the beginning and afterwards clouds the mind and restricts awareness, contributes to further ignorance and unconsciousness.

What is presumed to be happiness because of unconscious states or delusional behaviors does nothing to improve one's personal circumstances, physical or mental health, or spiritual awareness. A life lived under the influences of tamas guna is wasted until a degree of soul awareness unfolds. A life lived under the influences of rajas guna at least holds some promise because one may eventually tire of trying to find happiness by outer endeavors only, and be self-motivated to discover a more meaningful way. A rajasic lifestyle may afford opportunities for improving functional skills and acquiring practical knowledge about causes and their effects. The yoga way to facilitate spiritual growth is to overcome tamasic influences by engaging in constructive actions, and to master and transcend rajasic influences by cultivating sattvic, elevating qualities.

40. There is no one, either on earth or in heaven among the gods, who can exist free from these three qualities born of primordial nature.

There is no one, not here on earth or in astral or causal realms among souls which are more conscious, who can exist in relationship to the manifest realms without being influenced by these three qualities produced from the field of primordial nature.

So long as a soul is identified with a mind or body, both of which are formed of the constituent characteristics of nature, the actions of the qualities of nature will have some influence. This is true in physical, subtle astral, and fine causal realms. When the soul rests in awareness of itself, it is removed from the influences of nature. It is possible to maintain a calm state of awareness while expressing through mind and body even though they are still somewhat influenced by the actions of the gunas. When soul awareness is constant, cosmic consciousness unfolds, superior superconscious influences progressively purify body and mind, and sattvic influences prevail.

41. The duties of the brahmins, kshatriyas, vaisyas, and sudras are apportioned according to the qualities which arise from their basic mind-body constitution.

The duties of those who are spiritually aware with pure intellect, those who are dynamic and self-controlled, those who enjoy success and pleasure, and those whose interests and skills are related to material endeavors, are according to the influences of the qualities of nature represented in their basic mind-body constitution.

In ancient India, when Vedic scriptural influence was dominant, the belief was that one could best fulfill personal needs and the needs of society by adopting a lifestyle compatible with one's basic psychological and physical constitution—allowing for personal growth and improvement in skills to determine choices in making changes with the passage of time. Usually with the advent of Dark Age cycles, in many cultures people were forced by societal pressures to adopt the social status of their parents regardless of individual intelligence or ability. The ideal is for individuals to discover the functional abilities they have, or can acquire, and skillfully use them. By doing this, one is true to the basic mind-body constitution, and is able to function effectively while growing to emotional, intellectual, and spiritual maturity.

42. [The cultivation of] tranquility, restraint, austerity, purity, forgiveness, honesty, knowledge, wisdom, and faith in God, are the duties of brahmins [those who are spiritually and intellectually developed], born of their basic nature.

Devotees whose spiritual and intellectual capacities are already pronounced can more easily cultivate the virtues and believe in the grace-providing reality of God. An obstacle to soul unfoldment may be pride because of a degree of spiritual awareness or intellectual aptitude. This problem can be avoided if, while perfecting actualization of the virtues, one remembers to remain surrendered in God.

43. Heroism, vigor, steadiness, skill, not fleeing from battle, generosity, and leadership, are the duties of the kshatriyas [who are dynamic and self-disciplined], born of their basic nature.

This verse is particularly suitable for an Arjuna type devotee, who is encouraged to courageously confront the necessity of entering into a contest with, and overcoming, destructive mental tendencies and debilitating habits by self-discipline and meditative proficiency. One who is heroic, vital, firmly resolved, skillful, courageous, openhearted, and decisive can accomplish worthy goals—including overcoming of all obstacles by Kriya Yoga practices—efficiently when motivated to do so.

44. Executive endeavors are the duties of vaisyas [who enjoy life and are skillful in the use of resources], born of their basic nature. Service [and any other suitable endeavor] is the duty of the sudras [who are provincial and unskilled], born of their basic nature.

Individuals with a natural aptitude for organization can make rapid progress on the spiritual path by using their skills and energies to live effectively, while simultaneously cultivating soul qualities and sustained, meditative contemplation. They can easily focus on essential activities to accomplish noble purposes.

Devotees who, by nature or because of lack of experience, have limited understanding and undeveloped functional skills when they begin their self-improvement and spiritual growth quest, can make rapid progress by choosing a lifestyle which is entirely supportive of their endeavors and by being totally resolved on their chosen path.

45. One attains perfection by being devoted to one's own duty. Hear how one who is devoted to duty obtains perfection:
46. That from whom all beings have their origin and by which this universe is pervaded—by worshipping [reverently relating to] that through the performance of proper duty, one obtains perfection.

Applying intelligence and skills with focused purpose and doing everything in relationship to the Infinite is the master key to effective living and to unfolding innate soul potential. Regardless of our personal circumstances when we begin our quest for higher knowledge and spiritual growth, because we are all rays of God's light, we have the same innate potential to succeed. The way to do it is to use the talents we have while cultivating helpful skills by right endeavor and experience. When we do our best to help ourselves, God's grace will do the rest.

47. Better is one's own duty, though imperfectly performed, than the well-performed duty of another; one does not incur misfortune by performing appropriate duties.

We function most efficiently by doing what we are best qualified to do. In this verse we are informed that being true to ourselves, even if we have yet to learn how to be skillful, is better than superficially imitating the actions of another. What is most desirable is to learn so that our growth is authentic and we have a firm foundation upon which our lives can flourish.

48. One should not abandon the duty to which one is born even though it be performed with deficiency. Indeed, all enterprises are clouded by defects as fire is obscured by smoke.

The duty for which we are best prepared because of our inclination, knowledge, and skills, is the one we should fulfill. We should not do less than what we are capable of doing because superficiality is not conducive to growth. We are here to learn, to function skillfully, and to serve. We should give to life the best of which we are capable. We are not confined to the circumstances of our birth. As consciousness expands and our skills improve, we naturally become more insightful and accomplished.

49. That devotee whose understanding is unattached, who has self-mastery, and from whom desires are gone, awakens to the supreme state of freedom from actions.

With the unfoldment of Self-knowledge we are released from attachments of all kinds, become established in soul awareness and mastery of mind and senses, and actualize desirelessness. Enlightened desirelessness does not result in lack of interest in living or inability to accomplish meaningful purposes; it results in freedom to function spontaneously and successfully as directed by innate knowledge.

50. Learn from me, briefly, how one who has awakened to perfection also attains to Brahman, the highest state.

Learn from Self-unfolded knowledge how one who has awakened to perfection also realizes the Field of Pure Consciousness.

Having awakened to knowledge of soul and by remaining intent on discovery, further awakenings which culminate in final realization of the Absolute naturally occur.

51. Endowed with pure intellect, with firm self-control, abandoning sense objects, casting off attraction and aversion,
52. Dwelling in solitude, eating in moderation, controlling speech, body and mind, constantly devoted to yoga meditation, taking refuge in dispassion,
53. Relinquishing egotism, forcefulness, pride, desire, anger, and attachments, remaining unselfish and tranquil, that devotee is fit for realization of Supreme Consciousness.

Note that mere wishing for God-realization is not sufficient, nor is partial realization without follow-through a guarantee of success on the spiritual path.

Intellectual powers should be purified by error-free discernment and by superconscious meditation.

We should have mastered *self-control.*

Reliance upon externals for happiness and feelings of security should be *renounced.*

We should not be overly fascinated by anything, nor should we have to struggle to avoid misfortune. We should be established in *soul contentment.*

To dwell in solitude means to live a well-ordered life devoid of unnecessary distractions.

Nutritious foods should be taken in *moderation* and the mind should be nourished with only calming, constructive ideas.

Speaking, personal behaviors, and habitual modes of thinking should be regulated in accord with our understanding of life's higher purposes.

Superconscious meditation should be regularly practiced.

Dispassion is even-mindedness that ensures mental calm and emotional balance, essential to success on the spiritual path.

Renouncing egotism banishes vanity and arrogance.

Renouncing forcefulness, pride, desire (craving), anger, and attachments, actualizes selflessness and tranquility that results in soul contentment.

54. Absorbed in Supreme Consciousness, that one who is tranquil, who does not grieve or desire, and is impartial among all beings, has the purest devotion.

Devotion is pure when we are surrendered in God. Pure devotion devoid of emotionalism and dramatizations of psychological disturbances dissolves all sense of independent selfhood.

55. By devotion to me does one come to know me in truth; then having known me in truth, that devotee enters into me.

By devotion to the Absolute does one awaken to knowledge of Consciousness; having known it, that devotee awakens to wholeness.

Even if a person begins spiritual practices without an understanding of God, as soul unfoldment progresses, the reality of God will be apprehended. Because of devoted aspiration to know the fullness of God, intellectual powers increase, intuition provides direct insight, and dynamic, awakened soul forces accelerate unfoldment of soul qualities and knowledge.

56. The devotee who performs all actions with reliance on me attains, by my grace, the eternal, imperishable abode.

The devotee who performs all actions with reliance on the Infinite realizes, by God's grace, the eternal, unchanging state.

When we are so God-focused that awareness of God is effortless and constant, we are conscious that our every thought and action is in relationship to God.

57. Mentally renouncing all actions in me, devoted to me as the Supreme, taking refuge in the yoga of discrimination, have your attention constantly fixed on me.

Renouncing all actions in God, devoted to God as the ultimate to be realized, taking refuge in the samadhi of discrimination, have your attention constantly focused on God.

Living in constant awareness of the Presence of God is a happy, alert, creative experience that has nothing in common with the emotional, unintelligent, dysfunctional dramatization of devotion that one sometimes observes in the behaviors and mental states of people who, while perhaps sincere, are deficient in authentic spiritual awareness.

58. **Concentrating on me, you shall pass over all difficulties by my grace; but if because of egotism you will not listen, you will perish.**

Contemplating the reality of God, by grace you shall pass beyond all difficulties; but if because of arrogance you will not listen, you will fall away from the spiritual path.

By letting our attention be attracted to God, all obstacles will be overcome because of grace which supplements our right endeavors. Because the challenge of egotism can persist until the final stage of awakening, we should not presume to have awakened fully in God until our realization, knowledge, and demonstrated behaviors confirm our enlightenment.

59. **If you egotistically think, "I will not fight," vain will be your resolve; your own basic nature will compel you to fight.**
60. **Then, deluded, against your will, impelled by your own karma, you will do that which is contrary to your wish.**

If you egotistically think, "I will not confront and vanquish the obstacles to Self-realization," vain will be your resolve because your innate soul nature will compel you to do so.
Because you are deluded, you will desire to facilitate spiritual growth but because of inner conflicts you will practice ineffectively.

Even if we think that we can ignore our soul urge to have awareness restored to wholeness, our innate inclination will eventually compel us to endeavor to facilitate spiritual growth. If there is resistance to doing this, or if endeavors are halfhearted, our psychological conflicts will usually result in flawed practice that will not be soul-satisfying, and subconscious conditionings will determine our lives. To be spiritually accomplished we should surrender the mind entirely to right living and knowledgeable spiritual practice. We should enthusiastically affirm, "Yes! I will respond to my soul-call to awaken from delusion! I will, by right endeavor and with the support of grace, banish all obstacles to Self-knowledge and complete realization of God!"

61. God abides in the hearts of all beings, causing all beings to continue their experiences by the power of illusion.

Souls identified with primordial nature that produces the universe are impelled to continue to express because of their innate spiritual reality, and are compelled to continue their cycles of destiny in time and space because of the truth-veiling influence of primordial nature. There is no escape from unconscious involvement with circumstances until the soul awakens to the truth of itself in God.

62. Flee with your whole being to God alone for refuge. By God's grace you will attain supreme peace and eternal abode.

We turn to God by turning to the innermost core of ourselves, remembering that, because we are rays of God's light, our omnipresent reality is God. So long as we feel ourselves to be other than an individualized expression of God, we should cultivate awareness of God. When our sense of separateness dissolves, only God-awareness remains.

63. Thus the knowledge that is more secret than all that is secret has been explained to you by me. Having considered this fully, do what pleases you.

Thus the knowledge that is not known by ordinary people has been self-revealed to you. Having reflected carefully on what you now know, follow the leading of your inner guidance.

The *secret* here referred to is not information kept from souls. It is the truth about life that is not generally known by most people, which can be known by acquiring knowledge from others who have insight and by contemplating the nature of Consciousness until clear understanding unfolds from within. Once we know what is true, we have but to live our lives in accord with it.

64. Hear again my supreme word, most secret of all. You are dearly loved by me; therefore, I will speak for your good.

Receive again the supreme revelation, most secret of all. You are in the flow of redemptive grace; therefore, revelations will continue.

The love of God is the attracting influence of the omnipresent Field of Consciousness that unveils the soul's innate knowledge of itself and of God. The soul-liberating actions of this attracting influence is the purest expression of grace. It cannot be earned; we need only accept and surrender to it. This fact is "secret" only because it is not always understood by the devotee. When one is identified with the delusion of independent existence because of intellectual error, the general belief is that God is other than the soul and can only be realized by extreme personal endeavor or when God decides the time is right for the soul to be enlightened. God's grace is always available. Souls need only to turn to God and let the redemptive actions of grace be influential. All of our preliminary endeavors on the spiritual path prepare us for the final experience of liberation by God's grace.

65. Meditating on me, being devoted to me, making holy offerings to me, surrendering to me; in this way you will truly come to me, I promise you, for you are dear to me.

Be devotedly attentive to God, offering yourself by surrendering self-consciousness. In this way you will truly awaken in God; you have this assurance, for you are ever nurtured by God's grace.

When meditating, desire only to be lost in God. Merge in God with complete devotion. Let self-consciousness diminish and God-consciousness increase. This is the direct way to God-realization as taught by saints and experienced by surrendered devotees.

66. Abandoning all duties, take refuge in me alone. I will liberate you from all misfortune; do not grieve.

Abandoning all duties, take refuge in God alone. God's grace will liberate you from all misfortune; do not grieve about anything.

During the final states of spiritual awakening, contrived practices and personal endeavors to facilitate soul unfoldment are to be abandoned so that the actions of grace can be influential without interference. There is nothing to fear at this stage of final soul unfoldment, and nothing about which to mourn. There is no loss of anything that is useful; there is only the fullness of God to be realized.

67. Do not speak of this to anyone who does not practice austerities, nor to anyone who is without devotion, who does not render service, who does not want to listen, or who speaks ill of me.

Do not discuss these matters with anyone who is not self-disciplined, nor to anyone who is not devoted to God, who does not live to support evolution, who does not desire to learn, or who is an arrogant disbeliever in the reality of God.

We avoid conflict with others and utilize our mental, emotional, spiritual, and material resources most effectively when we live with enlightened purpose to efficiently actualize our noble ideals. We should not talk about our spiritual practices or about philosophy with people who are not prepared to learn, who are not interested in knowing how to learn, or who are resistant to learning. People who are doing their best to become more functional, who are willing to listen and learn, and who sincerely want to know about the reality of God and the way to Self-realization should, of course, be encouraged on their awakening path. Even so, until our experience and knowledge enables us to teach others, it is better to provide sincere truth seekers with books and other learning aids and to refer them to a qualified source for further learning. To try to personally help others before we have effectively helped ourselves to higher understanding and fulfilled living may interfere with our own spiritual growth and is not likely to be of real value to them. Good intentions are not sufficient to provide others the real help they may need.

68. That one who, having performed the highest devotion to me, teaches this supreme secret to my devotees, will surely come to me.

69. There is none among humankind who does more pleasing

service to me than that one; and no other on earth will be dearer to me.

That one who, having awakened to Self-knowledge as the result of surrendering self-consciousness in God, teaches this inner way to sincere devotees on the path, will surely realize the fullness of God. There is no soul that performs better service than the devotee who shows others the way to God-realization; and no soul in the realm of nature will more completely experience God's grace.

The God-aspiring soul's inner revelation is now almost complete and compassion inclines it to help others who seek knowledge of higher realities. When one is completely open to the flow of grace, truth is transmitted from the Source to souls who are receptive to it. The almost-free soul can now be a *satguru*, a truth-teacher whose every thought, word, and action is instrumental in removing the veil of delusion from the consciousness of souls prepared to awaken to Self-knowledge.

70. And who will study this sacred dialogue of ours, by that one I shall have been worshiped with the wisdom sacrifice; such is my assurance.

And that one who will study this sacred revelation of the soul, by that devotee wisdom will have been rightly applied; this is the truth.

The awakening soul now understands that what has been revealed should be examined during interludes of meditative contemplation until knowledge blossoms into wisdom and wisdom is replaced by complete realization.

71. Even the person who hears it with faith without disputing it, that one, also liberated, shall attain the joyful realms of those whose actions are purified.

Even the person who hears it and does not doubt, will also be freed from delusions and awaken to a clear state of consciousness.

Having learned of the way to soul freedom, one who accepts it on faith and lives in accord with it, will have delusions and illusions removed and superconscious states will spontaneously unfold. The reference to attaining the realms of those whose actions have been purified indicates that the soul that benefits from revelation, while experiencing exceptional freedom, still has to awaken through the final stages of soul unfoldment necessary for complete liberation of consciousness.

72. Have you heard this with concentrated attention? Have your ignorance and delusion been banished?

Having experienced self-unfoldments of revealed truth, the devotee is inspired to engage in meditative contemplation to clearly discern if understanding is complete and all erroneous beliefs have been dispelled. To ensure full liberation of consciousness, our awareness must be devoid of even a hint of egotism or self-deception.

Arjuna said:

73. My delusion is gone and I have regained wisdom through your grace. My doubts are removed. I shall do as you ask.

My delusion is gone and I have regained wisdom through God's grace. My doubts are removed. I shall do as you ask.

The fully awake soul is now error-free. Awareness is restored to wholeness. Forgotten wisdom is self-shining because of the redemptive actions of God's grace expressive in the soul. There are no more doubts. The soul now, without hesitation, will live and act intuitively and spontaneously to fulfill destiny.

Sanjaya spoke:

74. Thus I am thrilled to have heard this wondrous dialogue from Krishna and the great-souled Arjuna.

I am thrilled to have learned this wondrous revelation unfolded by Supreme Consciousness from the innermost core of the soul.

75. By the grace of Vyasa I have heard this most secret yoga which Krishna, the Lord of yoga, has personally taught.

By the grace of knowledge-wisdom I have been informed of this inner way to God-realization which the innate Divine Reality has Self-unfolded.

76. **Remembering again and again this marvelous and holy dialogue of Krishna and Arjuna, I rejoice again and again.**

Remembering this marvelous and sacred unfoldment of divine revelation from the depths of the soul, I continually rejoice.

77. **Remembering again that marvelous form of Krishna, my amazement is great, and I rejoice again and again.**

Remembering that marvelous reality of Supreme Consciousness, my overflowing amazement compels me to continually rejoice.

78. **This is my conviction: wherever there is Krishna, Lord of yoga, wherever there is Arjuna, the self-disciplined devotee of God, there, will surely be radiant good fortune, victory, well-being, and righteousness.**

I am convinced that wherever there is Supreme Consciousness which determines all outcomes, wherever there is a true devotee of God, there, will surely be radiant good fortune, victory over all obstacles, spontaneous well-being, and the establishment of righteousness.

In the Upanishad of the Bhagavad Gita, the science of the Absolute, the scripture of Yoga and the dialogue between Sri Krishna and Arjuna, thus ends the eighteenth chapter entitled Moksha Yoga: The Yoga of Liberation

Center for Spiritual Awareness

Founded in 1972 by Roy Eugene Davis, world headquarters is located in the northeast Georgia mountains, 90 miles north of Atlanta. Facilities include offices, the Shrine of All Faiths meditation temple, meditation hall and dining room, library, learning resource center, bookstore, and six comfortable guest houses. Meditation retreats are offered from early spring until late autumn, on a donation basis.

Truth Journal, Studies in Truth lessons, and a newsletter for kriya initiates are distributed internationally.

*For a free literature packet with a sample issue of
Truth Journal magazine, information about Mr. Davis'
books, CDs, and DVDs, and meditation seminar and
retreat schedules contact:*

Center for Spiritual Awareness
P. O. Box 7   Lakemont, Georgia 30552-0001
Phone 706-782-4723 weekdays 8 a.m. to 3 p.m.
Fax 706-782-4560
e-mail info@csa-davis.org
Or visit our web page: www.csa-davis.org
click on *Free Literature*